a Ros

Here is a fascinating and entertaining memoir of Edward Blishen's life as a conscientious objector during the Second World War. He superbly evokes that perplexing and traumatic period in our history while unfolding the story of his own personal dilemma as the war runs its course about him. This is a work of deep beauty and deep understanding: moving, robust and constantly illuminating.

'A warm personal memoir of those years, written with a gentle sense of humour. Colourful, evocative, and with more than a suggestion of nostalgia' *Manchester Evening News*

'Captures both the beauty and the boredom of the experience. He also succeeds in illuminating the relations between the conscientious objectors and the groups with whom they come in contact: the officials, the land-girls, the soldiers, and the prisoners of war' *Times Literary Supplement*

D1386668

Edward Blishen

A Cack-handed War

Panther

Granada Publishing Limited
Published in 1974 by Panther Books Ltd
Frogmore, St Albans, Herts AL2 2NF

First published in Great Britain by Thames
and Hudson Ltd 1972
Copyright © Edward Blishen 1972
Made and printed in Great Britain by
Richard Clay (The Chaucer Press) Ltd
Bungay, Suffolk
Set in Linotype Times

Contents

Author's Note

Autobiography is a severe art, requiring the writer to make what he can of the exact events of his life. The art I've tried to practise here is another one. All that follows is very close to my experience as a wartime pacifist. But I have merged and muddled scenes, incidents, people. No one was precisely like this or did exactly what I say he did. Yet the essence of it is as true as I could make it. To use a metaphor drawn from these experiences: I have been along the overgrown hedges of reality, trimming them to let the light in, and have given its ditches a rather easier flow than they actually had.

'Damn it,' said George, 'my hands aren't clean, and I'm going to fight. I have what you'll think is a weird sort of consolation. When it's all over, and if I survive, I'll come back and knock hell out of the people who dragged us into it.'

He stared at me, and I knew my face was pale and pinched. Only last week, Nicky Pellet had announced that he was joining the Territorials. I looked at things very simply, in those days. Pacifism had seemed to be the air we all breathed, when we were at the grammar school together. How satirical Nicky had always been about military matters! Well, we'd all read Remarque and Barbusse and Toller, and our views had always appeared so beautifully clear. War was black. Any war was black. And now it was upon us, and one by one they were finding reasons for taking part.

George's defection was the most unlikely blow yet. Fiercely radical George, who was so soundly intransigent on every imaginable issue. George who was against marriage, and the wearing of hats, and the possession of riches. George whose bookshelves were so different from mine. I accumulated books almost desperately, building them into a wall between me and the philistine world. For me, every book was a blow directed against the enemy. Take that, my suburban foe! – that being a novel of Aldous Huxley's, a collected Auden, a complete Chaucer. 'You're hemming yourself in,' George would say when he visited our house. 'A few more books, and they'll never be able to get at you.' I felt ashamed when he said that, ashamed of this fortress of books in the middle of which I lived. Because George was against possessions, too, personal possessions and that included books. He had Karl Marx, a volume of Donne, a Lytton Strachey and, oddly preserved from our sixth-form days, a copy of Gautier's *Voyages en Espagne*. God, I used to think, how marvellously discriminate he is! Here am I, using books to hide inside, and to affront the non-reading world with; and here's George, travelling light through life with four essential volumes! If anyone was going to hold out against the pressure to go to war, it would be George.

And now he was saying: 'Of course, you have your innocence. What goes for me doesn't necessarily go for you. I think you know what you have to do. And good luck!'

There was a searchlight jerking across the night sky even as he spoke. Since the Munich crisis this had become a common sight. George and I had duly made jokes about it. We knew who was handling that searchlight. It was T. H. Jones, our arch-enemy at school: Jones, captain of the First XV, whose grammar school accent tripped highfalutinly across his basic Cockney, and who, when we were lower down the school, had followed me around for a whole term shouting 'Poet!' Jones had gone into insurance, and George had referred to him in a letter: 'The other day, on the platform as we waited for that poisonous train, I caught a glimpse of a symbol of our times! Guess! T. H. Jones in a round bowler hat! T. H. Jones, with *The Times* under his arm!' And so on. Jones had been an early recruit to the Territorials, and we imagined him behind every searchlight, every suddenly glimpsed little parade of amateur soldiers, during those months of 1939. We imagined him hurling that light into the empty skies, like a rugger ball, and shouting 'Poet!' at each star he caught in its sliding glare.

But even as I looked up, that evening, standing at George's side, the image of preposterous T. H. Jones vanished, and that other one took its place, which had been in my mind a few nights before when I looked up like this. My companion then had been Jean Hopkins.

I had kept Jean carefully in a separate compartment from the compartment that George and I shared. Lord, George was against love, as I understood him: against the despicable emotionalism it certainly involved. Sometimes, for example, when Jean and I lay side by side in Hyde Park, in the company of the sheep that used to crop its grass in those days, I'd think of George and the pleasure would go out of our kissing. What would George's reaction be if he overhead that irrational vocabulary I used in Hyde Park: from that arch-inanity, 'I love you', onwards and downwards? What would he say if he knew that, not long since, I had in straining myself against Jean actually burst a button off my shirt! What would he say about all that brushing of hair with cheeks, that holding of hands, those endless teasing telephone calls? I had always known that I was unworthy of George, with my book-collecting, my enthusiasm for Chopin: but those were minor treasons compared with the secret making of love that now took so much of my time.

When we'd looked up at the searchlight, Jean and I, on that evening when we'd walked ten miles into London in the dazed excitement of being together, I'd suddenly seen that silent unsteady beam in the context of the vision of war we all had, then. It was a vision built up from reality partly – from Guernica – but also from the film of H. G. Wells's *Shape of Things to Come*. We knew what war would be, the moment it was declared: the fleets, the endless fleets of bombers throbbing into our skies, the cities exploding, the instant anarchy. Life would become a huge horror film. They wouldn't know how to bury the dead. I'd said, out of our happiness:

'Oh, *they* will spoil everything!'

Jean had taken her hand from mine, stared at me in one of her special ways. I knew what that stare meant. It meant: There you go, being a solemn political male! Oh, how very solemn men and boys are, when they slip out from under the spell that women lay on them! I dreaded, and was awed by, Jean's scorn for political considerations, her belief that holding hands, and being in love, was of such importance that the ways of governments were trivial and tedious by comparison. Darkly, genuinely, Jean rejected every intellectual approach to life. Life was emotion, life was laughing and kissing as much as you could. It seemed a sort of wisdom she had, and I hid much of my thoughtful life from her as I hid my emotional life from George. I felt unworthy of her warm acceptance of things as they were. So I stared back, shaken, as she stared at me, and as the searchlight flickered and went out: and she said, 'Silly Teddy – nothing can spoil it, unless we want it to.'

I hadn't even discussed my feelings about war, much, with Jean. Oh, the compartments one had to live in, the sense of guilt that arose from one's shifty capacity to be happy in each of these incompatible cubicles of the mind! I *had* once mentioned T. H. Jones to her – and his bowler hat. 'Oh, Teddy,' she'd sighed, 'you're intolerant! He's entitled to wear a bowler hat, if he wants to.' 'What would you say,' I'd protested 'if *I* wore a bowler hat?' She'd caught my face between her hands, then, and seemed for a moment to be measuring its incapacity to support anything so substantial as a bowler hat. I knew I had a small, narrow face, and that T. H. Jones had a very large, round one – the largeness of it had appalled me when we were at school together: it seemed somehow to suggest a sinister favourit- ism on the part of the creator of human beings, whoever he was. The Joneses of this world were given large faces, enormous reserves of face, so that it was harder to defeat them, in any way whatever: score a hit, verbal or physical, on any part of one of those faces, and there were still acres of face on which their self-esteem could survive. Hit my face, any way you liked, and it was done for! And as Jean spoke, I also felt the uneasiness that was a constant thread in my vivid relationship with her. Oh yes, she loved me for being small-faced, and for scorning hats: but wasn't there also a Jean who was drawn to the substantial Joneses of the world, to their big faces and stiff hats and the capacity that went with these things of ... ugh, supporting a family, creating a career? One thing I knew was very wrong with my relationship with Jean: it included no sense of an ordinary practical future, real as opposed to poetic mar- riage. I wanted to marry Jean, all right, but I thought of our life together as one long vague poem, in conditions of undefined colourful poverty. As a reluctant newspaper re- porter, I earned a pound a week: I was only just out of my apprenticeship, when in fact I'd been required to pay a weekly half guinea for the privilege of having my pieces for the *Monmouth Hill Standard* reduced, as I saw it, to illiter- acy. That was another thing Jean thought I was being too solemn about – my belief that I was being coached on the *Standard* for the role of a journalistic illiterate.

Jean gurgled and said: 'If you wore a bowler hat, I should capture it and drop it into the Thames.' Then she said: 'After that, I should kiss you – rather like this.' The demonstration made me forget the searchlight, the coming war, the vision I'd had of Jean sensibly confiding herself to a sort of super-T. H. Jones, whom clearly the title 'husband' would fit more securely than it would fit me.

George recalled me from that remembered evening to the

present one by saying: 'They'll set up tribunals for people like you, of course, just as they did in the other war.'

I didn't attend my tribunal, in fact, until more than a year after that conversation.

My time for registering came in the spring of 1940. France was falling, and on the morning when I had to go to the Labour Exchange, I'd read of the German units 'seeking to make contact' with the fleeing French: and I remember thinking *that* was such a friendly phrase for such a murderous activity: and I remember, too, the shock of knowing that France was finished, and the voice within me saying, 'You can't . . . you can't not be in it, now. Not now they've done this to France.'

But all that literature of disgust I'd read, bitter fruit of the Great War (as we'd called it till this greater war came) . . . the horror of it, the rejection it expressed, had run in my veins, until I could not think of fighting without a sense of shock. It had been horrible, they had all hated it, those chroniclers of the First World War, and one couldn't, having supped of their anger and revulsion, start it all again. If war began – I'd been very clear about this, in my last year at school – one would be tempted, the flood would seek to carry one with it; but only by intolerable betrayal of all those haggard men of the first war, I thought, only by turning one's back on Barbusse and Remarque and Sassoon, could one give in.

So as I made my leaden way to the Labour Exchange, I heard that voice within me, weeping for France, as the voice of disloyal temptation; and I registered as an objector. I was sent to the bottom of the buzzing room, alone, away from all the others; and it felt as though I were separating myself from the world . . .

And then came that brutal summer and autumn. I went on being a reporter on the *Monmouth Hill Standard*. There were – after the nights of gunfire, like someone slamming doors in a world far bigger than our own – the mornings of tramping over the remains of houses. There was the house that had come up with all the clay on which it stood still attached to it; like an uprooted tree, lying across the suburban road. There had been all the bits and pieces of lives, scattered around, the toys and books. There had been the night when they bombed the docks, and I had been covering a flower show and as we came away from that, from the incongrous decorum of flowers laid out for exhibition, there'd been that terrible flower of fire growing in the sky, and the bombers coming back again and again.

The tribunal had been like the flower show, an inappositely decent thing in the smashed world, polite voices asking questions in a shelter under the Strand; and I remember being surprised that they called me 'Mr —', since there was a part of me that would have dismissed myself far more brusquely. I was still drawn two ways, wanting to be in the maelstrom and then hearing the voices of rejection and disgust, and already I was so committed to the stand I had taken that I should have had to be clearer and harder and much maturer than I was to reverse it.

A cold voice said that I was registered as a conscientious objector on condition that I worked on the land.

I'd seen little of Jean Hopkins since the war began. She'd been moving about the country, on ill-defined errands, staying with friends, preparing to be a nurse, a WAAF, a nun ('But don't take me seriously, dear Teddy – *you* know that's not my *métier*!'), a spy. The passionate nature of her letters seemed to be in inverse proportion to her accessibility. A few days after the arrival of the most rapturous of them ('Silly Teddy! – what there is between us is more important than any war!') I received a copy of a newspaper containing an account of her marriage. Her husband, now in the Navy, was the son of a middlingly wealthy industrialist. His name was not, but might well have been, T. H. Jones.

I developed an instant allergy, itching from head to foot. I lay in bed, raw and weeping mostly, but with a corner of my mind available for a little laughter: *he swelled up, and was subcutaneously blistered from tip to toe, all for loss of his love.*

And George wrote from Chatham. The worst thing about being in the Navy, he said, was that you were deprived of a fly-front.

And then the letter came saying I was 'accepted' (I liked the word) for 'ditching, hedging and land clearance' in Cold Clapton, near the North Sea.

1

'Be very watchful. Very watchful indeed. *They'll try to separate us.*'

It was Pringle who said that. Tall, thin, his pale face marked with blue bristle, he was one of the six of us who'd met, that afternoon early in 1941, in a chill riverside town in Essex. We were sitting, now, in a café, drinking cheerless tea, and being warned by Pringle.

'I was *tipped off*,' he said, 'by someone at Peace Pledge Union headquarters.'

The rest of us were fairly clear that Pringle was attempting to make a drama where there was none. Here we were, waiting for an official of the War Agricultural Committee to pick us up. The little town, in peacetime a yachting centre, lay bleak around us. The tide was out and the river was a grey trickle through mud. The boats, heeled over, looked like toys in a nursery the children have abandoned. Many of the houses were of wood, lightly verandahed, meant for peacetime and then only for summer: now their emptiness was an ache. No: there was no drama. Pringle was warming himself up, trying to chafe some importance back into himself.

Oliver Cragg sat next to me. We'd come from London together. He was a tiny fellow, with a leathery white face under black hair, and tied to the case he'd brought were the most enormous gumboots I'd ever seen. Oliver was one of the Particular People, and the grounds of his objection to fighting, which he'd explained to me on the train, were so intricate, and rested on such a curious reading of so many unfamiliar parts of the Bible, that I regarded him with something like awe, as one might some eminent crypto-grammatist. He had leaned forward when Pringle began his warnings, as though he'd hoped that Pringle's information might have come from measuring the Pyramids: but now he sat back and sighed heavily and, catching my eye, gave one of his little nods. 'Oh, Jupiter!' he murmured.

Facing us, and crooning happily, was the Quaker, Billy

Grantham. He was, I felt, the most normal-looking of us all: a pleasant boy with a characterless face. The emotional orderliness which he derived from being a Quaker made him, in fact, seem almost conventional: a member of the pacifist establishment. The rest of us were first-generation objectors, and some very queer reasoning had gone on among us: but Billy was secure in the traditions of his nonconformity. This seemed to leave him free to croon, which he did all the time. We'd known him only half an hour, but it was already clear that Bing Crosby meant at least as much to him as George Fox. He smiled pleasantly when he saw me looking at him and raised the tone of his booby-o-dooping, as a sort of mark of friendliness.

'... separate us so they can do what they like with each of us ... victimization ...' Pringle was saying.

Pringle had been a bank clerk and, essentially, still was. The rest of us had gone some way to rising to the imposture demanded of us. Oliver had gone furthest, with his colossal gumboots: but roll-necked sweaters lassoed the pale city necks of us others, and we wore old sports jackets and dissolute flannel trousers. Pringle was dressed for Threadneedle Street: a hard white collar, a navy blue suit, a trilby hat as stiff as if he'd been a statue. His voice was like his clothes, hard and proper: and he put his sentences together as if each was a foundation stone he was laying. In introducing himself he'd explained that he was 'a muscular Christian': which, in a world of Particular People and Christadelphians and Exclusive Brethren, somehow didn't seem odd. It *was* odd, though, one saw on reflection, because plainly if Pringle had had any muscles he'd have got rid of them, as being inconsistent with city suiting.

A little brown van with a canvas hood buzzed into view and headed for the café. On the door we read the letters EWAEC. Pringle rose and gave us the look of a man bravely facing the scaffold.

'Remember,' he rapped, 'it will be essential to be *alert* ...'

As it happened, separation was not what we had to fear. We raced up an unexpected hill and down the other side and there was our destination, the little village of Cold Clapton, a church and some council houses in the distance and, as the van drew up, a bungalow, standing on its own, its roof an atrocious purple.

'Four of you can go there,' said the official. 'Who's it to be?'

Oliver and Pringle and Billy Grantham and I were at the back and we tumbled out. We turned, politely inquiring, to the other two, but the official said 'O.K.' and then, 'The farm you're working at is Goodacres. Down the road. Mrs Goss will tell you. That's her bungalow. Seven o'clock to-morrow you start. Sharp.' And the van had gone.

'Very clever,' said Pringle, picking up his neat leather case. 'Of course, you noticed what he did? *Gave us no choice . . .*'

Mrs Goss was a widow, a neat little woman of over seventy: and witchlike.

It was as if, when we walked in that day, we'd entered the sweetmeat house in *Hänsel and Gretel*. We were four toothsome delicacies, the little woman seemed to suggest, whom some time or other she'd pop in her oven. At the same time she made it clear, as she showed us to our rooms, that in agreeing to accommodate us she had run great social risks. Some of her friends in the village wouldn't like it at all, and we must understand that, and understand – and here she was vague – that her taking us was unenthusiastic. It was implied that somehow by telling us this she could save her face among the neighbours, and that it wasn't to be taken at all seriously, since, though of course she entirely agreed with what her neighbours said about us, she liked having us, and hoped we young men would be at home. In some such muddle of sentiments she expressed herself: and then, gleefully and with a quite extraordinary suggestion of sensuous pleasure, she pointed out to Oliver and me the bed we should share, and where we would grow plump and tasty for her oven.

It was Pringle, of course, who noticed the four white feathers in the vase on the mantelpiece.

After Mrs Goss had buzzed around us and noted hungrily where we'd put our cases and expatiated a little further on the social disgrace she was simultaneously embracing and avoiding, we asked her where Goodacres Farm was and escaped into the lane.

Goodacres, so the story went, had been taken over by the War Ag from a farmer who'd been lost in some impatient dream of scientific farming, and had goaded the authorities into expropriating him by causing an explosion in the farm kitchen. There was certainly a large singed hole in the farmhouse roof. For the rest, it was – or it struck me on that first afternoon as being – the usual arrangement of fields and hedges round the usual collection of sheds and barns: flat and very wet and very chilly, as everything was in Cold Clapton. The fact that its hedges were overgrown, and its ditches had all but vanished, didn't strike me: for the axes and spades of wartime agriculture had barely got to work, and a townee hardly knew, then, that what to him was the characteristic appearance of an English farm was in fact the characteristic appearance of long neglect.

We weren't the first arrivals. A batch of us had come the previous day, and we saw them at work in a field near the road, and climbed through a hedge to meet them. There was no difficulty at all in deciding that they were not normal land workers. One or two wore trilbies that had plainly been in tube trains and other urban situations. One was wearing a college scarf: another, plus-fours. They were all talking – another mark of the town – and there was, in that first moment when we saw them, something in the hesitations of the sickles and billhooks they were using, in the way they seemed to be hacking away without clear purpose, that marked them out from real labourers. Pringle was again busily in the lead, stepping forward like a man meeting a hopelessly small group of allies when desperately beleaguered. 'What,' he demanded at once, 'is the situation?' He was answered by a tall young man with a dreamily pleasant face, who rubbed his nose with the blunt edge of a billhook and said, 'Very cold.'

'No, I mean,' said Pringle, 'how are you being treated?'

'Well, not at all,' said the tall young man. 'No, you couldn't say that we're being treated at all. On the whole they just leave us out here in this rather big field, but they say we can leave at six o'clock.'

'Perhaps they're lying low, for a day or so,' said Pringle disappointedly. 'I have a pretty good suspicion what they'll have it in mind to do, after that.'

'And so have I,' said the tall young man, sighing. 'I think

18

they're going to go on leaving us out in this large field, until we've cut down all the blackberry bushes. That's what the foreman told us this morning, anyway. He is, by the way, the fattest foreman in the world. You'll see tomorrow.'

And at seven o'clock the next morning, we saw.

Bert Trott, the committee ganger, who was to be our master for some months, was the severest shock of all to Pringle's view that terrible things were to be done to us by specially chosen sadists.

It was cold when we first met him, and, for most of us, inexpressibly early. We had never known that there was *weather* at seven o'clock in the morning, enormous black clouds rolling over, and stars barely vanished, and a chilly fràgment of moon. Bert met us at the top of the chase, a great quantity of waistcoats, a small cloth cap above an immense face from which a moustache hung, seeming to be joined to the lips only by a thread, and, in a fat hand held forward, a watch, whose chain could be traced via innumerable pendulous loops back into that universe of waistcoats. This was Bert, the fattest foreman in the world.

'C'm on, owd 'uns,' he grunted, as if there were a tape stretched there by the barn, and we ought to run forward and break it.

We hurried to join him and nothing happened. The black clouds raced faster, the moon became colder, the stars flickered and died. But Bert did not move: except once, when, at great length, he poured his chain and his watch back into his great stomach of waistcoats. There were a dozen of us, now, standing around him, together with two real farm labourers, one very tall, with a long darkened turnip of a face, and black eyes and a black moustache: the other small and round, as if he'd been the prototype for Bert himself. There we stood, shuffling and whispering, and Bert as fixed and contemplative as a Buddha, but breathing heavily. Nothing happened for a long time, and somehow it seemed that one ought perhaps to scuff a hoof on the ground, or swish a tail. We'd become a still animal group. Then from the lightening end of the chase came two figures in yellow-brown: girls. One was neat and slim, one stout. They waved and came nearer and a huge sound came from Bert's throat. It seemed to be a sound of derisive pleasure. Then the tall dark man spoke:

'She's plomp, that Sally,' he said.

Words came from Bert.

'Yer need summat to get a 'oud on,' he said.

Their amusement spiralled inside them, noisily, and then they were silent again until the girls reached us.

' 'Mornin', m'dears,' said Bert then. 'Bed hang agin?'

'Go on with you, you old fat man,' said the slim girl, whereupon Bert, with a slow movement of his monstrous arm, seized her buttocks in his world of hand and squeezed.

'Ay,' he said. 'Get t'tools out.'

Into this highly ambiguous scene, Pringle stepped anxiously.

'I imagine, foreman,' he said, 'that you will take into account our unfamiliarity with this sort of work.'

Bert gave him an empty stare – as a bear might were someone to walk into his clutches too hopelessly skinny to be made anything of.

'You all come along o' me,' he said: and our agricultural experience had begun.

It was a very large field. There were far too many blackberries in it. The sickle I was using ('bagging-hook', Bert had called it) was blunt. I glanced at my watch: then cursed. Though I had deliberately not looked at it for what seemed hours and hours, the time was only 10.45. I listened to what Oliver Cragg, a few yards away, was saying to Pringle.

'They measure the Pyramids,' Oliver was saying. 'Very interesting. The devil will rule for —'

'I've heard it, old man,' said Pringle. 'But permit an Anglican to say —'

'It was just a thought,' protested Oliver.

'Spiritual stunts, if you'll allow me to be blunt,' said Pringle.

'Hmm!' said Oliver. His face – as I knew now always happened when he met with disagreement – went white and taut. 'But they've *measured* the Pyramids.'

'Any Egyptologist will tell you ...' said Pringle, but Oliver, unable any longer to bear the other's monstrous evasion of the Truth, began to prod Pringle in the belly, laughing madly.

'Ha ha,' said Pringle, his own mirth dry.

I noticed that as they spoke they were both of them battering a blackberry bush into a pulp. Now they sighed together and moved on from the appalling mess they had caused to the next bush.

There came another hideous breath of wind straight from the North Sea, bringing with it half a dozen gulls who let themselves be borne limply over the field like dead things.

From a distant corner came regular sounds: Clop, clop, clop. Tom was at work there, the tall dark labourer who, I'd discovered, looked after the horses. It was plain, from a glance he'd given us that morning, that he had nothing so subtle as an open mind about pacifists: and even at this distance I could feel the black warmth of his eye reaching me. 'Those ber-loody conchies,' Tom would certainly be thinking. 'Those – clop – ber – clop – loody – clop – conchies – clop – clop.'

All round was Cold Clapton. The little white upended carton of a church; the line of houses that formed the street; detached a little, Mrs Goss's purple roof, beneath which at this moment Mrs Goss was certainly going through our cases; and the trees that lay away, lean and leafless, from the wind. How, I wondered, could anyone have decided to live there? So close to the marshes, on this flat, aching peninsula that was only an inch or so above the sea? And who, having settled there, had kept so calm as to be able to call the place only Cold Clapton, instead of Bloody Cold Clapton?

I pulled myself out of my trance and turned and aimed a blow at a bush. The point of the sickle hit the ground and stuck there. A branch, set dancing by the blow, whipped my wrist. I pulled the sickle out of the ground and this time held the branch and managed to slice it off. Then I saw Bert's heavy feet only a few yards away.

'Hi, mate,' Bert sighed as he came. 'Keep low on they bushes, won't 'ee?'

He stopped, so thoroughly and heavily that it seemed he would never be able to start again. There was a long pause while I banged away at the bush.

Bert sighed. 'Yer cackhanded,' he said. And then: 'What's that chap doing?'

I took this as a cue for relaxation: looked up and followed Bert's gaze. Oliver and Pringle had not noticed the foreman's approach. Oliver was gesturing with his long slasher. Whatever point he was making seemed to need energetic physical underlining, and the blade of the slasher whizzed round close to Pringle's face.

' 'Ave the other chap's nose off afore 'e knows what,' said Bert.

Heavily he moved off, towards the unwary Oliver. Again he heavily halted. They still did not see him, and now Oliver's slasher made a most remarkable sally in the air, ending with a downward sweep that endangered Bert's knees. This brought Oliver's eyes round, and he saw Bert. There was a moment of lively silence, then: 'Cor damn and blast it,' said Bert. 'What d'you think you're doin', mates?'

The shock in his eye dwindled to perplexity as, at that moment, Billy Grantham went by, on his way to the bonfire, two or three tiny strands of blackberry bush dragging at the tip of a pitchfork.

'Booby-o-doop, booby-o-doopidy-doop,' Billy was musing, sadly.

It didn't take long for our degrees of promise as agriculturalists to emerge.

The four of us from Mrs Goss's bungalow gave Bert no cause for hope whatever. It must be said that this was partly because we were involved in the psychological shock of finding ourselves in Mrs Goss's clutches. She fed us badly, and to take with us into the fields she gave us each, every day, a little packet containing two sandwiches of a vague sort of meat savaged by her homemade mustard pickle. It is possible that before it went mouldy this pickle was not very wonderful: now the mist of green corruption that covered it put it outside the pale even of our great hunger, and we had a sad burying every midday.

For the rest, we caused Bert, somewhere deep in the barrel of his body, amazement.

There was the morning we were set to dig our first ditch and Bert came along and found that I had made my section curve to bypass the stump of a young tree. I was rather proud of this curve, which I thought beautiful, but I could tell from the heavings of Bert's frame that something was amiss, and at last he whispered, 'You dig that tree out, mister, and make 'n straight. Make 'n straight, mister. 'T'nt a bloody circus.' I looked at him helplessly and then at the stump, which I vaguely imagined to be removable only by explosive, and said: 'What! That, Bert?' For answer he gave me a glinting look and seized a mattock that stood nearby and struck the stump a huge easy blow that half-severed it. "T'nt a bloody circus,' he said.

Some of us were far more capable, and were soon promoted to lordlier tasks, and were known to Bert by their Christian names: or, were these too highflown, by names invented by himself.

The most successful of us all was the tall young man who'd spoken to us on the afternoon of our arrival. He was an artist, who had refused to fight, he said, simply because he preferred to paint. He was clearly not to be with us long, and friends were already at work arranging his transfer to a private farm; but while he was with us he gave us an air of distinction. He was quite the most sophisticated of us, and his habit of regarding the visible world as the raw material of art gave an unlooked-for glamour to Goodacres Farm. In those early days, when it seemed to us largely a sheet of flat green world, almost under the sea, bound into place only by its thousands of blackberry and blackthorn bushes, and drifted over by sad gulls or wild duck honking their impatience to be gone, it was a warmth and excitement to be shown that here were also, caught in the frame of Richard's eye, pictures: an oak strewing its pattern of branches above a ditch, a group of buildings so mossed over that they were halfway to being trees like the poplars that stood behind them and made the accents within his frame that Richard was seeking. But it wasn't just this: he was also so attractive a person that Bert, and George, the fatter farmhand, and even Tom the horseman, and the landgirls and the gaitered officials of the War Ag, courted his company and enjoyed his jokes and failed to think of him as a conchie: and we all benefited by this. Richard had charm, and it's fair to say that he was also well-off, and had a negligent ease that came from being well-off: and we were a herd of rather mangy and dubious mixed animals who happened to have a splendid lion among them, and so for a while were treated almost as if they were all lions.

Alas, he turned himself into a hedger and ditcher with no difficulty at all, and Bert had never to call him cackhanded. So that Richard was often on his own, or with one or two nearly as efficient as himself, and they were often a long way off, cutting bushes down in a tremendously neat way while we bashed and smashed in a huddle of the unpromising...

It was all thorns and icy water. We cleared the fields, and reduced the hedges to the simplicity of wounded stumps. We dug new ditches, and began to find some moments good: when, for instance, sections of a ditch were joined, and the dammned-up water began to sing down it. It was, I thought, like an enormous piece of spring-cleaning: slowly we stripped the surface of the farm of its old congestions, and the face of one field after another was ready for the plough, freed of bogs. The thin colour of the east coast sky reached down where there had been hedges, down to the new wet bareness we had made.

But it was, in fact, *winter*-cleaning. In the mornings I woke with fingers crooked in the shape they'd taken round the bagging-hook or spade the day before. The icy water entered my bones, and when Oliver and I went on Saturday evenings to the cinema at Maltford, five miles away, my whole skeleton would ache. I could feel the ice in every bone, a pain ready to shape itself to every posture, standing or sitting.

We were an odd rabble of men. There were the cussed adherents of strange varieties of puritanism: Christadelphians, Plymouth Brethren, Elimites, Particular People. Some of these were not so much pacifists as (I uneasily felt) complacent spectators of what they took to be Armageddon. The Bible, as they read it, gave a better blow-by-blow account of the war than any newspaper. It had been bound to happen: the devil, with his course mapped out for him, had invented Hitler, sparing time to invent Stalin also: he was now engaged in nudging the armies in such directions as would ensure that the final holocaust occurred in the places prescribed for it. When it was all over, I gathered, there might well be some sort of rapture in which all these colleagues of mine would rise, glowing, out of the ditches, leaving the rest of us —

'Leaving the rest of us doing – what?' I once asked Oliver.

But Oliver gave one of his Biblical answers – such a web of textual references, and gabbled glosses on each of these, that I was left feeling hopelessly uninformed.

In bed, night after night under Mrs Goss's purple roof, Oliver had begun to struggle for my soul. For a while, having heard him in argument, I had tried to keep the full measure of my paganism from him. I knew no rational means of answering assertions that were made on the basis of crazy cryptograms and odd little fervours springing from the discovery of quite outrageous meanings in the simpler – usually, indeed, the duller – verses of the Bible. In argument Oliver had habits that I knew would quickly drive me to the edge of hysteria, if ever I was at the receiving end of them. 'Ah,' he would say, after someone had opposed one of his declarations; 'Ah' – a sound full of impatient pity. It was like the warning growl of a dog that has its teeth in a bone. 'Hmm, yes. Of course, that isn't true at all. Mmm, you see —' And then he would proceed, very fast, with some grotesque assertion that made me want, as a mere bystander, to dance on the spot with vexation. Trying to argue with Oliver was like trying to enter a door held open invitingly by a man with his foot wedged in it. No little disputative push of your own was ever going to get you anywhere.

But my own brand of would-be rational open-mindedness was revealed a score of times a day in the long talk that made our labours tolerable: and Oliver must have sensed that he had serious work to do from the moment we met. He held his tongue for an ominously long time, and I had now and then a panic-stricken certainty that something was going on that was on the scale of preparation for battle. He was mobilizing – I was sure of it. The great guns of his texts were being rolled into position. At any moment now he would fire the first shot.

It seemed unfair to wait till we were in bed. My need of sleep was a lust. But suddenly one night Oliver said: 'The devil is near the end of his reign.'

I was already in a coma, and imagined he was talking about Wilkins, the War Ag's labour officer, whose appearance in the fields was always the cue for a quarrel. For Wilkins, the correct attitude of a labour officer was one of perpetual rage. He was aimlessly angry with us, and since, in these strange circumstances, we were perfectly ready to be tetchy ourselves, little disputes would break out, at the mere sight of him, that were, as often as not, wholly irrational. We simply responded suitably to his obvious ill-will.

So out of my half-sleep I murmured: 'You think he'll get the sack?'

'One thousand years was the term chosen,' Oliver continued, remorselessly. 'The text is very clear about that. Let me tell you about it. If you read ...'

Taking this reference to a millennium as the cornerstone of my sleepy reasoning, I decided he was not referring to Wilkins. I listened to the long exposition, which Oliver delivered in a remarkably uninterruptable fashion. The bone was between his teeth and he worried it ferociously, there in the slightly damp darkness of Mrs Goss's bungalow. 'So you see,' he concluded. 'There can't be any doubt about it.'

'Oliver,' I said, 'I intend to go to sleep, but I might as well tell you that I have the very gravest doubt about it.'

I'm not sure if Oliver had ever been trained in conducting conversions while sharing a double bed: if not, then he had a natural talent for it. He stirred sharply, so that the sheets whipped in the air and slid away from me. Then he twitched, with elaboration, and began again.

This second exposition approached the curious thesis – I was never very sure what that was, except that the logic of it was that I ought to attend Oliver's church – from what I miserably supposed might be a new angle. Some of the texts seemed unfamiliar. There was an increased freedom in the way he dealt with historical events. As I was to discover from Oliver and others among us who shared his views (though sharing them was not incompatible with their belonging to severely antagonistic religious bodies), the events of history had largely taken place in order to provide, as it were, a coded message for the believer. In such and such a year, such and such an event had occurred purely so that, taken in conjunction with this other event in this other year, the mysterious communication might be assembled – ultimately to be passed on to me, in what was clearly a definitive form, under that purple roof in Cold Clapton.

I badly wanted to mutter 'Twaddle!' or 'Superstitious

balderdash!' But somehow it wasn't possible to address Oliver in such terms. On this nonsense his whole life was erected. I had to suppress my yawns, my irritation, and stammer into the sheets:

'But Oliver ... even if it were true, and I must say I — I missed whatever proof you were offering ... even if it were all true, to discover that the world was constructed on a basis so *absurd* ... !'

Oliver grew stiff beside me and I remembered that he must believe it was the devil speaking through my lips. He believed he was in bed with someone devil-possessed. That was frantically annoying.

'Oh, look here, Oliver,' I groaned. 'I simply couldn't ... I couldn't accept an outlook that took such a poor view of the vast majority of us and —'

And, I wanted to say but saw that I mustn't — *and* brought the whole story to an end in a very tiny, dreary heaven filled with Particular People and Exclusive Brethren and Christadelphians, all textually rather cross with one another.

Oliver began again, and I had the odd impression that, horizontal though he was, he was clerically garbed — fully dressed for the pulpit, as he lay there gabbling in the night — and was clutching the corners of a lectern which ... which, certainly, I could feel pressing into my aching spine ...

I had time to tell myself that it was his knee I could feel, and to work out a theory that a preacher who, erect, might have his arms akimbo would, if recumbent, have his *knees* akimbo ... and then I fell asleep.

War had emptied the peninsula of everything but thorns and icy water, us and soldiers ... The soldiers dug huger ditches, in the form of tank-traps. Night came quickly, always, suddenly a shivering dimness in the afternoon, and complete dark by the time we put our tools away. It was through a black five miles that Oliver and I walked to the cinema, there and back. But often the blackness, on our way home, was broken by the melodrama of searchlights, aeroplanes, guns; and the frozen night of the country road and the fields was fringed with violence.

We discovered that Bert Trott was recently married. It had been late in life for him, and she was young, a plump girl like a gypsy. Bert never talked much, but about marriage he was always ready to talk. To make him happy you must give him an opportunity to say, 'Want to git yerself a wife.'

'Marriage is all right, then, Bert?'

'Ain't married, Ol'ver?'

'Haven't got round to it yet, Bert.'

'Ah. *Want to git yerself a wife*. Nothin' like 'un.'

'How d'you mean, Bert?'

And a shy gleam in Bert's eye. Scuffle of his heavy boot in the mud. Perhaps a wild swing of the stick in his hand.

'Warm. Soft. Merry thing. Wife's a merry thing. Want to git yerself one, Ol'ver.'

In all that ice, among all those thorns, Bert's shy intense delight in marriage was something to warm yourself by. Though, as the long aching days crept by, it was the moment of rest that was valued, to be gained always by provoking him into grunting out his hints of astonished pleasure. And best of all when the discussion took place round the bonfire, in the roaring redness and thick smoke: with the gulls blown over, and Bert gleaming, suggesting such merry things with his swinging stick.

2

The war grew enormous, all round us, and my sense of uncertainty with it. What was I doing in this freezing backwater, among lunatic puritans – in this very odd margin of a war?

George was on leave, disguised as a sailor. We met on one of my weekends at home. I was amazed that the Admiralty should have had the nerve to dress my old friend, that sardonic revolutionary of the sixth form, in a sailor suit. I felt an absurd need not to appear to be noticing those bell-bottom trousers, the collar round his neck that the children reached up to touch for luck when we went walking.

'I hope I'll get a destroyer,' George said. 'The Atlantic run. Might as well see some action, don't you think?'

'Hardly decent for me to have an opinion on that?'

'Oh come,' said George. 'As if we didn't know of your gallant engagement with blackberry bushes.'

He thought the real fight would come after the war. *This* war was only a prelude to *that* one. The British Empire would hardly survive such a drain on its ill-gotten resources. And who knew what disorders would come out of its disruption?

'Meanwhile,' said George, 'I learn to do without. I learn to live in a space about six foot by two. I'm cutting life down to the bone. That will help, afterwards – don't you think?'

To my dismay, he was now in favour of love. Or rather, of erotic pleasure. 'Met a girl you'd like. Middle-class – daddy's a senior civil servant. Rather an obvious trap, you might think. Deanna Durbinish. Angora jerseys – you know the sort of thing. Taught me to dance.'

I felt suddenly ready to confess to my own past, in this line. 'I once knew a girl who —'

'Took me home to meet her parents. It helps, don't you think, to have a table to get your knees under?'

'The Deanna Durbinish girl?'

'No, no. You're not listening. This other girl. Swedish mother. I suppose I might marry her, or someone like her. What do you think?'

'Marriage? But —'

'If ever I drift in that direction. I suppose you're having a suitably lyrical affair with a landgirl? Tell me about it.'

'No, really —'

'But I think I prefer this girl whose father has a fish-and-chip shop.'

I was in love, as it happened, but quite hopelessly and indeed speechlessly, with Joan Boulting.

She was the slimmer of the landgirls I'd met that first day : dark, with a boyish figure, and she wore her hair in a little cupola of a bun that seemed to me the most exquisite possible arrangement of hair. It heightened her beauty for me that she never wore Land Army breeches, which were all corduroy bum, but brown linen jeans. She was neat, a lively little parcel of a girl, and when I saw her mounted on one of the Goodacres tractors I trembled to think that anything so powerful should be in the charge of anyone so slight. At the same time I admired the wiriness that made her so – as it seemed to me – daring a driver. She always appeared to be heading straight for ditches and turning at the last moment. When she had finished work in a field and was racing in a straight line for the farm buildings, I thrilled at the speed and determination of her passage. It struck me from time to time that I was rather near to wishing myself a Fordson tractor.

But an innate gaucherie, broken down by Jean Hopkins in a brazen and obstinate seige, had returned, with doubled effects of dumbness and self-doubt, when my first affair ended. So that, whenever Joan Boulting was at hand, I fell into a desperate silence, and with agony envied those who could speak freely to her and even make her laugh. Especially I envied Jim Mace. He was a War Ag mechanic, whose real love was reserved for machines; he was celebrated – and, by his superiors, often cursed – for taking them apart when they were in perfect order. His hands were always oily, and that played a surprisingly large part in the rage I felt when I discovered that Joan favoured him. It seemed to me peculiarly important that her suitors should have decent fingernails.

I was spared the sight of them together, but Oliver had seen them sharing their lunchtime sandwiches. 'She talks to him about books,' he said. I laughed coarsely. 'Books! What does he know about books?' Inwardly I bled. Books were *my* subject. I could have provided her with talk, about books, that would have outlasted all the sandwiches in the world. Oliver said: 'I heard him arranging to take her to the pictures on the back of his motorbike.' I flung up my hands and attempted a touch of worldliness. 'The most surprising girls will do anything for a ride on a pillion.'

Then, even more wastefully, her attention turned to Mervyn Root, a Plymouth Brother: and my anguish doubled.

We'd already become, working in ditches, in the dusty hearts of hedges, unbearably conscious of one another's smallest tics and habits. I was struck by the rage they sometimes roused in me. Oliver, for example, had a concern for his appearance that would make him stand, sometimes, his spade leaned against the side of a ditch, scratching away at some tiny speck of clay on his trousers. I would look up, and catch him at it, and the inane rage would consume me: simply an anger at the way each of us, in terms of these tiny habits so dreadfully familiar, insisted on being himself.

But no one caused me so much secret wrath, of this kind, as Mervyn Root. His habits were all derived from a vast complacency. He belonged to the strictest branch of his strict sect, and was therefore opposed to all the gaieties of life: to cinema and theatre, to music and literature. How could *he* talk of books to Joan Boulting? How could *he*, indeed, justify the gleefulnesses – I supposed them to be that – of courting her? Or whatever the phrase was. 'He puts his hand over hers to help her turn the starting handle of her tractor,' Oliver reported. Courting must surely be the word.

Mervyn had a face that was secured against life. I would observe, with fascination, that his mouth was like the slot in the simplest form of moneybox: through it could pass only the smallest and dullest of coins. It was a face that expressed a certain locked-up triumph because there was such a limited world within – and no enlargement of that world was ever going to be permitted. Mervyn delighted, in a most unholy way, in the misadventures of those of us who stumbled about in that wider world, devised by the devil, of relatively free ideas, relatively unconfined experience. He would laugh, a small rationed laugh, when we slipped. He liked to catch us in some predicament, and to shake his head over it, the mouth thinly smiling.

His view on almost any topic was tethered to some pamphlet published by the Plymouth Brethren. You might be talking about trade unionism, and would try to bring Mervyn into the discussion: but he would shake his head, carefully, as if to avoid any dislodgement of small coin, and would say:

'It's against our belief.'
'What? Trade unions?'
'We don't join such things.'
'But why?'

But Mervyn could rarely give the reasons for such a belief. He was an acquiescent but not a studious sectarian. He would offer to show you the relevant pamphlet: 'It's all there.'

'But just let yourself go for a moment. Give us a reason of your own for not joining a trade union.'

The careful, triumphant smile. A sense of extra padlocks having keys turned in them. 'It's against our strict belief.'

But in time one came to see what was at work here. The world was God's achievement. All was as He had meant it to be. To attempt to make it better was to fly in God's face. All social and industrial action, all political effort, all artistic labour, all free thought of any kind was inspired by the devil in his effort to cause dissatisfaction and the evil hope of improvement. 'Better' and 'worse' were words of no meaning.

We were layering a hedge, once, on the frontiers of Goodacres. It was a strange day – a mist of rain all round our rainless centre. I was dragging the cut pieces of hedge to a bonfire near by, of which I was the proud originator and guardian. I knew how to make bonfires, now, beginning with the tiniest tent of dried twigs: laying a slightly larger tent over that, when it was really aflame: and so building up and up, until there was such a roaring heart in the fire that it would burn anything. It had travelled, in the wind that morning, several yards from its first site. I was happy, watching the way the fire would suddenly fly snapping flags of flame from its summit: how, in a gust, a storm of fine ash mixed with sparks would leap into the air. I was thinking of fires good and bad, and was wondering, against all philological probability, whether 'bonfire' could mean 'a good fire'. And then, snatching hastily at a complicated branch of hawthorn that was twisting in the wind, I drove an immense spike deep into my hand. I dropped the branch, cursing, and as I raised my hand to my mouth I caught sight of Mervyn's face: it bore that tiny, locked-up smile of intense satisfaction. He was glad that I'd been hurt.

The strange thing was, as it seemed to me, that, though he rejected all efforts to make the world a better place, he had no objection at all to its being made worse. A view that intensified when he became Joan Boulting's favourite courtier.

I was beginning to think that women had no sense of fitness at all.

32

Had all my fellow-conchies been of Mervyn's stamp, I think I might have run for it. Or even Oliver's. *He*, outside his special religious thinking, was at least a little of the world – of the puzzling, absorbing, tragi-comical real world. But to be wholly in the company of men who, having a monstrously apocalyptic view of things, were able at the same time to lead rather dull private lives – this I could not have borne. I could not understand how, believing in Armageddons and in millennia dominated by the devil, my companions who held these opinions could trudge equably – as most of them did – from day to day: or bother about the running of water in a ditch. Surely if they saw existence in terms of such enormous supernatural melodrama, they ought to match in their daily conduct the raving amazement of their beliefs?

But there were others whose attitudes, like my own, had roots in relatively ordinary kinds of thinking: and some who simply seemed gentle, rather conventionally churchy men – though it was more often chapel than church that bred them.

Pringle was alone in being a lofty, rather recondite Anglican. The ascetic Pringle, absurdly but sometimes touchingly alarmist in his view of our situation – he did so much long for a world of black and white – was hardly the same kind of human being as Alan Fisher, whom you'd have taken at first sight for some particularly agreeable young scoutmaster.

Alan always put me in mind of fruit – there was something sweet and, as it were, edible about him. His hair was thick and corn-coloured, and his bright face was covered with freckles as an apple might be. There were freckles, too, like patches of over-ripeness, on the backs of his big, square hands. He was stocky but quick: with an immensely musical voice. Always he sang – sentimental airs out of the musicals of the 1930s. The light true sound he made gave extraordinary virtue to these songs. In all weathers he wore the brightest of green hats. It was impossible to imagine him constructing political or religious or metaphysical reasons of any subtlety for being a conchie. Nor was it to make any insupportable claim for pacifism to say that it must have been some fundamental, inalienable decency that took him in that direction. It was a particular kind of decency – too good for the world, or too simple for it, perhaps: but it had made him, unfussingly, incapable of going to war. Yet there was certainly nothing holy about him. He had a natural, light wit, like his natural, light tenor voice. He judged people shrewdly; he had that sort of general ability that made him an obvious resort whenever a practical problem arose. And talking one day of situations that would call for supreme courage – we were thinking of the man who in a submarine that had sunk would be the one who could not escape, because he would operate the escape hatch for the last but one and so would have nobody to operate it for him – we suddenly knew that there was among us one person of whom we were certain he would show just this courage. And Alan would not only have insisted on being the last man, but he would have done it with such unfussing, sensible charm that he would have overcome every objection. It was odd for a group of conchies to divine that they had among them an example of that very rare class of human beings, the natural heroes.

Alan's landlady was Mrs Rollings, who lived up the hill, in the next village, where you looked down into a narrow cold river imprisoned between shoals of mud. She drove Alan nearly mad, for though she was the kindest of women, and didn't know what a conchie was, she had for her solitary lodger an ideal of regularity that not a saint could have lived up to.

Once, when she had asked Alan to be home at 12.30 for Saturday lunch, he arrived at 12.29, and she cried: 'Oh, I can't have this! It's impossible! If you're going to play fast and loose with time like this...!' Alan's dismay was great at finding this most amiable of women unendurable. 'I'll go out of my mind...' he'd cry. He would come down to Mrs Goss's to escape, and sit for a while, speechless, struggling with his fury over the gossamer exasperations that Mrs Rollings caused within him. For as a subdivion of this one strict intellectual conviction of hers, that no one ought ever to be less punctual than the very clock, she insisted that nothing in her house should ever, once having been touched, be replaced in anything but obsolutely the same position, to a millimetre.

Alan came into Mrs Goss's late one evening, tossed down his green hat, and groaned: 'I knocked a vase on the mantelpiece half a degree out of true with my elbow, without even noticing it! And the fury! Oh, that woman! "I can't have people kicking my best vase all over the living room," she said. As if I'd jumped up on the mantelpiece and played football with it.'

All her everyday kindliness, all her bumbling fondness for him, couldn't make Mrs Rollings tolerable to Alan. He hadn't the heart to seek a change of lodgings. It was an unexpected situation – the pleasantest man among us being tormented beyond all bearing by one of the nicest old ladies in the east of England.

The winter turned, leaf by leaf, into a spring at first hesitant and then – one morning, as it were – full of a bright green confidence. It was painful to watch the soft shadows of trees blown across the fields as we worked, and to know that spring, now, meant only offensives: that it lit up the world for brisker sorts of carnage . . .

It had been the wickedest winter I'd ever known: in many ways, the first I'd ever *really* known. It remains in my memory now in terms of that sharp icy ache in every fibre: of my self-doubts, sharpened by contact with the shaky or (as it seemed to me) simply monstrous nature of the opinions of many among whom I found myself working. But always, as I tried to straighten out my own thoughts, I came to this belief – an innocent belief, George had called it – that I must not kill. Oh, surely you could kill in the most indirect ways: the chain of events you set going by standing in a ditch might result somewhere, far off, in a killing? But, struggling with a problem too big for me, still so strongly charged with those young revulsions, I clung to the step I'd taken.

And exhaustion helped: helped, that is, to bring the tangled thinking to rest. Because what I also remember is the way we were swept through that winter, first through the wilderness of Goodacres, and then – as that grew more trim – to other farms around, in villages that all seemed to have names like Sharp Midwinter: and there, too, we rooted up trees and hedges, and burnt the huge tangles of shrub and bush across the breast of many a cold field, in the bitter light of that long season. I spent many weekends in Cold Clapton – often alone, the others having returned to

35

their homes – and the melancholy of the place struck into my soul. It was submerged, so much of that low-lying wing of England, thrust into the North Sea – it was submerged under winter water, cold streaks and pools of it in all directions: and on such hills or small rises as there were, you'd stand and see everywhere the villages, rheumatic clusters of cottages, and the damp towers of little churches.

The people were secret souls. There was Bill, for example, who worked on a distant farm, and came some evenings to tend Mrs Goss's garden. He'd brought up the larger part of his family – seven sons, three daughters – on ten shillings a week. His youngest was eight, a thin cheerful child who seemed to spend much of his life perched on the carrier of his father's bicycle. 'My little old boy', Bill called him. Bill talked of time in terms of moons. 'That was when my little old boy broke his arm – seven moons ago, it 'ud be.' Meeting you, Bill would beam with a strange effect of sadness. I never knew anyone smile more broadly and create so melancholy an impression by doing so. 'Ah – it's goin' to clear up – I reckon. Be no more rain this week. Wee bit o' sun, even, if we'm lucky.' He'd beam. And you'd struggle with a great desire to weep.

Bill can't have been more than fifty, but he was already bent. So much of his life had been spent hoeing, reaping – bending in a field, in his allotment, in other people's gardens. He moved always like someone measuring out his effort: it was impossible to imagine him moving swiftly, impulsively. But then we'd noticed that those who'd laboured all their lives on the land had this characteristic of careful deliberation. With all your life to go, without let-up, you had to adopt a methodical, rhythmic pace, and keep it up, in everything you did. So, later, I'd see old men hoeing – their backs bent from beginning to end of the day, not spoiling the rhythm with talk, with more than the occasional stretching of the limbs: slowly, steadily, working through the day, bent, because there were all those other days to come, and all those other days behind. We, newcomers to the land, wore ourselves out with the bored irregularity and the fits and starts of our effort. Even our groans were an added exhaustion. When the old men looked disapprovingly at us, it wasn't, I think, because we were conchies: it was because we brought such heresies of working habit to the fields. I noticed that even when they pissed, they didn't leave their jobs – didn't, like us, hurry to a hedge. They stood where they were and performed – often with girls present – in perfect decency: making little hoods for themselves with their hands ...

One day, we heard that Bill was in hospital. He had blood poisoning. Oh, he would recover. With so many dependent on him, he could not do otherwise. 'The old fool,' said Mrs Goss. 'He's such an old fool ... Do you know what he did? They're so ignorant ... He chopped his thumb off with a billhook. That was last week. But nobody knew. He wrapped it up in a rag and made sure no one noticed. Old fool! And do you know what he did with his thumb? He *buried* it! They're ignorant *and* superstitious. Otherwise the evil spirits would get it, or something. If you cut a bit off yourself, you have to bury it. Have you heard anything like it? And then, of course, he collapsed. He just collapsed at work!'

Mrs Goss's delight was great at having such a disaster to report, and especially one that demonstrated such ignorance *and* superstition.

'Had to race him off to hospital,' she told us, happily. 'Got him there only just in time.'

We were busy still, on Goodacres and beyond it, in this suddenly shining world – making new ditches: or remaking old ones. I was amazed anew by what we were doing to landscape that, all my life, had been familiar only in its decadent form. The wild fat hedges, running alongside those faint dips that I now knew had once been ditches – these had been the typical background of picnics, of long boyish strollings. Now we'd razed the hedges to the ground. In their place were the lines of stumps, white from the axe or the saw. The light spilled, and the air raced, where for fifty years or more they'd had no place. The farm was striped for action. And now we were completing the work of draining the water from it.

I loved the ditching. We'd be strung out along the side of a field, one pair worked towards the next: a man digging, another shovelling up. You stood in stale water. The clay came up easily, one spit and then back for the next: two spits wide, three spits wide. The clay was a clean orange in colour. The new banks we were making were bright with it. Down you went, deeper and deeper, caring for the angle of the walls as you dropped. The water rose. When two sections were joined, then the water began to run, making little singing sounds, forming tiny eddies where it met with some unevenness on the bottom. I was desperately against unevennesses, on walls or bottom. I carved and sliced away with an unnecessary thoroughness. And then came the moment when the whole ditch was working – a moment always of great joy – along its length. For then suddenly the whole run of water would begin racing – would pour, at first, fiercely along the new channel, becoming cleaner and cleaner, until it had settled down to what it should be: a low unbroken flow. It was the best of plumbing.

Bert Trott moved among us, slow and heavy, growing happier with the growth of the spring and with the discovery that, as farm hands, we were not so grotesque as he'd feared. His jokes remained, all the same, variations in the main on his astonishment at our cack-handedness. We were like self-taught musicians who had never learned to hold their instruments correctly. It was impossible that, holding a spade or a shovel thus or thus, we should dig at all. Yet it was done. You'd look up and see Bert enjoying his own incredulity. And when a joke came ('No wonder you an't married, Ol'ver, ef you 'oud a woman like you 'oud a spade') it was never accompanied by anything so free or swift as a laugh, though sometimes by a smile that took so long to develop it always disappeared before it was complete.

We felt a complicity, now, between us and Bert as against the War Ag officials who came spritely into the fields. Bert would groan when he saw one of these approaching, brisk in his breeches, his jacket split at the back, the usual porkpie hat.

'Trouble, Bert?' one of us would hint.

Bert would roll his eyes, and slowly heave himself in the direction of this agricultural bureaucrat. As often as not it was Wilkins, the labour officer. Wilkins would bring irritable little problems connected with timesheets, with pay packets, with inquiries about whole missing teams of workers. Bert had no love for all this. He would frown in the sun, ready for the effort of understanding this ill-tempered man, who confused the programme of practical work in the fields by trying to make it match with dossiers, plans, minutes written in the office. Bert took a simple view of War Ag officials. They were all failed farmers, or opportunists with dubiously relevant backgrounds who had wormed their way into their indefensible jobs. And there was in them an anxiety to be punitive that irritated him. They wanted to achieve an uncomfortable discipline: they felt it necessary to receive, and to deal with, complaints about their motley employees.

'They all working well then, Trott?'

Bert would fidget under the question. Then he'd run his eye along the ditch, from man to man, as if half-inclined to make some comment on our versatility as to cack-handedness. But Wilkins would not understand that sort of joke. So Bert would grunt and say:

'They'll do.'

'Him?' Wilkins would point perhaps to Oliver, who'd be leaning on his spade, listening, grinning. Oliver had a great affection for Bert, and expected much from these colloquies between our foreman, so simple and direct, and the labyrinthine official.

'He'll do.'

Wilkins baffled. 'Well, Trott, you do know – any man whose work doesn't satisfy you – don't hesitate. We have all the powers we need to sharpen him up.'

Bert would stand and allow such a speech to circulate through his great bulk, as if testing it there for relevance, good sense or merely for meaning: then you had the strong impression that, somehow, he expelled it completely, rid himself utterly of it.

'Ah,' he'd say.

There were other officials – drainage experts, who worried Bert no end with their habit of making a mid-field conference of something that was a matter of farming instinct: such as the slope required on a ditch to ensure its fair running. Equipment officers came: experts in ploughing, in the maintenance of tractors, in the use of fertilizers and pesticides. There were days when Bert was summoned to what looked like board meetings, in the centre of a field. He came back from these, always, short of temper. ' 'Oud that bloody spade straight, Ol'ver!' It was anger, really, at the invasion of his world by men clutching papers ('More bloody papers,' he'd say, as one of the little vans hurried importantly up the chase), at the general air of politics the officials of the War Ag brought into the fields. There was a fierce rivalry of officers and officials: there were matters it was improper to discuss with one because they should have been discussed with another. 'They think I'm a bloody clerk,' said Bert, and then almost completed a smile at the idea of it.

They pestered – that was another word of his. The whole village was pestered with papers, plans, orders, tetchy points of protocol. If it wasn't the War Ag, then it was the Army.

The Army was busy digging an immense tank trap on the edge of Goodacres. This, from time to time, brought officers into the field, carrying papers. It also brought us, now and then, face to face with angry soldiers.

They'd plant themselves squarely in front of us and address us in perfectly square terms. We were yellow-bellies, weren't we? Wouldn't we like to admit that? What were we frightened of? We *were* frightened, weren't we? Perhaps we'd like to confess to that, too, before we parted?

I never knew what to answer. They said what they had to say, and there was no hope of a dialogue. I could only shrug, smile. 'It's not quite as simple as all that...'

I thought of photos of my father, taken during the First World War. He had looked like this – so young, so fit, so bronzed: driven by the masculine ebullience – oddly, by the masculine boredom – of soldiering. He had stood with legs apart, like this – and the huge obscenity of the battlefield was waiting, as it was for these young men in the Essex lanes and fields.

I had no inclination to quarrel with them, about the elaborate backgrounds of experience that had led them one way, us another. Pity for us all – that seemed the only reasonable attitude. So much angry talk revolved around that phrase about turning the other cheek: and did the phrase spring from any belief but that one could have no certainty of conviction on which to found a quarrel? And I did not see how any of us could stretch his mind over the whole huge problem and be sure that he had come up with an answer of any real adequacy.

So I would stand in the midst of the angry, contemptuous

young soldiers, feeling this philosophical modesty that was too complex to be discussed in such circumstances, where it was all jeers expecting counter-jeers: and there'd be, perhaps, some barging with shoulders – the first step in what, at other times, might have become the beating and stoning of the outsider – and then they would go their way, their cries of derision turning even as they went into the jesting uproar that was normal to them, the noisy amusement with which they filled the long boredom of military life.

3

In the late spring, we sowed the Goodacres fields. We did this by hand, in the old fashion, scattering the seed as we swung in arcs, this way, that way. It was like dancing. We followed this up with a sowing of arsenic, to kill the leather-jackets. Bert Trott was impressed by an official, for the first and only time: the man told him there were fifty million leather-jackets on Goodacres. Bert seemed to conclude that a strict count had taken place. 'You wouldn't think there was room,' he said, staring across the farm as if he were trying to spy the village over the jostling heads of fifty million doomed crane-flies.

The sun bloomed everywhere: spring became full summer without changing gear. Farming began to fill with pleasures. We piled on to trailers and went here and there to cock up the cut hay. Inspired by his dislike of Wilkins, who wished us to be caused the greatest possible inconvenience, Bert insisted that we be driven about in this way, even when small distances were involved. 'Short ride's better'n long walk,' as he put it. The days spent among the sweet smells of the hay seemed designed as some sort of reward for the wounding winter. We left field after field like primitive townships, strewn with the rounded huts of the hay. At one farm we were presented with an unusual objec-

tion to our pacifism. The farmer, a woman, was a spiritual-
ist, and she seemed to argue that the war was some kind of
huge and happy recruitment on behalf of the other world.
Since it was best to be dead, nothing but good could be said
of a war: and a vast war was better than a small one. We
needed the smell of her hay after talking to her ...

George came home one weekend and talked angrily
about the distribution of space in a destroyer as between
officers and men. He was very tired. We went to hear a
concert. George was dismayed to discover that it would be
chamber music.

'I have a crude ear,' he said. 'I like something large and
noisy. I don't qualify as an eighteenth-century gentleman,
would you say?'

I glanced at his ocean-reddened face and assured him
that he didn't. 'Your point is —?'

'Haydn,' said George, stifling a yawn. The members of
the quartet took their places on the stage of what, during
the week, was a cinema. I looked at them, there in the pool
of light as the other lights were dimmed. Four men, the
glowing instruments, there in this quietening building, on
the fringe of a city tormented by war. It was a long way
from my fields, from George's dangerous sea.

'Of course,' said George drowsily. 'I listen to these things
as a philistine fighting a tendency to go to sleep.'

The first small, orderly statement from the stage. I
thought how scarcely bearable some contrasts had become.
The intelligence of music, especially, was so often, as you
began to listen during those years, almost something that
could not be endured, in the context of murderous folly
provided by the war.

George was already asleep – made unconscious, not by
Haydn, but by the long nights as a signalman on the bridge
of his destroyer ...

Now came weeks of hoeing. The peninsula suddenly
seemed to be covered with millions of sugar beet, and we
hoed them all, bent day after bent day. The sun beat down
and we knew a fresh dimension of boredom. 'If only,' said
Oliver, 'they didn't all look the same.' The similarity of one
beet plant to another was certainly difficult to bear.

There arrived among us an elderly Londoner who, having
retired, had decided to seek a new and rural lease of life,

and had been taken on as a general labourer by the War Ag, with promise of elevation to the post of hostel warden when a vacancy occurred. Through Sid's eyes we saw agriculture afresh. It amazed him beyond words. He'd always longed for a garden, he said – the longing had lain behind his decision to come into the country – and now here it was, the huge garden of Goodacres and of the whole peninsula beyond, and he was dismayed by it. 'Goes on and on, don't it?' he'd say, as we bent to the hoeing of the sugar beet. 'Goes bloody on and on.' He'd stare round at the flat immensity of Essex. 'I'd thought of little fields, really.' He struggled to tell us how little the fields had been, in his imagination. 'Much more like gardening.'

'With flowers?' someone asked once, and Sid looked caught. Of course he'd known it would be corn and sugar beet and potatoes, and not flowers: and yet...

But the real blow was that he actually had a garden, now, the wild, overgrown stretch of long grass and forgotten flower beds that lay at the back of the decrepit cottage the War Ag had found for him. Being rather the opportunity for a garden than a garden in healthy being, this had disappointed Sid from the beginning; he had not thought of the digging and weeding and planning that would be needed to make anything of this patch. His dream of a garden had been of an instant one. 'I thought I'd just be pottering,' he'd sigh, as we ached our way along the tedious rows. But the disillusionment had been worse even than this: for Sid had trouble with what he called 'my shit'.

The plumbing in the cottage was primitive. There was not even a cesspool. His waste he must bury, and the only place for it was his garden. The problem was that he had more waste than, before he had this involuntary opportunity of measuring it, he'd ever dreamed that he produced. He was opening up his ground, and hurriedly closing it, at an alarming rate.

'I'm awfully worried about my shit,' he'd groan, day after day. 'I'll 'ave to get the War Ag to do something about it. Who'd you think I ought to talk to?'

We tried to decide to which of the dapper officials who came to glare at us at work such an application might be addressed. There was none into whose department it seemed naturally to fall. 'I daresay there's a form to fill in,' someone said heartlessly. 'That's not what I need forms for,' said Sid, gloomily. He was now convinced that he was given to producing waste on a quite abnormal scale, and that he needed amenities to match.

An attempt to solve Sid's problem was one of the uses of an odd activity we embarked upon one evening at Mrs Goss's. Billy Grantham had come back after a weekend at home with news of a curious game he'd played. But not a game really, he urged. It was both simple and queer. You needed a tumbler, and the letters of the alphabet, each on a separate piece of paper. You placed these pieces of paper round the edge of a table – in a circle. The tumbler should stand upside down in the middle. Then you all sat round and each laid a finger on the tumbler. You asked a question – any question – and lo and behold, the tumbler would begin moving about the table, from letter to letter, spelling out an answer.

'I don't want any gambling,' said Mrs Goss, having half-listened.

Mrs Goss was always ready to nip in the bud anything any of us should propose might be done. It was clear that she'd come under sharp fire from some quarters in the village for taking us in. She tried to make up for that by watching us with a fidgetily suspicious eye. We could imagine her saying to her critics: 'But I'm *watching* them, you see – it needs someone to watch them – see they don't get up to anything. They won't find it easy in "Bella Vista".'

We knew now the story of the building of 'Bella Vista' – the bungalow. It accounted for some of Mrs Goss's sourness. Her first husband had left her sole owner of the village store – 'a little goldmine', everybody said. It was soon after she was widowed that Mr Goss appeared upon the scene. According to Mrs Goss's own indignant story, of which we were always hearing fragments, he – himself a widower – had wooed her most romantically. He would leave on her doorstep titbits from his garden: always the largest marrow, the sweetest carrots. He must have been a man of some penetration: for he knew that he must subject Mrs Goss to the humblest of sieges. When he had established quite clearly his sense of his own unworthiness – we imagined him nodding his head happily at the most unreasonable of her opinions – she had allowed him to marry her.

From that moment he had changed. He sold the shop over her head and had the bungalow built. *He* did the shopping – she merely carried the basket. *He* decided what should go into the garden – she did the sowing and weeding. The only slip in his strategy occurred after two years, when he suddenly died of a chill. Mrs Goss had lived ever since in a condition of astonishment, relief and indignation, all of which she expressed freely.

'An awful man,' was what she called him . . .

Billy patiently explained that it was not gambling. Then he patiently explained that it was not black magic. He rashly added that it was not a way of communicating with the enemy. Then he talked his way out of that . . . At last we had the pieces of paper cut out, had obtained a loan of one of Mrs Goss's most dispensable tumblers, with the condition that it must be back in her larder within the hour, and we sat down to try out Billy's non-game. Alan Fisher was with us; and Pringle had agreed to take part – but hesitantly, and when he took his place it was rather as though the Archbishop of Canterbury, fully robed, should have seated himself for a particularly shady seance.

'Honest,' said Billy, as we each laid a finger on the tumbler. 'You ask your questions and the glass moves. I'm telling the truth. You'll see. It moves and spells out the answers.'

'What did you ask it?' asked Alan.

'Well,' said Billy. 'I asked who was the best singer in the world —'

'And it spelled out Bing Crosby,' I said.

'Must have been using a tone-deaf tumbler,' said Alan.

Oliver was impatient. 'Come on,' he said, crossly. 'Let's start. You never know.' This was clearly very much in Oliver's line. It smacked of measuring the Pyramids. He had always believed the truth, the great answers, lay in some such psychic eccentricity as this. 'Come on.'

'You may laugh,' said Billy. 'But it was right about Bing Crosby.'

'But we need a question,' said Alan, reasonably.

I thought Oliver might succumb to apoplexy. You could see that he was trying to formulate a single, apocalyptic query which, being answered, as there was every chance the tumbler would answer it, would alter everything, at once.

Here, in the sitting room of 'Bella Vista', the world would turn a corner. But it didn't seem that Oliver could hit upon this prodigious question.

Alan caught my eye. 'This *is* the twentieth century!' he murmured. 'Well, let's make practical use of this informative tumbler. Let's ask it what should be done with Sid's —'

He shot an eye in Mrs Goss's direction.

'– with Sid's special problem.'

Oliver groaned. This was not the road to the reign of all the saints.

'Right,' said Billy. 'That'll do to begin with.' He addressed the tumbler in a thunderous voice – evidently uneasy that, if not tone-deaf, this one might simply be deaf. 'How do we deal with Sid's – ah – problem?'

We let the weight of our fingers register on the tumbler. There was a moment when nothing happened: Oliver tutted, cross and flushed: and then, having presumably computed the general tendency of the pressures we were exerting, the tumbler began to shuffle across the table. At once fingers grew knowing, or flustered, and the tumbler began to skid in one direction and then another. It exhibited at first a clear abhorrence of going decisively towards any of the letters. There was giggling: Oliver called out vague and passionate remonstrances. 'Give it a chance! Give it a chance!' he shouted. Whereupon the tumbler shot towards the letter E: touched it, and made off in a tremendous hurry towards the letter O: then, after marking time again in the middle, collected the letters P, A, M and U. It then fell over, largely because Alan's finger was trembling with amusement. Mrs Goss had left her chair and was staring over our shoulders. 'A dictionary!' Oliver was calling. 'Has anyone got a dictionary?' And Alan said:

'I always knew that's what Sid should have done.'

We tried several other questions, and were answered to much the same effect. Oliver was certain there was a foreign language involved, or perhaps a dead one. 'VXGOWAPL?' Alan inquired. 'Or a code,' Oliver urged.

So Sid's problem went unanswered. As did mine. Alan had suggested: 'Let's ask who loves Ted.' The answer had been: FTOKWLPV. It was no help to me, in a field where I should have been glad of help. I knew no one of that name.

Small jobs. The many small jobs of summer. We cleaned machinery. We carried fertilizer: were whisked, once, in an atmosphere of inexplicable administrative furtiveness, half across the county to paint half a dozen caravans. Then Oliver and I were sent in quite another direction to clean a pond on a huge farm that seemed to belong to no one.

I learned to ride a bicycle. I was riding with Mervyn Root one morning to hoe on a farm in the next village, and our attention was caught by a pair of very charming legs protruding, waveringly and frankly, from a ditch by the side of the road. I allowed Mervyn to dash forward and investigate; by the time I'd shyly arrived – young women the right way up were bad enough, but young women upside down! – he was on good terms with the girl to whom the legs belonged. I thought a Plymouth Brother should have been rather more aloof from the thanks she was showering upon him. It turned out that there were bicycles with fixed wheels: if ever you stopped turning the pedals, the bicycle put its brakes on. The young woman had borrowed her brother's bike, which was of this kind, and had forgotten his warnings. She was confident she would have suffocated but for Mervyn's intervention. He was complacently convinced of this, too.

I rode on, now uneasy about bicycles as well as about girls.

But I loved the rusty bike Bert Trott had found for me, abandoned in one of the Goodacres barns. I loved my dirty clothes – the general grubby raggedness of the labourer. I began to believe that I could never again work indoors, never again dress respectably. I was groaning my way through this year, crying out against my fate every inch of the way, and then bitterly assailing myself for considering my own condition of any importance – or, indeed, a particularly uncomfortable or frustrating one. But, for all the groaning, I found it beautiful, standing day after day, from dawn till near sunset, in the open world: aware, as I'd never been, of every tiny change in the weather. I had acquired the small violent vocabulary of labouring. I swaggered a little, in the queer pride of *being* a labourer.

And then came Goodacres' first wartime harvest.

The harvest astonished me. Here were these fields that in

the dark winter we'd provided with ditches and, by chopping our way through the hedges, with air: and now they were warm and golden with corn. They were our surprising creation. And reaping them – I could not have guessed it would be this way – was like a gala.

There was cropping the headlands first, to make room for the binder. We turned our wondering attention to a new tool: the scythe. 'Blast me,' said Tom the horseman, reduced by the occasion to a rare good humour. 'They'll have all their dam' legs off, way they're going.' I was reminded of a story about Harpo Marx: that he'd been misled in his approach to the harp by a sentimental picture of an angel. Behind our handling of the scythe lay similar pictorial fallacies: we sketched our huge swings, intended to be graceful, that took no account of the inert weight and wilful sway of the long blade. Ideas drawn from golf and cricket also led us astray. Bert lumbered among us, aghast. 'Ye're cack-handed, the bloody lot of yer!' Tom worked up an immense joke. 'Leave 'em, Bert – let 'em make *tripods* of 'emselves.' And we knew that we'd have pleased Tom mightily, earned his utmost gratitude, had we left the headlands littered with pacifist legs. 'Let 'em be, Bert!' he counselled, with the sincerest urgency.

But we mastered the queer art of it, and felled the first thick heaps of corn. And then the binder came, with its clattering sails, and we moved on to other headlands: in one field, deep into the corn, since this was spoiled with thistle; and the same in the field next to it, where a curious eddy of wind had laid low and tangled the tall stalks. Then came stooking-up.

I don't know if it has always been this way: that harvesting has released laughter in those who work at it. Everyone was suddenly happy, taking in his arms these whiskered and intricately whispering sheaves, and propping them together. Even the discomforts were deeply pleasurable – the scratches inflicted by stray straws, the malice of thistles. The sun was warm above us, and a companion warmth came up from the corn, from the bristling soil. And if this flat Essex world was, in winter, a host for wind and water, it was equally receptive in summer to the shining heat: it hardened and cracked around us, a huge and radiant dish of clay.

The landgirls went into shorts, and I was sharply shaken by this view of Joan Boulting's lean brown limbs. There was a sort of immemorial connection between the heaps of corn and the shape of a girl that made the fields, for me, arenas of hopeless desire. All that larking! Over there I would see them – Alan Fisher and Jim Mace and the girls, and such laughter, and such obscure tumblings! Obscure to me, since my prior notion of such activity, drawn from reading, imposed itself upon what actually happened: so that I half-believed splendid rapes were occurring, among those encampments of sheaves. I longed to be part of it.

At one late day's end, in the yard, Joan ran a hand over her shirt, making a face because so many grains of corn and other fragments had worked their way into her clothing. She leaned forward and I saw the small white heaps of her breasts and retreated further into my impotent shyness. Alan said: 'I get rid of them like this,' and rolled up his shirt and let the grains and dust fall from inside it. 'But, he said, 'you can't do that.' Someone said: 'Why not?' And a sense of brilliant provocative extensions of this dialogue passed across my mind, and faded into what I was sure was my weak and even frosty smile.

And then came the carting and the making of stacks. The first stack we built grew to be a vast golden monster, in the Goodacres yard. We ran alongside the carts, sending sheaves twirling up to the loader on our pitchforks, which became more and more expert. Fewer and fewer were the moments when, at the end of such a twirl, we were left with a sheaf absurdly still clinging to the tips of the fork, because we'd speared the string or for some other amateur's reason. The air was thick with flying sheaves, and the loaders ran from side to side, catching, dropping, trampling into place. The carts took shape, like great loaves, sheaf locked with sheaf so that the walls of the load dare grow at increasing angles. To be a loader, when your turn came, was to mount towards heaven: to catch your breath at the outrageous height of the swaying cartful.

Joan called, at a moment when I was up there, as high as a tree: 'Oh, Ted – that will do! Don't risk any more!' And though she was laughing, and the sheaves continued for one or two layers yet to spin up to me, I felt a ridiculous emotion: as if she had expressed some special care for me – as

49

if she had betrayed a concern that till that moment she had been most successful in masking. I strode around my load for a while as if I'd been the most reckless of heroes, defiantly increasing the concern of the little woman who waited for me below, her heart in her mouth. Then I found time to peep down again, expecting to see her merry face turned up and a little secret pallor in it – only to observe that she was barging hips with Alan, each intent on being the hurler of the next sheaf.

But the loveliest moments of all were when carts completed their loads at the same time, and, as we lay on warm beds of sheaves, watching, we saw the tractors and the loaded trailers converge slowly – bumping, swaying – on the opening to the yard. Best of all when they did this at the day's end, in the dusk – a long, pausing encounter, till one lumbered away in the lead. Beyond, at the top of the yellow stack, now higher than the trees around it, tiny men were catching sheaves: with one in a niche halfway up, bisecting the high throw from the cart. Sweating, silent, watching across the cropped fields, we'd lie between the corn and the sky, feeling boundlessly content...

Of that first stack I heard Tom say, he being its chief architect: ''S like the one I built ... many year ago at Summerhill.' I thought it such a perfect proud statement that my last resentment of Tom's hostility died altogether. A man who could say that had a right to indulge himself, when he was not making cornstacks, with distance for conchies.

4

Now that Goodacres was a farm in working order, that had yielded its first wartime crops, much of our work lay outside it, in one place or another on this peninsula that was again cringing under the autumn winds. Oliver and I were sent to work for a farmer called James.

He was a deeply depressed man, this farmer, who always wore a white coat and cloth cap, and was always peppered with a white-and-black bristle. He had some vast, unaccountable but quite unelated detestation of his workmen. Everything filled him with gloom. The very size of his farm, nearly a thousand acres of it, spilling across wet fields to the marshes, where it drowned itself at last in the desolate mud of a creek – the very scope of his empire made him gravely uneasy. 'I can't be watching you,' he'd say, as if we might be nursing some grievance because we were not perpetually spied upon and inspected. 'I'm too busy. Got all this big place to look after.' And he would look away, over the meadows sheeted with glinting water, down to the yachts that stood, in the distant creek, waiting for the war to be over. 'Go and help Willy, Ted.'

Going and helping Willy always meant standing about while Willy tried to start his tractor. He was a tall, silent, dark man, very gentle, who would tut over the machine as if it were some moody woman. 'Hmm,' he'd say, as the raw jangle of the engine died away once more into silence. 'Come on, old girl!' He'd take the plugs out and dry them, tenderly. He'd do coaxing things with oil. 'Old lady's in a bad mood.' I would stand by and say, insincerely: 'Damn' and 'Terrible'. Sometimes he would smile at me, as if he regarded these murmurings of mine as unusual but not unhelpful kinds of engineering. 'We'll get her going,' he'd say, as the morning grew around us.

Such mornings they were! Imitations of spring! To the eye, it was all springtime: light leapt off the water, and ran along the hedges. Only the skin understood that this was a warmth that was diminishing on the earth, not growing. All these autumn days that began so beautifully were moving towards afternoons of frantic chilliness and cloud.

The tractor would respond at last, and Willy would smile at it forgivingly as he let the engine run at full pelt, and the rough anger of the sound went roaring into the North Sea. 'It's been cold for her all night,' he'd say, deeply compassionate. And then we'd go seed-drilling, in fields that felt infinitely lonely at the creek's edge.

I'd stand on the drill, making sure the seed flowed freely. It filled the long box that made the drill look rather like a

51

perambulant chest of drawers, and it ran, with an endless hiss and rustle, out through pipes into the ground. A slight dampness or a stray bit of straw, and there'd be clogging: I had to see this didn't happen.

The seeds themselves bewitched me. Each so tiny, delicate – pinched, like microscopic peaches. Pinched, as a woman is between her thighs. In their dancing heaps, as they joined the eddies above the pipes, they displayed, so briefly you hardly believed what you saw, an extraordinary range of colour: brown, gold, green, blue, purple, scarlet. They bubbled and argued as they were drawn to the point of their disappearance; and because, at this time of destruction, they were symptoms of life – tiny particles of creation – I felt strangely moved by that sound: by the endless rustle of what so soon would be standing corn.

Over there – the basin of mud reticulated with water ... The light was so clear that it made a minute pit of radiance in each of the little hoofmarks left by James's wandering heifers. Old posts leaned out of the mud, this way and that, making crosses with their own shadows. And the birds passed over, going away, in a lovely confusion of movement. There was a secret rhythm, it always seemed, in their blown and wheeling and scattering manoeuvres; they'd die, thousands of them, in a moment of windlessness, and then rise and cohere in the encouragement of the next gust. One moment, a thick mass: then they'd turn together, in a new direction, and become the thinnest pencil-strokes in the white air.

Willy would look round and smile, sometimes: even make a remark. 'Cold old day!' It was cold, always, down by the marshes, even when the sun shone. Rheumatism leapt at you out of the earth. I'd grin and fall back into the trance of watching the seed in its box. Or I'd look up at a gull and feel again the curious sexual excitement that so much of this world of fields and sky seemed to prompt. The wings of the gull, so white, suggested armpits, legs spread ...

And when we stopped to eat our sandwiches, Willy would now and then speak of the only subject that made him remotely talkative: the subject of Bob.

Bob was the farm's clown. He had no intention of causing

amusement. He was simply made for blundering. It was Bob who, for no physical reason clear either to himself or to the onlookers, once fell on his face in the dung-water that made a greenish pond of most of the farmyard.

'Gawd's truth,' he'd said, picking himself up. 'I'm going to look a sight all day.'

'Better nip home and get a change,' someone suggested.

But Bob frowned at him, puzzled. He seemed to have been born without the faculty of recognizing that steps can be taken to modify the effects of most disasters. If Bob had suddenly lost a leg – and it was likely to happen at any moment – he would have hobbled about on the other, cursing in his perplexed way, without giving a thought to surgery and certainly none to the existence of wooden legs and crutches. He walked about all that day, stinkingly green and bitter.

Tales about Bob brought a thin smile even to the farmer's lips. He'd been delighted by the story of what happened when Bob went home to his cottage and found his wife had failed to make the fire.

'I told the silly cow of it,' Bob had said. 'I didn't swear at her, mates. I just told her . . .' He shook his head over the memory. 'And afterwards I told her I was sorry I told her.'

Mrs Bob was always being told of it, and then apologized to. She was so like Bob himself that all their disasters were doubled. She had a habit of sending her husband to work with an empty sandwich tin. Neither of them thought there was much that could be done about such calamities of forgetfulness – except, of course, that Bob would tell her of it, without swearing, and afterwards tell her he was sorry he'd told her . . .

Apart from driving tractors into ditches, and falling into them himself, and layering the wrong hedges, Bob had powerful, confused political emotions that, since he was always confiding them to James, were another sort of disaster. It had never struck Bob that it was undiplomatic to express radical views, in tones of rural certainty that had surely seldom been devoted to such opinions, in the ear of an employer who worried so deeply about his inability to give his hands the constant, whip-cracking supervision suitable for serfs.

'After the war, guv'nor,' Bob would say, 'the working

classes will be above the rich.'

In a flat, dangerous voice James would say: 'Do you think so, mate?'

'Big places like this – the workers'll 'ave 'em.'

'Is that so, Bob?'

'Ah.' Bob would search for an extention of his theme, since the guv'nor seemed so interested. 'An' tied cottages – they'll be agin the law. Right agin the law.'

'You reckon that, mate?'

'Ah.' Bob was now convinced that the happiest of expositions was under way, in the presence of the happiest of listeners. 'This lot in parliament – they'll be out, the lot of 'em. Hark at 'em on the wireless, any day! Plenty o' praise for the farmers, but the farm labourer 'ud go and shake hisself in hell afore they'd think on him.'

'That's your opinion, Bob?'

'Ah.' Bob would resume his search for more stirring matter, but James would have had enough.

'You can go bloody down on the bloody marshes, then, and cut that hedge down there, and I'll be down to see how it's going, and don't let me find you having more than half an hour to eat your bloody sandwiches – if there's any in your bloody tin.'

'My!' Bob would exclaim. 'That's a rotten old job and bad weather for it!'

But down he'd trudge, with his dubious sandwich tin – once more unable to associate a disaster with any possibility of providing against it.

There was a day when the sky changed constantly, building up huge dramas of cloud and then dispelling them in favour of perfect sunshine. Never, never had I seen the world so exquisitely coloured. In the periods of cloudlessness, everything seemed to have been swept amazingly clean; it was as if every corner of the scene had been dusted and polished. All one saw had an incredible particularity. The black-and-whiteness of the heifers, fidgeting on the marshes, was of such a purity that it was as if actual shapes of white had been locked lightly into corresponding black shapes – as if someone had a moment ago pressed the pieces together as part of some jigsaw. I seemed to be seeing cattle for the first time: found myself, oddly, trying to shake off my old memories of such animals, in order to accommodate this feeling that they had been invented that morning.

Willy even halted the tractor for a moment to say 'Lovely day!' I smiled and we both stood for a moment, looking all round us and round again: then, apologetically, Willy set to work once more. I noticed that he looked across to the farm buildings in the distance: it was as if he was saying, 'Sorry, Mr James, to have admired the world in the boss's time.' Willy's gentleness made him a helplessly conscientious workman.

In the afternoon, the weather became involved in even vaster uncertainties, and at last a rainbow appeared, intensely coloured. We drove towards it, along the headlands, past ranks of little trees that, in this light, were brightly green of stem and a profound bronze of leaf. The rainbow was like some immense proscenium arch, and the clouds within it, hugely dark, were like the setting for some great drama. I tried to memorize all the colours – tiny fragments of colour, quite unexpected, leapt to the eye from all quarters. Far away, sea gulls hung in the sky, dazzlingly white. As the sun behind us came out of the clouds, it threw on the ground a light so pure that we seemed to be moving over a quite unreal earth, made up of black and white cubes of clod and shadow.

Then the rainbow, in a matter of seconds, sank away and disappeared – there was a moment of dullness – the gulls turned instantly to black hooks in the air, and again the sun flared, and a whole hedge ahead of us became a long run of green flame . . .

I thought of George, riding through the fields of the sea. 'I should have written to you a night or two ago,' he'd said in his last letter. 'There was a sun going down like a spread of plum jam on one quarter and a dusky moon stealthily trailing her tattered silver train on the other. You could walk on the upper deck, letting the cool evening breeze chill the tiredness out of you, and take your choice – splendid decay of the daytime on the one hand, bewitching promise of the night on the other. Such moments are rare at sea, despite the novelists, but they make the rest of it – stench and squalor of messes down below, strain of eye and mind and muscle when she pitches and rolls her way through heavy seas, constant necessity of obeying orders without questioning their validity – they make such things seem not so very damaging after all.'

God, I thought, what will happen to us? – what *is* happening to us in this queer moment of time? We passed under a tree as Willy made a loop to take the tractor and drill back up the huge field, and one or two leaves, loosened by the puff of the exhaust, spun down in front of me. Where, at this moment, was George, in that murderous ship of his . . .?

The sun set under great orange dramas of cloud; and as it did so, one cloud after another, all round us, burst into flame. Then the sun sank away, and the clouds cooled into a soft damson glow: the naked sky itself became intensely blue. Change of colour, second by second, and the clouds shrinking away from the roof of the sky, subsiding on to the horizon: until we were surrounded by a low foam of them, faintly lime-green. The last seeds of the day fell through the pipes: the world became, quite suddenly, very cold.

'I think I'll volunteer for one of the nastier runs,' George had written. 'Don't you feel this – that with the normal emotions of life gone, you need excitement?'

'Not finished that bloody field yet?' groaned James as we drove into the green stink of the yard.

Next day, perhaps in his eternal suspicion surmising that I'd acted as a drag on Willy, James sent me threshing and put Oliver on the drill. My dismay at having to master a new job was increased when I saw there were two landgirls on the cornstack. I was certain by now that girls regarded me as a quite ludicrous representative of the male sex.

It was a windy, shabby day: the strawstack, as it rose slowly, bent at the corners and seemed to dance. A squat little man called Charlie was in charge; despite the proximity of so much inflammable corn, he was warming a piggish nose with a very tiny pipe. He'd grunted, on my appearance, and handed me a pitchfork. I blushed and tried to impale the heap of straw Charlie pointed out to me where it lay, constantly added to, at the grumbling rear of the threshing machine. My fork came up with one or two wisps weakly caught on it. Charlie groaned, took the fork and speared with it what looked to me like a fair-sized stack. 'Quite,' I muttered, and hoped the girls hadn't been watching. The tinkling of their laughter, from the top of the corn-stack, seemed to be flighted at me. Even when I made out that it was really caused by the presence on the stack of a burly labourer who found it necessary to fall against one of them every time he tugged up a sheaf with his fork – even when I found that this simple amorous by-play was occurring up there, I couldn't be sure that some of the squeals weren't directed at me and my embarrassments below.

It was a long, desperately blushing day. I found myself hating the straw. It set out – so I felt – to make a fool of me. It was in complicity with womankind. I watched Charlie. Quickly rake the straw into a heap – then rush at it with your fork and bear down hard. Up it would come, all of it. I did this. The rushing, I was convinced, was the important thing. Don't give the straw a chance to think things out. I rushed and bore down hard and up came my few wisps.

But to my surprise it was not I who was censured. On the strawstack was a boy: a short, stout boy with a kind of naked pertness about his eyes, and a very runny nose. He was never in the position Charlie wished him to be in.

'Lazy little sod,' Charlie shouted at last.

'Oi,' cried the boy, rushing to the edge of the stack and peering down. 'I don't sleep in the ditch like you did, Charlie.'

The little pipe nearly dropped out of Charlie's mouth. 'You're a bloody little loy-ar!' he called.

He turned to me, ignoring quite remarkable squeals from the other stack. 'No one's going to give me a lazy character,' he mumbled.

'Quite,' I said.

'If I was down there,' hooted the boy, 'I'd stick this fork in your eye.'

I edged away, nervously.

'I'll—!' cried Charlie, making frantic gestures with his own fork.

The rape, or whatever it was that had occurred on the cornstack, came to an end; and the two girls tinkled and leaned against each other, now giving their flushed attention to the war across the way. I blushed.

'Oh, get on with your bloody work,' said the boy, and returned to the back of the stack. Savagely Charlie speared an enormous ball of straw and sent it spinning upwards. To me he muttered:

'I don't know why I didn't go bloody up and knock him bloody down!'

'Mmm.' I sounded as impartial as I could.

'Don't understand him,' said Charlie. 'His father's one of the best bloody men that ever walked in a pair of shoes.'

'Really?'

'Not counting his uncles – fine fellows!'

'They are?'

'How,' Charlie inquired fiercely, from the other side of another ball of straw, 'did they come to have a bloody little old boy like that? I ask you – *how*?'

'Well —'

Gusts of wind raced up between the two stacks; we worked in a painful mist of odds and ends of straw, chaff, mouldy dust. The cornstack tittered and shrieked constantly, as though there were hundreds of bottoms up there, being pinched. And as the sad day wore on, I was surprised to sense, in Charlie's very special friendliness, that I'd come out of this puzzling affair with credit. He tolerated even my continuing ineptitude with the fork. 'You'll pick it up,' he said, tenderly. 'You got time to pick it up.'

Oh God yes, I thought – I had war's infinite suspension of time in which to pick it up . . .

James sent Oliver and me water-furrowing. In this wet region it was always necessary to provide channels for the winter water, if the fields were not to become lakes. As you moved through the peninsula, you saw everywhere fields striped with silver, where the furrows – specially dug – had taken the water, and were funnelling it into the ditches. This was to be our job, now, on a hillside at the far end of the farm from the buildings.

The wind shook the air, there, as if it were thin paper: you could hear the crack of the papery air, all round you. The major colour in the scene was the dark brown of the earth; and it was seconded, more and more as your eye travelled down to the creek, by the sharp grey of water. In the hedges, summer was in stained and almost colourless ruin; the last leaves rattled, there. It was desolate: and to warm and cheer ourselves, we talked. In the daylight, Oliver consented not to talk of religious riddles. He told me the story of his life: I told him the story of mine. He advanced opinions on a wide range of subjects: I repaid him with opinions of my own. We shivered, and talked, and now and then, almost absent-mindedly, I worked at the furrow. I knew at once that I was doing it wrong. It had always been a fault of mine, from the first ditching, to work with a sort of exquisite accuracy, as if I were sculpting rather than engaged in rough husbandry. As I'd lovingly given the walls of my ditches a precise slope of forty-five degrees, and had shaved every roughness off those walls, so now I provided this immense soaked field with furrows of the most beautiful symmetry and straightness. Oliver had no such instinct, and I found myself, still absent-mindedly – for our talk occupied the whole forefront of our minds – giving a polish to his work in between spurts of original labour of my own. But spurts is not the word. We made our way back and forth across that field with amazing slowness. Day after day, more and more slackly, we arrived together for what was primarily a conference. There were mornings when it was so cold, so dark, that we thought we could not bear it: we must run away; but then the sun would come out of the tree-dark distance, and though it was to be seen rather than felt, and the wind was sure to return, still it made it possible – even if barely possible – to use that field as the venue for another daylong conversation.

We saw nothing of James. Some major activity was occurring at the other end of the farm, and when he caught sight of us, morning or evening, his eyes would leap about in his head, as if we were the one final element in his complex life that threatened to overturn his wits. 'Finished down there?' he'd snap; and then, when Oliver had vaguely replied 'Nearly', James would turn away, hurrying towards some other last straw, leaving behind him the words: 'Can't be everywhere! Have to trust you!'

There came a weekend from which Oliver did not at once return. I spent a whole day out there alone, and was suddenly almost crazedly conscious of the nature of the scene. It seemed to be at some bitter tag-end of the whole world. I felt, in some monumental sense, out of place: even the spectacle of a huge yellow dawn slowly evolving over the black earth could not reconcile me to being there. I was persecuted that day by a phrase I'd read, of Stephen

Spender's: all poets could do in wartime, he'd declared, was 'to shout messages of hope into the mists of an uncertain future'. It seemed to me that I stood, on that hillside, in the centre of a very model of the uncertain future. Would it not all end in some such scene, all man's summers in ruins, the cold glint of water?

I crept like a worm along the furrows. After some hours I began to see horses, men in the hedges. The illusion was curiously powerful. I was borne down by the monotony of the earth, of this tough, fibrous earth, now soaked. And I began to have the sexual feelings that sprang from being alone in such a huge space, so that you had a tormenting sense of your body as the only warm, ingenious thing in the whole visible world: the only thing capable of passionate action. In the hedges I began now to see the crouching, tempting shapes of girls.

And the birds were going away, in sudden congregations. There were little wheeling troops of them, everywhere in the sky. It felt like being deserted.

Oliver returned the next day. A great gloominess of cloud came with him. It had rained all night. The spade was a sticky mass, pushing helplessly at another sticky mass. We made scarcely any progress. And then those clouds burst, like great paper bags, and we ran up and back to the buildings: into one of James's great barns. The other hands were there – Bob, Charlie with his tiny pipe, even Willy. The farmer suddenly appeared, rain dripping from the peak of his cap. 'Hallo, hallo, hallo,' he snapped, and his own men scampered out through the door, like schoolchildren. 'Finished down there?' he demanded.

The others had gone to make a pretence of working in one barn or other. 'Always something needs cleaning', was James's view of what should happen when it rained. We should dash up and begin spring-cleaning a tractor. Now we stood in his huge barn and scorned him. We scorned this man with his tractors and his buildings and the puddles in his yard and his thousand acres. We sat in the centre of decades of smells, adding up to an intense sweet-sourness, and I looked up at the splits in the roof, a broken roof-strut. I flinched. One of my nightmares was that I should be required to perform herculean tasks, and now I imagined James demanding that I set this immense ruined barn to rights. The thought of the effort of such tasks was always, in these black fantasies of mine, heavier than the worst labour itself. It was a form of anxiety, I knew. And I was more and more anxious these days, surrounded by such an unexpected, insistent immediacy of objects and scenes, but really reaching out for what lay beyond, out of sight – the war, the future. Everything was so near, and I was deeply worried about the distance.

And next morning the explosion came. Oliver and I had declined to the exchange of extremely recherché sensations, and I was commenting on the thin clean feeling your hands had when you took them out of warm gloves. My spade lay on the ground: Oliver was using his as a shooting-stick. 'Try it, Oliver,' I was saying. 'Try *suddenly* taking your glove off. Feel the air *defining* your hand. Golly, how conscious you become of the bones! It's worth trying, Oliver!' And at this moment we found James at our side. He'd come over the field, two hundred yards or more, and we were so pre-occupied that we'd not seen him. The cap was thrust back on his humourless head. 'Good grief! What have you been doing? You must have spent two days on one furrow! Good grief! I can't afford to pay you for that.'

We stood, helplessly penitent. Of course he was right. It was bad of us. They'd say this was what conchies were like. How to explain the immense boredom that had driven every thought out of our heads but the need to rouse little interests in one another? 'But' – one could hardly say this – 'we've covered a huge field of autobiography and general comment on life!' Our incapacity to react in any of the ways that might be usual in such cases reduced James at last to a great sadness: he was simply sad that we were such special obstacles to that aim he could never achieve – that of running 'this huge place' with the amazing efficiency, and great financial success, that was ideally possible. It was, we thought afterwards, wondering why there was no talk of reporting us to the War Ag – it was as if, after he'd made the usual gestures of anger, James quickly reached a point where sadness was, for him, a happiness. He was only happy when his expectations of frustration and disappointment were realized.

'My goodness,' he wailed. 'If I only had to concentrate on a little job like this.'

61

Looking back, I see that he was too glad to have even this bad labour to make a fuss, unless absolutely driven to it ... I think of those days on James's farm as the nadir of my experience on the land. I had a conscience about work, really. I didn't want not to work. But the fields of this soaked, sad farm spoke of the serfdom that made grown men, Bob and Charlie and Willy and others, scamper guiltily beyond the boss's eye. With our urban background, Oliver and I reacted against this servility. And we were tired, we knew, of this melancholy edge of England, of the endless wind.

Tired, yes. Had we any right to complain, I wondered, when so much that was worse was happening to so many of our peers?

The next day began with sunshine: I stood in it and felt as though I were made of the thinnest possible wires of bone and muscle. The wind, after weeks in the east, came now from the west: it grew during the morning, and suddenly, in the afternoon, switched off – you could hear it happen – and let the rain fall. We ran away from the farm, to an old building on the edge of the marsh, and there, stretched out in old mangers and feeling like Arctic explorers in their bunks, we talked of applying for a transfer – nearer home, perhaps: certainly as far as possible from the North Sea.

Letters to National Service Officers. Applications to our home county. If we were accepted, we could live at home. Pringle wanted to leave this frigid peninsula, too. Mrs Goss hastily raised our rent. Wilkins, the labour officer, searched through official orders for some provision that might balk us in our quest of a transfer ...

And our home county wrote to say that, provided the relevant, almost insuperable intricacies of procedure could be gone through, we should join a certain threshing tackle on a certain date ...

The official tensions suddenly snapped. Essex let go. We had no time for farewells. Mrs Goss suggested that we might have infringed innumerable strict rules as to the treatment of a landlady whose care for us could not have been exceeded, and hinted that the payment of a fairly large sum might inhibit legal action on her part. We smiled at her, and swiftly round on the world that had been ours for almost a complete cycle of the agricultural year – on all our ditches, cornstacks, water-furrows and such sugar beet as had survived our hoeing.

We found time only to visit Bert Trott. He said:

'Want to git yerself a wife – Ol'ver – Ted!'

Part Two

1

The traction engine was a gross and greasy monster, and Jimbo was its master. He had another name but we could never remember it. When we first saw him, that morning, the first of the week's soot garnished his face and gave a clown's prominence to his wicked eyes. For a quarter of a century he had shunted his tackle from farm to farm in this corner of the county. There was nothing he didn't know about threshing: and he knew nothing about anything else. He was the soul of his own apparatus. So much was he part of it that when I came once upon the engine standing untended, on a rare morning when snow had delayed Jimbo's arrival, I seemed to be in the presence of a husk. The engine had a melancholy visage at any time: the big brass handle that held the boiler door in place looked like some sad yellow moustache on a round dejected countenance. But, with Jimbo absent, the sadness was intensified, became unbearable. There were some who held that Jimbo from time to time slept with his machine. It certainly gave the impression of a sort of marriage. Man and engine, they'd been together so long, riding from farmyard to farmyard during long autumns and longer winters. It was a hard, black, uncomfortable life, and they embodied it, Jimbo and his engine.

Besides the engine, there was the barnworker, which did the actual threshing: like some hulking dull red perambulator, bristling with the wheels to which the various straps were attached when the threshing began; and ending in the shakers that sent the straw dropping either to the ground or into the trusser. A separate piece of tackle, the trusser tied the straw into convenient bundles, and when we took to the road was followed by our perambulant toolbox, filled with tarpaulins, spare straps and a host of curious devices whose use was necessary whenever the tackle found itself on wet ground.

A factory on the move: and in his mastery of it, Jimbo had an assistant – his nephew, Fred. It was, we were to discover, a rather odd relationship: ratty, much of the time.

Emotionally, they worked neatly together, cog with cog. Jimbo was laconic, watchful, malicious – the perfect machiner, master of his small black world. Fred was loose and foolish, with the emptiest of laughs. If things went wrong, Fred was bound to let his laugh slip, and Jimbo, eyes narrowing, would pounce upon it, frugally angry. 'What's funny, boy?' 'Oh, but uncle —!' And the laughter would spill out of Fred's helplessly loose-knit nature, while Jimbo tightened his lips and made his blue eyes look like stones. 'Get on with it, *boy*! And grumbling, grinning, Fred would hurry off to deal with the trouble : while Jimbo kicked out – very tiny, unwasteful kicks – at the nearest surface of the tackle. It really did seem a planned part of the machinery, this tight fury of Jimbo's and Fred's slack foolishness: when one cog meshed with the other, then trouble could be dealt with. But not before.

Oliver, Pringle and I arrived together in the farmyard where the tackle stood ready to move on to its next job. Steam was building up, and Jimbo and Fred sat round a brazier in the shadow of the engine. The farm was part of a very expensive girls' school, and very expensive young ladies in farm clothes of careful cut were moving to and fro in the background, carrying out small tasks. Fred was in such ecstasies of social and sexual delight that he could barely bother to greet us.

'You come to help us out, then? ... Hey, uncle, look at 'er! Seen a bum like it? Bloody princess, she is!'

Jimbo followed the progress of the young woman in question with his cold blue eye, encircled with soot: but was plainly not ready to issue a comparative statement about bums. 'Floppety, flippety,' said Fred, referring to another aspect of his princess. Jimbo directed his cold attention at that, too: then he said:

'Now, my lucky lads! We're off to Farmer Jones – the meanest farmer in the county!'

'Mind they don't drop off!' Fred spluttered into the girlish distance. His uncle gave him a quick cooling glare, and within minutes we were on the road – a long, slow, puffing procession, bound for Farmer Jones.

His was a farm on the edge of a very large, confused estate. The yard itself was backed by the walls of a convent, and had a now-familiar, dreary untidiness. Fragments of machinery lay around, rusting. On the rain-wet roof of a Dutch barn, birds were sitting in their own shadows. Our snake of a tackle made a coil of itself in the lee of the barn, and Farmer Jones stood waiting.

He was a tall, weak-faced man consumed with anxiety. 'Ah, 'chiner,' he called. 'You've come. Thank God! I'm spiking! Look at 'em!' He pointed with a trembling stick at four stacks that huddled together on the open sides of the yard. 'The autumn sowing failed. Well, it did everywhere, didn't it? Had to tear it up and sow again in spring. So they were late. The stacks were late in building. Couldn't lay hands on a single straw for thatching. So they've spiked!'

He stared at his stacks with horror, and then back at Jimbo. The 'chiner gave him a small cold smile, then turned his own gaze on those huddled heaps of corn, green with growth where the weather had soaked them. 'We'll do our best, mister,' he grunted. The farmer shuddered, then hurried away. 'I'll send my men over,' he called, without conviction.

'Men!' muttered Jimbo. 'When did Farmer Jones employ *men*, I wonder? Little lads and skelingtons!' He came down from his cab and began to pull at the nearest stack, ripping out tufts of rotten wheat and flinging them to the ground. 'What dreadful stuff!' A sour smell came from the wounded stack. 'He ought to be locked up! How disgraceful!'

Fred cackled: and Jimbo gave him the benefit of a very long, bitter stare. 'Setting up in a bog like this?' he grunted. 'With the stacks arse to arse?' Fred choked, took the point, and the great work of setting up began.

As was often to happen, Jimbo made satirical heavy weather of the farmer's ineptitude in stack-making. The yard was stickily wet, the ricks were built too close. An essential exercise was to align the big flywheel on the engine with the driving wheel on the barnworker. The unevenness of the ground made this difficult; the mud seemed to make it impossible. Jimbo, cursing with his eyes, drove the engine backwards and forwards, an inch here, an inch there, while we rammed planks, bricks, sacks under the huge wheels. Jacks were produced, and the engine rose into the air. Then it was decided that the engine must be sunk, instead, and we dug deep trenches for it. Jimbo spread about him an atmosphere of malicious gloom. When Farmer Jones's men appeared – a very fat, empty-eyed boy and an ancient fellow whose chief contribution took the form of groans, hollow groans that might have been an eccentric form of breathing – Jimbo suspended activity for a whole minute: staring, with an elaborate effect of disbelief. Now and then we caught sight of the farmer, peeping out from behind the barn: beating a leg ferociously with his stick and blinking with alarm. He emerged once and called, already on the turn: 'A little top moisture, I'm afraid, 'chiner!' Jimbo was directing us as we attached the straw binder, which could hardly be made to cohere with the rest of the jacked-up, blocked-up or deeply sunk items of the tackle. He turned his eye on the farmer, who finished his turn feverishly and hurried off, flogging himself without remorse.

There was time for only half an hour's threshing, that first day. The real work began the next morning. It was an eternity of a day – we were threshing for ever, enclosed in dull mist. For ever and ever we tossed that dry dusty barley, which had been stacked loose, from a dwindling rick on to the barnworker. The half-hour for lunch was a dizzy, aching break. Half a dozen farmers appeared during the day, hurrying across to Jimbo where he bent over his engine, busy with his oilcan. Jimbo did not work: he reserved for himself a general vague supervisory role, given an edge of activity by constant use of the oilcan – so that he appeared like some black Aladdin. The farmers all spoke hoarsely, all in much the same words. 'Don't go to the big men, 'chiner. They've got enough money. Come to us little 'uns.' Jimbo made non-committal use of his all-purpose eyes. The day went on and on, until it was queerly time to cycle home – wondering how it was possible to recover in time for the morning.

The third day was an intenser prison of labour. This was my first experience of physical activity so unremitting, so ruthlessly mechanical. Oliver said he'd woken, in the middle of the night, from a dream in which he'd loaded and emptied his fork time after time, and had found himself crying aloud: 'You needn't do it now! You needn't do it,

in bed!' There were all the furious irritations of imprison-
ment; it seemed that the day, the world, must be almost
unbearably rich, amusing, various, just beyond the corner of
one's fixed eye, blinded with the mouldy dust of that bad
corn. The convent bell tolled the hours; astonishingly, in the
middle of yet one more upward thrust with the fork, from a
stack now very near to the ground, I caught the eye of a
nun, watching from behind a barred window over that high
wall. She looked to me incredibly beautiful: but she vanished at once.

Farmer Jones was always in the corner of one's eye, too:
but now that Jimbo had really set up, now that the stacks
were really being munched by the barnworker, he began to
creep into the dusty light of day. He began to move around
us as we worked, suspiciously. He began even to make
obliquely critical remarks. 'Thought that stack 'ud have
gone by now' – but Jimbo had a glare for that sort of thing,
a flash of the eye which seemed to say: 'I could up and go
at any moment – off to those other little fellows who've
come creeping to me for help.' The farmer leaped away
then, beating his own shins black and blue.

There was a sort of pause, that day, when we had to
move the tackle to a new stack, and the engine was bogged
down and tore up huge lumps of black earth with its raging
wheels. Farm children were suddenly under our feet, helping with the movement of pieces of wood from one boggy
hole to another. The engine filled them with wonder. I
smiled at them, and they smiled back, and the world seemed
for a moment a tenderer place. Or rather, they seemed to
stand in some airy space to the side of our black cursing
world, seeing it admiringly as a marvellous source of smoke
and predicaments. A tiny boy asked what would happen if
the engine fell over. His small sister, with a happy smile of
knowledge, said he would be killed. No, said another boy,
angered by the unspecific nature of this suggestion: he'd be
squashed flat.

I was, by now, the middle of the week being reached,
almost drunk with tiredness. I couldn't sleep. If I slept, the
thought hammered at me with the pulse of the tackle itself
– if I slept, then one day of toil would simply run straight
into another. It struck me that, elsewhere, people were being agitated by, and passionately involved in, the proceed-

ings of parliament, the progress of an immense war: but such things seemed to me intellectual sophistications of improbable loftiness, occurring in some other world outside the yard that pulsed and shrieked and gulped with threshing.

But the stacks were devoured at last, digested and delivered as sacks of corn, mounds of chaff and cavings (odd loose rubbish), hurried hills of straw. The farmer gave a last demonstration of self-flagellation under Jimbo's unimpressed eye, and suddenly it was Saturday, the gates of the suffocated week flew open, and as I rode home that midday I passed two acquaintances, who looked at me and through me. I thought they might be late recruits to the ranks of my enemies, until in a mirror I saw the black, wild thing I'd become, with my nostrils stuffed with corn dust, my hair full of the tiny spears of barley.

Jimbo had said, as we left the yard: 'You'll do, mateys!' Fred had laughed, helplessly: 'Look more like it now, they do. Like a lot o' girls, beginning of the week.' Jimbo dowsed him with a stare of middling length, and then said: 'Monday, then. Sharp.' And we felt an absurd sense of triumph as we cycled away. Certainly, when we thought of what the fat boy and the old groaning man had contributed to the week's work – the grumbling evasions of their activity – we saw that we might have small competition when it came to the assessment of our worth as threshers. But all the same, it was clear that acceptance by Jimbo was an honour of some rarity; and *that*, as much as the weekend, did a deal to ease the fearful ache in our bones.

The weeks that followed were, as much as anything, an anthology of farmers. There were a number of repetitions of Jones: we quickly discovered that he was not alone in being, in Jimbo's judgement, the meanest farmer in the county. The general niggardliness of farmers was as central to Jimbo's view of the world as the need to maintain steam in his engine. Nasty, agitated small men made necessary enormous manoeuvrings of the tackle: we seemed always to be trying to draw alongside stacks that had been built on specially chosen hazards of slime. And at last we came to an intemperate, furious man who'd been obliged to farm a field he'd purchased for jerrybuilding purposes, just before the war began. Brown was beyond even Jimbo's talent for satire: he roared up, day after day, in his saloon car – it was the exact description for it, a sort of saloon bar on wheels – and ranted around us, as if we perfectly represented those forces that were preventing him from covering the field with ghastly houses. It was evident that corn, as a specialized form of grass, filled him with passionate distaste: he raged at it, even pounding the stack with his fists, a man at odds with history. It occurred to me that he was the most convinced conscientious objector I'd ever met; though this didn't prevent him from reserving for us, actual conchies, a shrill, jumpy hatred that was too frantic to have any bite.

And it was at Brown's that I met Reg and Frank.

The week had begun with Pearl Harbor. We tried to talk about that, on the dusty square of the rick, tossing to Fred on the barnworker mouldy flat sheaves of oats that looked like the beards of old crushed men. But that uproar in an ocean – it was difficult to relate to our tiny scene . . .

Reg had his own view of it. He was a slack young man, more naïve than anyone else I've ever met, with a mind quite astonishingly boneless. He rolled rather than walked, in overalls that were too large: his mouth was always loosely open, his eyes always puzzled. He was wet: I have never known anyone whose character was marked by such an anxious dampness. In some ways, he seemed a ruthless take-off of the rest of us. Of Pearl Harbor, Reg said, ineptly tugging at a sheaf that could not be removed till others binding it in had been taken:

'It's jolly rotten, isn't it? They're rotters. It's an awfully rotten thing to do.'

'By Jove,' someone said. 'Fearful cads, these Japanese.'

Reg paused in his impossible struggle with that ill-chosen sheaf. He blinked enormously. Then his voice rose in a wail of complaint:

'Oh crikey! No one takes me seriously. Why are people rotten to me?'

I was to know Reg for some years, and he worried me: at times he worried all of us. It wasn't so much his phenomenal weakness of spirit and quite exceptional flabbiness that caused us distress – though this was bad enough. It was rather the ease with which we all made a butt of him. No

one was more made for teasing: and we, who had registered an obvious claim to special humaneness, teased him
endlessly. The phrase, 'He asked for it', might have been
invented purely for Reg. He said nothing that was not a
reduction of some idea to ultimate dampness. For example,
he was opposed to – he slackly campaigned against – all
expletives.

'You can't take that bloody sheaf yet, Reg! All the others
are bloody well binding it in! For Christ's sake have a bit of
sense and watch the way the stack's built. Take that bloody
sheaf there – *that* bloody one, you fart!'

Reg would halt his feeble scratchings at yet another irre-
trievable sheaf, and roll his wounded eyes. 'I don't like language like that. I've told you already. Oh crikey! It's rotten,
talking to a chum like that.'

'A *chum*? Oh my God, Reg.'

'Oh crikey! Why do you fellows have to take the name
of the Lord ...'

Fred then, from the impatient barnworker: 'Oh let's have
it, Reg, you silly bugger.'

'Oh crikey! Why do you all have to talk that way?'

Even common helpfulness was reduced by Reg to a form
of unacceptable conduct. Someone would remember that
he'd left his lunch lashed to a distant bicycle. Reg would
lumber to his feet.

'Hold on, old chap. Stay put. I'll go and get it.'

'For the Lord's sake, Reg, don't always be doing things
for people. I'll get it. I bloody well left it there ...'

'Oh crumbs! Must you? ... Look, we're supposed to be
helpful to our chums, aren't we?'

'Reg, stop calling me your chum. If you hate swearing, I
hate being called anyone's *chum*.'

'All right – all right. You don't want to be my friend,
then.'

'For Christ's sake, Reg ...'

'Oh crikey!'

We had conferences from time to time, at which we discussed the atrocious way we behaved to Reg. We must stop
taunting him. We must listen gravely to his attacks on the
BBC, which revolved round the charge, almost daily levelled, that he'd heard a broadcaster say 'sod' or 'bloody hell'
– 'I did hear it, I tell you. Crikey, I've got ears, haven't I?'

Life was clearly an endless torment to Reg. He fell back, after every clash with it, into his own soft pulpy assurances: but that didn't excuse our own teasings – our *intolerance* ...

We would stare at each other, shocked, when that word emerged.

But it was no use. Reg asked for it, and we were less cruel than Jimbo, who waited like a cat for Reg to roll between his claws,

'Brown's a rotter, isn't he, Jimbo? He swore at me this morning. He oughtn't to do that, you know.'

Jimbo would stretch himself, blackly, flex his wicked muscles.

'No, matey? Is that your way o' thinking, then?'

'It's what the Bible tells us, isn't it?'

'That's what it says in the bloody Bible, is it, matey?'

'Oh crikey ...!'

'There's some bits in the bloody Bible ...' And Jimbo would tell an anecdote – about what he alleged to have been his schooldays. The story of Susannah and the Elders could be indistinctly discerned. 'Having a peep at this tart in her bath.'

And Reg would groan, and exclaim, and at last rise and roll away from the neighbourhood of the lunch-time brazier, round with despair.

And Jimbo, for some reason, would turn his eye to the heavens, and give the clouds a slow wink.

It was as a replacement for Reg that Frank joined us, just before we moved to a huge farm owned by the least pleasant farmer to date. Jimbo had begun to talk about this man, Curry, from the moment we joined the tackle. 'We'll be going to Mr Curry's soon, mateys. You'll have to watch out there. Nasty customer, Mr Curry. Nastiest farmer in the county.'

'And the meanest, Jimbo?'

If Jimbo was aware of the mild irony, he ignored it. '*And* the meanest, matey.'

A word in the ear of a War Ag official, and Reg was gone. Gone to ditching. *Drainage* – that was the word. The drainage gangs were the Pioneer Corps of agriculture. We had come already to dread the idea of demotion to drainage. Reg had gone, moistly miserable —

'Oh, Jimbo, crikey! Why? Why d'you send a chum to drainage?'

'Kindness, matey. It's a kindness. Mr Curry would make mincemeat of you. Off you go, and be grateful to old Jimbo!'

And so Frank joined us – as it turned out, a man made for matching with Curry.

The farmer, when we lumbered, hasty and sober, into his immaculate territory, and briskly set up alongside his first highly competent stack – Curry turned out to be simply a man of quite monumental ill-nature. He was clearly an able farmer, who couldn't endure anything in the human character that even verged on inefficiency, less than optimum, unsmiling speed and thoroughness of execution. He came to survey us, frozen-eyed, and demurred at once at the presence of conchies on his land and their use in the service of his corn. 'Bloody rats, traitors and yellow-bellies,' he observed to Jimbo, crisply. 'I don't want them.'

'They're hard workers, mister,' said Jimbo, deeply respectful. His tone was sympathetic: of course, it implied, he quite understood that he was straining the farmer's credulity. Yet: 'They're a good team, Mr Curry. And you won't get any other labour worth the name.'

Curry breathed fiercely through his nose – and looked widely round at his farm, as if inclined to call for disinfectant: or a firing squad. Then he said:

'First sign of slackness – out they go. War Ag or no bloody War Ag.'

And the tackle began to gulp down his corn.

Frank was appointed to look after the bound straw, taking it from where it fell from the binder and delivering it to the men who were building the strawstack. He came from one of the great shipbuilding towns that during the thirties had been derelict. His face was northern, the cheekbones making sharp angles: a high, narrow brow and eyes brightly alert. Much in his manner and appearance was a direct product of the experience of growing up in a dockyard town when the docks were empty. The quick movements, like those of a cock, strutting, arrogant. He was ready to crow, at any moment. Any victory over a farmer, a foreman, an official – for any such victory his crow was held ready. I thought of him as, essentially, an urchin – as the perfection of urchinness. A resentfully poor childhood had given him practice in every kind of impudence. He had smuggled himself into football grounds, he told us, gathered up the discarded evening newspapers on one side and sold them afresh on the other. Like all the boys of the stricken town, he had stolen from shops. They would ask for two ha'pennies in exchange for a penny, and would knock off what they could while the assistant's back was turned: then go next door and ask for a penny for two ha'pennies. The family had escaped at last when his father found employment in the south. But old habits died hard, and when his mother had taken Frank's younger brother on a first shopping expedition in London, she'd been astonished to find, reaching home, that her basket contained far more than she'd purchased. It had not been easy to persuade the boy that shopping might, from then on, be conducted along lawful lines.

But what had hurt Frank most, during those years of his childhood, had been the mock of further education that had been offered when statutory schooling was over. 'They wanted us off the streets. So they bribed us. They bribed us with two bob a week!' Frank's fierce eyes seemed to spit. 'The dole schools! Ugh! And the teachers! Old wrecks they'd dug out – poor old fools on their pensions! We gave them merry hell! Poor buggers! But it wasn't funny. Christ, it wasn't funny! They took us through the old stuff again. Tried to. *Simple* fractions! Decimals! Punctuation! Spelling! But – two bob! You couldn't turn it down. They knew that. The buggers!'

His being a conchie had followed directly enough from these experiences. He wasn't going to fight at the behest of a government that had invented the dole schools. 'In the army,' he said once, 'they don't even buy you with two bob. Do they? Your value's dropped to a bob, when it comes to the army, hasn't it?'

The job he'd been given seemed the right one for Frank, with its requirement that you stab the straw with your pitchfork as it flopped or flew (according to the weather) out of the rear-end of the tackle, and then turn and send the prickling mass spinning up to the man on the stack. Quick, treating the straw as if it were a farmer, or the official who'd handed him that weekly florin – quick and cocky, Frank would stab and wheel and thrust for hours on end; but we would talk all the time, as I crouched by the chaff bags, or drew the chaff loose with my rake endlessly, endlessly, towards the cliff of it by which I was so often trapped. We'd talk: and Curry, on his visits, would glare, equating talk with idleness, with treason.

He couldn't complain, since the tackle worked at amazing speed: even Jimbo, on that farm, moved about briskly with his oilcan and infused his unnecessary inspection of the many straps with an appearance of astonishing activity. Yet for Frank, hardest worker of us all, Curry had a particular hatred, sharpened by his inability to find any real cause for complaint. That empty dockyard town had left on Frank a mark that was recognized by all authoritarians. And a day came when Curry approached the straw binder, leaned on his ill-tempered stick, and glared at Frank. It was not a casual glaring; he made an occupation of it. Stationing himself a yard or so from Frank, he fixed on him a stare of vicious distaste. Frank looked surprised, but went on impaling the straw on his fork. It was barely manageable, short stuff, and he had to bear down on it, and screw his fork into it; even then he came up, from time to time, with only a few wisps. He laboured on, coughing through the dust. Curry's glare grew more intense. Whirling round after he'd thrown each wretched forkful upwards, Frank found himself face to face with this sharpening expression of hatred. He glared back, with hurried bafflement, and bent down and speared and screwed and then wheeled and thrust upward; and turned again to find Curry still there. At last Frank stopped, and met glare with steady glare. They stood for a long moment like this, as if they were wild animals ill-met; and then, very slowly, Curry said: 'If I were looking for the laziest man in the world, I needn't go further than you.'

The whole threshing tackle burst out laughing. A wild pleasure was felt, there in the dust: the malice, the total absence of justice, Frank's amazement – impossible not to laugh! Frank looked wildly in all directions, as if in search of something more probable than this encounter: then he spat dust on the ground between the two of them, gave his fork a helpless twirl, and said:

'*Sod you!*'

A moment which brought Jimbo into action, and another of his machiner's gifts: that of diplomacy. The main belt flew off the machine (Jimbo could make it do that with a touch of a spanner): he throttled down the engine. Curry whirled round. 'What's that? What're you stopping for?' Jimbo clambered down from his cab, made his unhurried way across to the dangling belt.

'Blown off, mister. Wind. These stacks lie in the wind, y'see.'

Great respectfulness; and Curry could do no more than half raise his stick; then, with a glare that took us all in, and spread beyond to the sky, to the source of the weather, he hobbled back to his car . . .

He was deeply opposed to talk, and a day or so later I managed to distress him most deeply by speaking. It was suddenly very hot, that day, and in the burning air the smell of oil and smoke, the eddying dust, the hot odours of the stack, built up within us all an implacable misery. I found some words of Macbeth's jumping around in my head, and they were there when Curry appeared at my elbow, glaring. So I spoke them.

'Time and the hour,' I informed him in a suitable croak, 'run through the roughest day.'

Curry beat the stack with his stick. 'Oh, get on with it,' he groaned. 'Get on with it, you talkative bastard!'

Out of the dust, Frank would gasp: 'They hate us talking! You know why? They're afraid of it! They know that talk is dangerous. I mean talk like ours. Not flabby chatter – not grunts. Have you noticed – they grunt! They can smell the ideas, and it makes them afraid!'

I was always a little uneasy about this lofty value Frank placed on our talk, his feeling that we were a cell of potential revolution, or at least of considerable philosophical advance. I'd had a proper schooling, he said. I would understand how he longed to master all the branches of knowledge – so that at last he could turn and cock the most learned of snooks at those who'd invented the dole schools. We'd convert the back of the tackle into a classroom. Despite the Curries of our dusty world, we'd do that. We'd teach each other.

One morning he said:

'D'you know – as I come along now, as I cycle to this bloody place, I think over subjects for us to talk about. I think – Ted will tell me about music. Ted will tell me about things in A flat or B minor, or whatever it is, and I'll laugh and say it's all just noise to me, and then you'll tell me all about – what the hell is it? – scales, tonic solfa – *sonatas!* – that's a good word! – *sonatas!* – and then it'll be time for me to tell you about algebra . . .'

Frank had been teaching himself mathematics, and had been delighted to discover that I was a mathematical moron. So I was to inform him about writers, and philosophers, and music – and he would repay me in algebra . . . and shorthand: through a course in which he'd been taking himself, before he turned to mathematics.

'You see in me, Frank,' I tried to explain, 'a man who knows a hundred things vaguely. Honest, don't take me seriously! I'm just your average woolly bookworm —'

'Must be some kind of caterpillar . . . We ought to bone up on natural history, Ted. There's a subject for us . . . D'you know, at school they called it nature study! *Nature study!* I tell you what – they just try to make it sound like stuff for kids. They want to keep us ignorant. They want to keep us kids for ever. Like calling it arithmetic instead of mathematics.'

'But Frank —'

Frank glared up at the man on the stack. Enthusiasm sometimes interfered with his rhythm, as it had done now, hitting upon this new definition of the conspiracy that had kept him in ignorance; and when this happened, then the stackman, working like a pendulum, would reach out for the next clutch of straw and find himself stabbing at the air. He would totter a little, come out of his trance and fix Frank with a bitter eye. And Frank would always glare back. So much of his childhood, you could see, had consisted of glaring – at policemen, officials, teachers.

'Tomorrow I'm going to bring a bit of chalk and we can use the back of the tackle as a blackboard. Then I can write up equations for you. And you can show me about music – what do they call it? – the *stave.*'

Jimbo was sourly tolerant of the academe we set up in the midst of the threshing. 'If you could put your tongues to work, mateys, you'd be bloody rich!' And when Curry made one more attempt to complain – 'You've got a couple of sodding members of parliament at the back there!' – Jimbo spat and fingered the soot on his chin and said: 'They'd do as well if they left their heads at home, but you'll go a long way to find better men on the straw and the chaff – not a blockage this week, mister.' And Curry had to content himself with striking out with his stick at one of his own workers, a boy filled with the careless and obtuse merriment that seemed characteristic of so many farm lads. It was such boys who normally looked after the chaff; but they were always away, sketching out cackling and complicatedly unpractical approaches to the dishonouring of landgirls, if we had any with us, or chasing rats – usually imaginary ones. Jimbo, alas, had discovered that I hadn't their gift for allowing the chaff to accumulate till the tackle was choked and came to a halt.

It amused me that both Frank and I, those advanced thinkers, were taken aback by the very direct and elementary depravity of most of the farm boys – together with the simple-minded lechery of Jimbo's nephew, Fred. The effect of such things on Frank was disconcertingly powerful. There was a day when one of the boys caused a positive puritanical explosion in him.

We had a landgirl working with us that day – she stood alongside Fred on the tackle-top, taking sheaves from the man on the cornstack and handing them to Fred, who fed them into the drum – the revolving metal that whipped the grain out of a sheaf. Fred's delight in her presence had brought about a welcome slowing down of the tackle – welcome, that is, to all but Jimbo, who stumped around his engine sombrely, shooting sharp glances up at his nephew and angrily oiling whatever offered, as if in doing so he might be diluting Fred's sexual juices.

But Fred was in his element: gross simple teasings were occuring, up there on the idling and juddering tackle.

'I'm going to lie down in a moment,' the girl cried. 'I'm tired of this.'

Fred paused, a sheaf half-offered to the drum, and his jaw dropped with delight.

'I bet you love *lying down*,' he said thickly, and with a tremendous suggestion of wit.

She screwed up her nose, and Fred worked upon his idea,

while his jaw hung and the machine went unfed: then, 'Like me to lie down with you?' he bawled.

'Trouble up there, boy?' Jimbo's tone was sepulchrally ironical.

Fred's jaw fell further. Then, flushed with the pride of humorous invention, he aimed an elbow at the girl's ribs and inquired: 'Like to get into trouble up here, would you?'

Frank, deprived of straw, leaned on his fork and exclaimed bitterly: 'The stupidity of it, Ted! He's like some daft dog! Slobbering...'

It was then that the boy joined us. Staring up at Fred and the girl, he remarked flatly: 'I'd like to 'ave a good look at 'er bum. Eh?'

It was as if Frank had been offered another florin. 'Get away, you filthy little boy!' he shouted. He pushed at the astounded lad with the safe end of his fork. 'Get out of it, you horrible-minded little bugger!'

I puzzled often over the origins of that deep distress caused in Frank by almost any display of sexuality. It was a ferocious disgust – rooted, it seemed, in an immense refusal of physical knowledge that was odd in someone so intent, in other matters, on becoming fully aware. Whatever its origin, it had plainly been sharpened by the conditions of conflict in which he had always lived. He had resolved that there was no future in softness. He might come round to music, because there was a science to be discussed, but to any of the orders of submission to the demands of hearts and body he would not be won. 'Wet' and 'messy' were his words for all that.

'You'd really like to *kiss* a girl, Ted?' he cried once, aghast, at the end of one of our discussions, having in some way wrung from me this elementary declaration. 'You'd *eat* your girls, would you? All that wet flesh!' And for an hour or so thereafter he was moodily silent, except for occasional wry shouts of: 'Don Bloody Juan!'

The dislike of romantic activity seemed to be spread throughout his family. One morning he told us of a visit to the cinema he'd paid the night before with a younger brother. The film had been largely romantic, and there had been kissing, and then more kissing: and at last Frank's young brother could bear it no more, and had uttered his protest in a groan that, Frank said, shook the cinema.

'Oh,' he'd cried. 'Oh, why don't he kiss her *arse* for a change?'

Of all of us, still not really at home in the rural scene, Pringle was least at ease. He had never truly ceased to be a bank clerk. He lived in a respectable suburb, from which he thought it impossible to depart in the morning dressed in labourer's clothes: so he carried his overalls in a brief case, and changed behind the stack on arrival: still somehow contriving to look as if his day's work lay behind a bank counter. But to this unsuitable decency of appearance he added a flow of words on monetary matters, very difficult to staunch. He would soliloquize gravely about finance even on the top of a cornstack, with the dust flowing and the threshing tackle shrieking and munching a few feet away. And this, in the end, was to bring about his dispatch to the ditches.

It might not have done so alone: but Pringle also managed deeply to irritate Jimbo, usually during our lunch breaks. Partly the trouble lay in the formality with which he addressed the old man. Accustomed to being called 'old 'un' or ''chiner', Jimbo did not respond happily to Pringle's cry of: 'Oh *driver* ...!' Pringle meant no harm: it was part of his general dry precision. 'Oh driver – I must draw your attention to an error that seems to have crept into my time-sheet!' Jimbo's eyes would bulge: the meanest farmer in the county had never dared to 'draw his attention' to anything whatever. 'Oh, matey. Is that so?' 'I'm sure you're as anxious as we are to keep the books straight, driver.' It was a fair guess that this was, in fact, an anxiety as remote from Jimbo's mind as one could get. The books, in so far as they existed, were inside his sooty head, helped out now and then by chalk marks made on the wall of his cab. 'Oh. That's how it is, eh?' he'd reply, vague and dangerous at once; and bend to his meal, with brooding ferocity.

I found that meal difficult to contemplate, during those first weeks. We'd sit round an old tin of flame, and Jimbo would toast his sandwiches on the point of a penknife. Pressed to the black holes in the brazier, they'd emit a broad fatty stink. His hands, black and oily, would seize a fragment of meat: the knife would scrape at a bone. Bread would fall to the ground but Jimbo would pick it up, rub off the dust and chaff with a screwing motion of the palm of his hand, and introduce it into his mouth according to a principle, not of mastication, but of continuous stuffing and gulping. His tea he made in a can of the profoundest blackness, and he would inject condensed milk into it as a long white worm blown through a hole in the top of the tin. The meal was plainly two parts of soot, dust and engine grease to one part of meat, bread or tea, and my queasy surburban stomach was turned.

Pringle – and this made things worse between him and Jimbo – would sit slightly apart and eat a meal that seemed a rebuke addressed at the machiner's. Mrs Pringle would have wrapped everything in greaseproof paper, and each heap of sandwiches in paper serviettes of the sort used at parties. His tea came out of a very fat, expensive thermos flask. I'd catch Jimbo staring at him, sometimes, under those eyelids thick with dust, across some bone from which accidents of dust and grease were being approximately wiped. He'd be paying special attention to Pringle's hands which, since he always worked in gloves, were spotlessly white. It was plain that trouble was brewing.

It was a bruising winter: Pringle was finding it fairly intolerable. To him, bad weather was a kind of uncouthness. We were held up for several days by snow – had to sit in a barn, waiting for the enchantment to go away. Dreadful coarseness welled up in us all, in that long frozen idleness: Pringle sat apart from us, rather, stiffly uneasy, reading a book on banking, trying not to frown at the loose banter that occupied us. He did mean to be worldly, to demonstrate that this curious mix of high churchiness and nonconformity that had driven him to be a conchie was capable of the common touch. But here was more commonness than he could bear.

This farm, like many, had a butt, a very simple old man called Dave who was the target of much elementary jesting: and he loved it.

'Hi, Dave! Didn't I see you last night down in 'atfield – looking between a girl's thighs with a torch?' Vast laughter in the barn. 'Damned old fool – hadn't the sense to feel for it!'

Dave torn between delight and the formal necessity of

resentment. 'Oi!' – oi! – they do give me some damned characters round here.'

'You like a bit o' dick then, Dave?'

'Ay – but she were a damned tight fit!'

'Didn't think there was any tight fits down in 'atfield!'

We fell about the barn with delight. Dave's face was afire with the happiest indignation.

Pringle flushed at the page of his book on banking.

It was the excitement of the iciness outside, perhaps, or of the sudden long licensed idleness: but the noisy amusement in that barn was roused by the mildest of jokes. A cowman came in, his shoulders white with snow, followed by his large, corpulent dog: they golloped him down at once as comic fodder.

'That bloody dog's no bloody good! He gets the cat to kill the mice and takes all the credit.'

The barn shook.

Enormous fun was squeezed out of an account of the building of a strawstack which fell down the moment it was finished. 'All sorts they were building it – a Czech —'

We laughed hysterically at the idea of a Czech building a strawstack.

'– a Pole —'

Not a Pole! We pummelled one another with joy.

'– and God knows what —'

Pringle observed to Oliver: 'Jokes at the expense of other nationals seem to me – especially at this moment in time —'

But laughter buried his protest.

After that there were days of thick dust. It settled in my nose like glue. I came to hate the two chaff bags, which so many times a day I had to empty and hook back in their place on the chaff box, the skin of my fingers irritated beyond belief by the perpetual combination of dust and sacking. I hated even more the two places under the barn-worker's belly where the chaff, on occasions when it was not suitable for sacking, was shaken out in heaps that reconstructed themselves as quickly as I flattened them, constantly threatening to rise so high that they would block the opening, drive the chaff back into the machine, bring the whole enterprise to a standstill. I hated most of all the dust-blind alley between the shakers and the trusser, where with two stabs of the fork I impaled the cavings and bullied them into a lunatic pile as far from the pounding machine as I had time to take them. In the wind it was necessary to deal with both chaff and cavings with the awful restraint of someone humouring madmen. At times I would have persuaded the cavings to the top of the heap and the whirling air would instantly return them to their point of origin.

When the corn was very bad, having been stacked damp, the stink of the dust would not leave me: I'd lie in bed, breathing it, the clatter of the machine still in my ears: and fire would squeeze out of my eyes, where the dust had left them deeply sore. Sleep itself was painful, fitful: to sleep was to swim against a tide of time that only too soon reached 6 a.m.

On the windier days, or when the dust was thickest, Frank and I were too grimly occupied to talk. But there were good moments, even when things were at their worst. There was a time when the wind took my careful pile of chaff and threw it high into the air, and for long moments I stood under it, under the confetti-like fall of those tiny coloured fragments, like some absurd bridegroom. There were times, too, when I'd have gone behind a tree to pee, alarmed at the thought of the situation that would await me when I got back to all that accumulating detritus, and suddenly I would feel a wild and not unpleasantly tormenting sense of freedom, having snatched myself out of that stinging dusty vortex of labour: and I would look back and see, for once as a whole, as a distant whole, all this golden tossing, this swimming mist of grey dust, the black *agitato* of the driving belt, the men locked together in a single, drowned, deafened process ...

And then back, perhaps, to barley. Barley was worst of all, though followed closely by rivet wheat. Both these crops were spiked, and the spiked bits, threshed out and set freely floating, would make a storm that left your face sorely red; and the bits would drive themselves deep into your clothing, so that you seemed to be wearing an infinity of pins. But so often, even when it was barley, there were odd beauties to redeem a wretched hour; as when once a whole stack was full of Scotsmen, sheaves more thistle than corn, and the thistledown was beaten out and formed a white moss on the ground, as if the earth had grown suddenly very old. And there were moments that were not beautiful, but had a dream-like oddity about them, because they happened in the dust and the fierce discomfort and against a background of unrelenting toil: as when, suddenly, I saw white-bellied rats leaping, scores of them, from a stack and straight into the jaws of a tiny, nervous dog.

When the day's work was over, and the machine incredibly shuddered to a halt, and everything had been tarpaulined, and the moment came – the moment that perfectly spelled release – when Jimbo wheeled out his black bicycle and cried: 'That's all for now, then, my mateys' – then you'd suddenly be aware of a drop, a vicious decline in vitality that was all the more intense for the fixing of that vitality at the high pitch necessary for work. It was precisely like being drained. Jimbo, always fresh after his day's oiling, would ride away, and you would lean against the barnworker, a tree, anything, and feel utterly empty.

It was no world for Pringle, so unconvincingly enacting the labourer in his cloth cap: which was chosen to bridge his two worlds of the polite suburb and the coarse farmyard. The end came for him when we were threshing on one of the farms on a large, ducal estate. It was named, the estate, after the family surname, which was a hyphenation of titles that sounded like a clash of swords: and the night before Pringle's downfall, walking back across this feudal park, he and I lost our way and blundered into the house, a former royal palace. I found myself shaken by its sudden appearance, by the severe secretive pillars, the enfolded courtyards – its air of unmistakable power, even at this moment, when the world it had played some part in shaping was falling bloodily to pieces. Political white beards seemed imminent in the courtly gardens, among the empty rose-arches. 'Damn its insolence!' I cried. 'You may not associate the family with banking,' observed Pringle, 'but in point of fact, in Elizabethan times . . .'

The farmer here was a particularly tetchy one, given to rages of which it was difficult to discover the cause: though a major one might have been those narrowed eyes through which Jimbo contemplated a particularly unhelpful positioning of the stacks. 'What's wrong! – what's wrong!' the farmer cried: and Jimbo's instant smooth answer, that nothing was wrong – 'No, mister – nothing wrong – no, *that's* all right!' – hardly put him at his ease, since it was delivered in a tone of which Jimbo had made himself a master, and which suggested infinite and insulting disparagement of the stacks, the way they'd been built, their siting and the intellect of the farmer. When, two hours later, we were still nudging and wearily urging the tackle into place, the farmer cried: 'What's all the fuss about?' and Jimbo went so far as to remove his cap, which had always seemed an organic part of him, and muttered grimly: 'We can't move these things about like wheelbarrows, mister. If I'd got stuck for two days, who'd have paid me?'

The farmer took it out on the rest of us. I demurred at having to walk twenty yards with the chaff and cavings. 'We had an old man of eighty to do it last time, and he didn't think he was worth his pay,' the farmer growled. And at our sore midday break, the day after we'd blundered upon the great house, Pringle said: 'He injures himself, you know, driver: if we were fairly decently treated, we'd work all the harder.' The use of the word 'fairly', with its meaningless effect of precision, was characteristic of Pringle. It – and the whole speech – angered Frank: who spat into the brazier and said: 'I shouldn't! I don't feel like working so that a man can get more out of it than he pays me. I feel I'm the sap.'

'Hardly the way the economy can be made to work,' observed Pringle.

But it was Jimbo who was most angered. I'd already noticed his wizard's eye fixed on Pringle that morning: for even in this desperate place, where threshing was monumentally difficult, Pringle had continued his grave soliloquies on financial matters, as he tugged at the steaming sheaves on the stacktop. 'Of course, the validity of a cheque ...' I'd heard him saying: a sheaf hanging forgotten on his fork. 'Oi,' Fred had shouted, empty-handed on the drum. 'Oh, sorry, old man!' Pringle had struggled to rid himself of the sheaf, which he'd contrived to get caught on the fork by its string. But even in the midst of the struggle the unreality of farming had faded away from him, the realities of finance had returned. 'I *would* like to make it quite clear about cheques ...' he'd panted; and then, 'Oh, terribly sorry, Fred, old man. Miserable thing's got caught. Half a mo' ... 'Oh Gawd!' Fred had grunted, in despair: and Jimbo had peered up glintingly from below.

'What's 'oldin' it?' Jimbo had called; and Fred had jabbed a disgusted thumb in Pringle's direction. 'Oh, come on, old 'un,' Jimbo had cried. There was venom in the upturned black face. 'Come on, old' un! You want to leave them tarts alone o' nights, you know. Save your puff for yer work!'

It was carefully chosen, that jibe. So many of Pringle's contributions to our discussions round the brazier had crackled with purity. He had told us how he had seriously considered becoming a monk. We gathered that his very marriage was an affair of immense severity. Now he paused in his wrestling with the sheaf, his face scarlet. 'There's no need to be insulting, driver!' 'Come *on*!' Fred yelled, and suddenly everyone was glaring at Pringle – even the farm boy.

At the end of break Jimbo suddenly gave orders to un-hook the trusser. 'Too wet to bind,' he mumbled. The straw-stack itself was ten yards distant, and Frank had been hard put to it to stagger that distance with the bound trusses and return quickly enough to prevent a pile-up. Now Jimbo said, pointing to Pringle: 'Let *'im* 'ave a go at the straw, for once.' Then, turning to Frank, who looked as though he'd been pitched out of the premiership, he added, soothingly: 'A change, matey! A change does yer good!'

I've never known a threshing tackle work faster than ours did that afternoon. There was an unceasing dusty avalanche of straw at the back. No hint had been given big enough for Pringle to observe. Picking his words with care, he lectured away in between absentminded jabs with his fork and lurching journeys across to the impatient and horribly distant strawstack. I, trying to staunch the stuff, was his audience, most inattentive. 'Look out,' I managed to gasp, now and then, but the words were flowing from Pringle, and it was some time before he noticed that he was taking away only one-tenth of the straw that was dropping round him. Even then, and even when he was trapped in a little bay of straw, he went on elaborating various points about, I think, the Swiss franc. He could only push the straw from him, now, to give himself space to survive in: but his mind was busy. He didn't see what, now, everybody saw: what the idle men on the strawstack saw and did nothing about, because Jimbo had winked at them: what Pringle's friends saw but could not avert, since the tackle was still pounding madly away.

Pringle was building his own tomb.

It was curious to watch him disappear: silent at last, inside a towering hut that suddenly grew a roof and then tumbled in on its unwitting architect. Only then did Jimbo stop the machine. When we freed Pringle, black with dust and bristling with straw, he uttered, before collapsing, one haggard remonstrance: 'I say, driver!'

It was poor Pringle's last day with us. We heard, the following week, that, after passionate petitions from many quarters, including from himself, he was now with drainage. Jimbo was content with a single comment, over the brazier – earnestly spoken, there being no doubt that Jimbo had a very real conviction of the link between daintiness in respect of eating, and debility in respect of threshing.

'It's them little sandwiches that done it,' he said.

2

We arrived, together with the spring, at a farm run by a bailiff: a remarkably unpleasant man, who displayed a sort of lazy, loose viciousness towards conchies. Within minutes of our arrival he had announced that they ought not to be allowed to marry. He enumerated several desert islands to which they could be sent. Jovially nasty, he watched while we pushed the trusser into position. 'I'd like to put you through that – and then the prisoners of war,' he carolled. Frank walked across to his bicycle, took a bottle of water from his rucksack, and drank. 'Real 'chiners,' called the bailiff, 'drink straight out of ponds.'

The sun was with us, at last – not sunshine on which shadows are black, but a mild penetration of the atmosphere by a lemon-coloured light. 'Spring is the opium of the people,' I called out to Frank. He stood, blinking in the light, gazing contentedly after the bailiff. 'Must be,' he said.

Birds sang in every bush. The light leapt at us from the

face of a pond. It was a light in which the little clots of chaff I threw into the air with my fork made green clouds. And as the sunshine searched through all things, we seemed suddenly to be living in a world where nothing had its probable hue. Painted green shreds hopped among the yellow chaff. There were chinese reds and sky-blues, and the whole brilliant splash of the heap on the ground made me tremble. In those first days of pure confident light, even the tackle seemed to have a sweet smell, as if of flowers. And subtle tremors, whether of colour or of scent one could not tell, caused shiverings in the air . . .

The bailiff's laziness meant slow working. There were no chaff bags. When I asked for them: 'Well, lookie here,' he said. 'I haven't got them in my waistcoat pocket.' This was correct: he did not have them in his barn, either. It took an hour to uncover sacks that were like fustian pillowcases, very small.

Two or three girls had been added to us, and the bailiff moved about among them, aimlessly lecherous. 'Don't wear yourself out, dearie.' 'Shouldn't bend over like that, love. Not with these conchies around. But they wouldn't know what to do, love, would they?' Frank thrust his fork in to the ground and leaned back against its head. 'There'll never be any straw again,' he called . . .

That was the beginning of a great April: the April of 1942, full of the lavish sweetness of the moment between spring and summer. There were days when a wholly blue sky would be filled, in a moment, with white clouds and grey hasty ones. The sun leapt in and out. Suddenly, there were air raids again: in the sunlight, so much less credible than in the winter darkness of 1940. We moved from farm to farm, stack to stack: from oats to barley to wheat, and once to beans. There were many days when we spat black. At one place the hard little shells of wheat pelted me as though I were under fire from a hundred peashooters. I continued to note that there were in nature a great many colours that were not obvious colours for the objects in question: purple fencing, for example, the gaudiest reds and blues in straw . . .

And, like a background of grey canvas for the splashes of pleasure, monotony. The growth of a strawstack was the very movement of monotony. The rapt monotony, I thought often, used the hours of the day much as a top spins. 'The spinning top of monotony,' I'd say to myself, as I laboured in yet another narrow passage between stack and chaff box, the wind blowing again and narrowed to a force that flung chaff, straw, thistles in my face. Once more, for yet another long day, the hot irritation of chaff, striking the face, rushing up sleeves, penetrating my clothes and forming round my collar a burning ring. There was no time to separate one action from another. And when I undressed at home, I'd find that chaff had made two lung-shaped burns on my chest.

And such longing for experience, springing out of the new summer as it grew. Absolutely anything – a bicycle passing on the road outside the farmyard, an old milk bottle lying in a dip – perhaps something only half seen, a dab of colour or twist of shape caught by the edge of the eye as I swung from one hasty act to the next – anything whatever seemed the starting point for some adventure there was no time to formulate, even ... Frank shared this torment, inflicted by war on all young people, alongside its more specific cruelties: the torment of natural experience utterly arrested. I did not forget that so much worse was happening everywhere, and to so many, than the discomforts of threshing. Yet, I'd feel, wasn't it a symbol of that general vast tedious arrest of natural development – that day after day I did nothing more than poke my head into a cavernful of flying pepper?

But underlying each of these days there was this excitement for which one sought a reason in vain – behind one's back, intently in the far corner of a field. You were aware of a magnitude, but not of what constituted the magnitude. The hours knocked you about the head; you tried desperately to hang on to some sense of a sequence of thought and time. And every day ended with frustration – with a feeling of having come close to something without recognizing it. In the first moment of the day, the very reopening of life, the accumulated expectancy of it, brought about sharp disappointment. And the evening's fatigue was in a sense a gratefully, if uneasily, accepted escape from the need to satisfy that expectancy. Morning and early evening were the worst periods of uneasiness. But this was all confused, anyway, given an extra dimension of uncertainty, by a characteristic of continuing great tiredness: that one had, throughout the day, a very strong intimate memory of one's dreams. Altogether, reality and dreams – the actual and the might-be – were hopelessly tangled.

Many days seemed either not to have happened or to have been quite without meaning. And at times the revulsion from monotony and repetition was an actual pain. I remember such an occasion, when even Frank's passion for argument and discussion seemed beyond bearing as one more familiar feature of what had become so hideously familiar in general. It was a day with sharp ten-minute periods of vast rain, with the sky divided into sections of livid cloud and bright blue. There was snivelling of rain, in between, not making threshing impossible, but making of the dust and thistles a sticky mass that coated everything near the tackle, including hands and face and clothes. There was every kind of uncomfortable weather, that day. For an hour or so there was a wind that seemed to have an actual intention of malice behind it: it blew the driving belt off, over and over again. Insupportably weary, I stumbled away from the tackle at one point and stared at it, hardly seeing it at first, and then noticing how it leaned down a slope and stood, a heap of blunt red angles, against the dark sky: it was foreshortened, as if Stanley Spencer had painted it ... Suddenly, indeed, it seemed to me like a Stanley Spencer come to life, surrounded as it was with foreshortened men in big boots and caps, having that comic, squat relationship to the tilted tackle that you find between men and machines in Spencer's paintings.

Frank said: 'What's wrong with the chap? He's not in the mood for anything.' And there was an anger between us for a while – a really deep, black anger; and had we spoken we should have said things difficult to forgive.

The threshing season was driving towards its end: we began to realize that what awaited us beyond it was drainage.

There were three weeks of a fierce wind in that May of 1942. It blew off even the new leaves. Each massive day, the straw streamed back on to the stack, while the refuse that should have collected beneath the tackle was raked out by the wind and blown fiercely against the side of a stack, where it formed a limpet-like growth. We worked on two little heaps of corn on a stony smallholding; then, at the next farm, in the middle of our first day, the wind suddenly went, leaving a heat that flashed from Frank's tall forehead, and a radiant light in which my hands moved red and golden. But even here, where full summer burst upon us, I had my dark office of dust between stack and tackle: the chaff blown from under the machine rose up and up, drowning the little door leading to the fan, and lifting me until I was towering over the bags into which the chaff should have poured, and the bags themselves, instead of hanging in their places, were lying out horizontally. Our distress was dramatic. It occured to me, as we nevertheless managed, that there was a Hercules in us all.

'Frank!' I cried at one point. 'I'm haunted by my cleaner self – radiant and pure in a white shirt.'

Frank gave me a token of a smile through eyes half-closed with dust.

There was a little rain, suddenly, curiously smelling of old books and fried bacon; and then the full heat came down again. Sweat closed our eyes altogether, gummed the dark dust to our chests, made our faces shine like polished wood. A huge pail of water was placed in the shadow of trees. Even the smoke of the engine was welcome for its function as an umbrella. As the bulky sheaves of wheat were raised and thrown from the stacktop, we flinched from the golden glare of it in the sun...

It was there that Jimbo gave us a rare glimpse of his past, as a lifelong 'chiner. The story was told over the brazier, during a break, and it brought Fred, usually slumbrous, to life: for Fred always acted as master of ceremonies, chairman and, as it were, signalman to his uncle's stories. He made sure that Jimbo took the story along the proper line, to the proper junction.

'Ah!' said Jimbo, on this occasion. His stories often began out of the blue, with an 'Ah!' 'I worked up at Mr Snape's place once. Not fur from here. Millionaire, he was. Rollin'.'

'You was rollin' too,' said Fred.

'Steamrollin',' said Jimbo, impassively: it was clearly an old joke in the family. 'We'd be at it, mornin's, an' the steward 'ud come along. "Stop work, my man. Stand by. Mr Snape's comin' on 'is meal."'

'Like a donkey, they are, these meals,' Fred explained.

'So I stood by. Four hours I stood by, mateys, waiting ... Then you could see Mr Snape comin', on this meal. Big fat man on this little donkey, like. An' a man runnin' in front – sort o' butler. Runs up to me an' says, "Mr Snape's comin' on 'is meal. Shut off that steam, my man. Mustn't frighten the meal." '

'Four hours,' Fred recapitulated. 'Then my uncle 'ad to shut off the steam. For fear o' frightenin' the meal.'

'But there was still a whisker o' steam comin' out o' the valves —'

'You listen to this,' said Fred.

'So I popped a little bag over it. And then I stood by th'engine and touched me cap as Mr Snape went by.'

'On 'is meal,' Fred clarified.

Jimbo blew an enormous worm of milk out of his tin and into his teacan.

' 'E'd 'ire you for a time,' he said. 'For a fixed time. Like it might be two months. Well, you might not finish the work in two months. Never mattered. Off you'd go, once it was up.'

'But if you done it in a week —' said Fred.

'–then you'd stay till the two months was up. You'd just come and sit by the engine till the fixed time was up. That was Mr Snape. Millionaire, 'e was.'

'That was when my uncle worked for Mr Snape,' said Fred, to make all clear.

And so we came to our last farm. It was the quietest, friendliest place of all, owned by two brothers. One was tall and skinny, with a red face whose ugly receding architecture, decorated with sparkling white eyebrows and moustaches, might have interested Rembrandt. The other was small and round, with a ready sentimental fondness for people. He was the only man, during those long months of threshing, who praised Frank for his deft way with the straw. Both brothers were there to greet us, courteously, each morning – something that had happened at no other farm. But the real delight, for me, of this last threshing was that a boy miraculously offered to do the chaff and cavings, while I, winking at the wicked dust, flew to the clean height of a stack that was half-oats, half-wheat.

I stood in the sun and breathed deeply; and slowly, slowly, we tossed away the stack.

But towards the end of the third afternoon, when we'd moved to a stack of oats, Jimbo whispered to Fred, and we guessed at once what was to come. We knew Jimbo's mind now, through and through. It was a mind simply furnished, and most of the furniture consisted of calculations as to how to make most profit from hastenings and delayings, between farms and on them. So now Fred whispered to Oliver, and Oliver to me, and I told the next man who passed the news on to Frank, that we didn't – for reasons provided by that calculating machine in Jimbo's skull – wish to finish the stack that night. It was perilously close to the ground: the tall brother was eyeing it thoughtfully. I placed the sheaves to the extreme left of Oliver, then to the extreme right: he stumbled and sent some of them back: we blew our noses and pursued imaginary rats. It was hard on such rarely nice farmers: but by Jimbo's calculations our world had long been ruled. Still the stack went down. Then, suddenly, chaff fountained from the blower.

'Look!' cried Oliver. 'A block!'

Jimbo concealed a grin for all of us, and stopped the machine.

But I was not to come to the end of my experience of threshing with a grin. There'd been very little grinning in it; it was not to finish with one. The blockage was very severe. It exceeded Jimbo's purpose. Looking down from the clean airs of the stack, I read the old 'chiner's lips as he conferred with the courteous brothers. 'Give it to *him*,' he was saying – and a nod in my direction – 'no one can do it like our chaff and cavings man – not a serious block since October.'

I gave up my fork, I went down, and there I was, for the rest of that day and half the next, the last of our threshing days – there I was in the worst dust I'd ever known, blowing out like the smoke of a fire, the interior of the trusser invisible, my spittle blacker than any previous black ...

We went to drainage by way of a short experience of potato riddling.

The War Ag had lost any sense of us, Oliver and Frank and me and the rest, as mobile workers. We must have been firmly set down in the office as a threshing team. To re-establish us was not the work of an instant. For a morning we even found ourselves polishing and purging the tackle, under Jimbo's orders, cleaning the autumn and winter and half a summer out of its dusty innards: we began to dream that we might be allowed to go into retirement with it, until the start of the next season. But suddenly the little War Ag van arrived, the little War Ag official sprang out, distempered by his impression that we were momentarily loose and unassigned; and an hour later we stood in a field beside a clamp of potatoes, which had been left late for lifting, so that when we broke the end – like forking your way into some immense Cornish pasty – it was to discover a softness of potatoes, a taut tangle of white shoots. We dug into the heap with the special fork, and poured the potatoes into the riddle. One of us turned the handle of this infernal machine; the wire cylinder revolved, the potatoes bumping round inside it, and the smaller ones fell out and the larger ones climbed a moving rubber staircase and dropped into a sack. An expressionless farmer stood among us, doing some sorting of his own, by hand.

The riddle! – ye gods! – it seemed an insult in an age of machines. First one and then another of us worked the handle, turning it until he was only half-conscious. The effect seemed exaggerated for mere potato riddling; but it was agony. You closed your eyes – grew aware only of a leaden circle with a centre of pain situated at your side – your body reduced to a circle of tightness where your belt dug into your belly. Behind your eyes, an alternation of a vague light and then soft darkness as you bent and then straightened up. Once or twice, as I turned, I sharply opened my eyes, and was startled by the grey dry light of day and by the spectacle of the potatoes, which in my self-induced darkness I'd imagined as golden, rolling dingily inside the cylinder.

Thousands of brown dirty spheres, then, for several days – locked together by white shoots: the black and yellow mess of a bad potato: the sickly blue smell of rottenness...

We were working on a new clamp, which looked like some monstrous grave, richly covered with poppies, daisies and cowparsley a yard high, when the War Ag van came buzzing among us again. Oliver and I were to go ditching one way: Frank in the opposite direction. 'Tomorrow, seven-thirty sharp,' said the official. He shook together the papers in his hand and frowned, as if somehow he had failed to be sufficiently menacing.

Frank said: 'It will do us good, to be separated for a while. We're beginning to grow on each other, Ted – like these damned potatoes.'

George was home, briefly: longing for colour, after half a dozen crossings to Newfoundland.

'After the Atlantic,' he said, 'you want bright things. I suppose that's why the sailor likes coloured parrots – and coloured women, too.'

Still, I thought, talking of women.

'... large, noisy, brassy. Perhaps that's why I liked her. I expect you are cutting swathes among the ladies of the Women's Land Army?'

I made the noise of a man who might, perhaps, be cutting such swathes.

At sea, said George, a convoy looked exactly like some industrial town: it was a mass of chimneys, which happened to be afloat.

'This Rommel,' he said turning his attention to the war on land. 'Perhaps Hollywood will snap him up?'

I wanted badly to tell him about Frank, Jimbo, the colours in the chaff. But it seemed small beer – lemonade – beside the huge grim adventures which, while stressing their tedium, he was hinting at.

It was a hurried leave. We clasped hands and I heard his slow hesitating footsteps going away once more into the darkness. 'Ditching?' he'd said, puckering his forehead. 'It sounds like hard work to me.'

Part Three

1

Tusk was in charge of drainage. He and other top brass had established themselves on a large farm that the War Ag was bending to its will. We presented ourselves, that first morning, to Tusk in his caravan.

He had the most curious nostrils. They addressed themselves directly to you – black holes that fixed you, as in more normal faces you might be fixed by the eyes. Tusk's eyes were cold, a dim blue, and baleful enough: but they were mere supports to those menacing nostrils.

We all exchanged glares of instant dislike. Then Tusk grunted: 'Sign on. Sign off. Seven-thirty to seven-thirty. Not a minute after. Not a minute before. No miking. We do things with mikers. Fix yourselves with spades and shovels. Report yourselves to Buttery. And let's see you really moving down that field.'

As we walked through the dipping spaces of this already severely-trimmed farm, at what we hoped was a dignified compromise as to pace, Oliver said: 'Sauce!' He was a master of comment that was inadequate in this old-fashioned way.

The farm was being mole-drained; gangs here and there were digging pipe-lines to receive the water that would gush through the narrow channels made underground by the mole. This, like a small shell, was drawn through the fields, this way and that, by a curious cultivator commanded by an old man wearing a very high hat. Or rather, it was the cultivator that was tugged across the fields, on a system of wires. It was odd to watch it: the old man, sitting high under his towering hat on the immense, black machine, seemed to be dragged across a field much against his will: from a distance, his manipulation of the simple controls when he reached a turning point resembled feeble gestures of protest; and then he and his machine were whirled round, at rude speed, and whisked back across the field.

Buttery, our foreman, was a sad, gentle, ineffectual man, bespectacled, who clearly found it difficult to hit the note of brisk brutality struck by Tusk, and exacted by him from all his underlings. He was, we discovered from one of Tusk's jeers, a farmer dispossessed by the War Ag for inefficiency. He did his best to be unpleasant, grunting his own version of Tusk's orders. Then, half-turning away as we stared at the ground we must break open, he murmured: 'It may interest you to know that in that caravan up there are half a dozen *agricultural geniuses . . .*' He whirled round again: 'At all times, have the sense to keep your bloody tools in your hands.'

He tried hard then to be beastly to Oliver who, boiling still with his sense of the sauce of it all, was chipping away with the half-hearted tip of a spade. Then, looking away from us once more, Buttery murmured: 'Spies everywhere. The great Tusk uses field-glasses. Beware . . .' Back then, and sharp bark at me.

This was the pattern of it, with Buttery. He'd face you, to make his attempt at nastiness: turn away, to cancel it with some seditious murmur about our masters. He was a man who longed for things to go well, for amiability to prevail. He was back with us in the afternoon, when we'd cut two or three yards of pipe-line – it was slow work, with a top spit of gravel – and began with a very large tape measure to gauge the hole we'd made. Then he stepped back. 'Best cut I've seen here.'

We mumbled amazement.

'Oh yes. The one with the most sense behind it. Commonsense. At least you know that water runs downhill.'

'Do we?' Oliver was surprised into asking.

'Squint here. Get down here and take a squint. See! I reckon it'll come out in the ditch – just over there!'

'So it will,' said Oliver: slow to assume the role of gifted ditcher.

'The better and more quickly you do your work, the less you'll see of me.'

'Ah,' said Oliver; and Buttery glared, sighed, suppressed some pleasant farewell that had almost slipped through his guard: and went sadly away.

Later still, Tusk appeared, surrounded by half a dozen orderlies: they came on an eddy of shouts, as they expressed their dissatisfaction at this pipe-line or that: and then they were standing above us, as we laboured away in our narrow cleft. I struck a stone, and picked my way round it with the edge of my spade: Oliver stood, observing me sympathetically.

'Here's another couple of 'em,' Tusk observed jovially, 'who'd not be shot in Germany.'

I let my stone be and said: 'Eh?'

'You have to dig your own grave there,' said Tusk, 'and you'd be so long at it, they'd give up and go away.'

'Sauce!' said Oliver, but his observation was lost in the appreciative laughter that spread through the ranks of our overseers.

I've no doubt, at this distance of time, that the War Ag had a difficult working force under its alarmed command. Most of us conchies would, in fact, have presented few problems in a less inflamed atmosphere: we were rather solemnly efficient workmen, by temperament. But there were other members of this ragged army of ditchers: men with queer histories – ancient ex-soldiers, nondescript refugees from urban life, boys not yet called up: one or two sad madmen. The War Ag might well have felt of us as Wellington felt of *his* army. And the conchie, with his horrible habit of asking questions and his general passion for talk – he must have made the War Ag feel curiously nervous. But the absurd Tusk compounded the edginess of officialdom with his bully's outlook. And so Ridgemount Farm seethed with angers, with jumpy watchfulness.

We had among us a man who'd been a trade union steward in peacetime, and who fairly welcomed Tusk's tone. He had a language to match. 'Tusk,' he would say, 'and the *parasites* who hang around him . . .' 'Parasites' was a word he used so pat when speaking of officials that it sounded like a formal title. Sometimes he would relax a little and call them 'the intelligentsia of the civil service' or 'things in clean clothes'. 'Ah, there,' he would cry, 'are the parasites, in conference over some important piece of mud': and instantly he would call a conference of his own. 'There's some filthy motive behind this overtime! I think the parasites receive some kind of bonus for it.' A term he used frequently was 'so-called'. It might be the War Ag itself that was 'so-called': or some National Service Officer: or, often, the farm. We were absurdly excited by this rhetoric. We would buzz with approval when, at some lunch-break ('this so-called break allowed us by Tusk and his para-sities'), our leader read extracts from his latest letter to County Hall. 'Adverting to the contempt emanating from your office...' he would read; and we'd nudge each other with pleasure. And when, one day, we found he had used the term 'Prussianism' to describe the conduct of Tusk and his tame intelligentsia, our glee knew no bounds.

It was all very silly: in the context of what was raging around us, the smallest storm in the smallest of teacups. Yet it was my first introduction to industrial angers – and I felt that our spokesman's phrases, with their stilted conven-tions of irony and scorn, were drawn from a vocabulary that had been real enough in the bitter years before the war. The boss and his representatives were the Enemy: it was as simple as that.

I learned much about this sort of thing, but in more reas-onable terms, when I met Mike Ferrini.

We came together in another of Ridgemount's pipe-lines; our union being the whim of a foreman called Wal.

Buttery had never revised his view of Oliver and me: we had once seemed to be executing the best cut on the farm, and whatever we did thereafter could not take the value out of that. We gave him grounds enough for disillusionment. There was an occasion when, at his behest, we dug deeper and deeper – 'Well, you'll have to keep on going down, won't you?' – and at last he came and asked: 'Found any-thing yet?' Oliver said: 'No. By the way – what do you expect to find?'

Buttery whistled with dismay. Then he clearly decided to disregard this evidence that we'd been quite unaware that the monstrous depth of the dig was demanded by the elu-siveness of a mole-drain. He made his whistling rise, into obstinate cheerfulness: then he said, 'I don't bother you chaps, do I?'

'No,' said Oliver, a little wearily – Buttery's way with conversation, which was to proceed along a sequence of simple, self-answering questions, lay strains upon his inter-locutors.

'Do you know why?'
'No.'
'Can't you really guess why?'
I took the burden from Oliver. 'No.'

'Because you get on with your work and do it properly.'

But Oliver had decided that very day to defy the inflexible demand that we work overtime till half-past seven. He looked at his watch: it was six o'clock. Smiling at Buttery, he vaulted out of the gulch: gathered his tools and slung them over his shoulder. Buttery stared at him, wholly bewildered.

'Where are you going?'

'Home. I'm tired. I've had enough. I just want a free evening!'

Poor Buttery! It was a hard moment for him! At the very instant when he'd been handing out prizes, one of his best scholars had decided to behave like the worst. He turned away, desolate. 'Oh well. I won't bother to come tomorrow, then – seems there's no need for me.' Oddly, the misery of working under Tusk must have been softened by the quite absurd feeling he had about Oliver and me: we had been a glimpse of that utopia of simple, orderly, friendly, unexacting achievement he longed for. One saw why he'd been broken, as a farmer. He assumed then a sort of heart-broken gaiety, making a cricket-stroke with the spade in his hand, crying: 'Well, well, well ... that's how it is, then ...'

Oliver had a brief shouting-match with Tusk up at the caravan; and the next morning he was sent to Jack Bone's gang. It was the worst thing that could happen to you, they said. All the awkward ones were pushed in his direction: the protesters against overtime, the slow ditchers, and anyone who was impertinent to an official. I had a clear picture of Jack Bone: a huge, savage man whose gang was always in some Siberian region of the county. The mud there was muddier than anywhere else, and to reach it you had to dig down through granite.

It was as I stood about, mateless, that I was seized upon by Wal and yoked to Mike Ferrini.

Wal was a tiny, baffled man, who'd once worked in sewers, and liked to describe his experience in a long monologue that consisted largely of exclamations: 'Phew!' 'Ugh!' 'Gawd!' and 'What a ponk!' These were accompanied by reelings, to suggest the near-faintness that had been his condition much of the time underground. His face was perpetually screwed up, as though these smells had never left his nose. Mike Ferrini had once spent a night in one of the War Ag hostels, in a bed next to Wal's. From Wal, all night long, he said, had come a fitful, bothered little chirrup.

Worriedly, now, Wal put me on the shovel behind Mike's spade. 'I've got you a good shovel man here,' he said – on what grounds I could not guess. Mike, as one of the older conchies – he was nearly forty – had Wal's confidence. This was, he said, one of the more difficult pipe-lines under his jurisdiction, and having secured in Mike a dependable, because middle-aged, digger, he had been anxious for some time to cap the achievement with a shoveller at least of promise. Mike solemnly listened to this statement: then, when Wal had gone, he said: 'Well, here we are, then. Crack ditchers both, eh? Distinguished Ditching Cross!'

He had a very long body topped by a small, thin face: curly hair looped out of his cap. He was a political conchie – a member of the Independent Labour Party. He had a sense of comedy that was wry and dry. To find himself ditching – he was a skilled cabinet-maker by trade – filled him with constant wistful amazement. 'Could you,' he asked me that first time we worked together, 'could you look at this ditch at the end of a day's work and say "*I did that!*"?' He pulled at the peak of his cap and added: 'Or bring your friends round to see it? "Just a ditch I put together the other day."'

He was much struck by the primitive character of the agricultural scene, by the monotony of its labours. He had a fear that the war might go on and on, and that he might grow terribly old, ditching. 'Like one of those old jossers of ninety you see – they must know every blasted twig in the county.' He would attack himself sadly for the sequence of awkward beliefs that had led him into this predicament. 'Just because I stuck to what I was pleased to call my principles. Why should I have wished to be different from the rest of the crew!'

I knew, a hundred times that first day, that I'd met a mate who would brighten the hours of ditching, as long and slow as the ditches themselves. It was partly that sad comedy, usually at his own expense. Throwing his spade down, he cried: 'There's one other thing I'd like to fling down on the ground – myself...' And when we left that evening, and his spade and mattock rattled together over his shoulder: 'Is that my chain or yours?' he asked lugubriously.

Mike was married to a girl of whom he spoke with a tenderness touched with comic exasperation. He discussed critically, and lovingly, her lack of any sense of direction: her deep, easy jealousy. It worried him that so many working-class marriages, as he'd observed, broke up over questions of money. 'I hope to God I never reach that stage ... Though it's not easy for the poor kid, on a farm labourer's wage. When she gets a bit sharp, I tell myself the strain's on her more than on me. She has to do the shopping, poor creature.'

Mike and I worked so often together, over the next months, that we came to know each other's life-stories with crippling exactness. It became dangerous to invent or vary a detail in any story you might have told before. When that happened once, in a story of mine, and I was able to convince Mike of the truth of the new version, he cried: 'Damn! That's twenty pages I'll have to tear up and rewrite!' ... This first day I learned of his great love of Dickens; of his impatience with religious conchies ('My God, when I think how the working-class leaders of the past, often alone, stood up and won their battles – and then hear *these* people discussing the political struggle .. .'); and of his impatience, also, with practically helpless people. I'd confessed that I wasn't really able to maintain my own bicycle. A puncture would take me clumsy hours to trace and repair. 'My God,' said Mike. 'I can't help it. That enrages me. I'm enraged when I see a man who can't knock a nail in a wall. Well, that's how it is. I think he's twopence short of a bob. Or he's lazy. Usually he's lazy.' He told me of an occasion when, at work, he'd been asked if he would drive a nail into a ceiling. His employer had stood by and watched as he did it, exclaiming: 'Wonderful! Amazing how you do that! How you knock the nail upwards, I mean! Must be incredibly difficult.' 'And all the really intricate carpentry jobs I'd done for him,' Mike groaned. 'After all the work I'd done, he had to admire *that*!'

It was a good day: I'd stumbled on an amusing mate. When we'd checked our tools in, Mike found his bicycle had become entangled with a hedge. He dragged at it, wearily: then addressed it – as, I guessed, he might have addressed his jealous, compass-deaf, much-loved and loving wife.

'Don't you wanna go home?' he'd groaned.

Then, suddenly, the day came when I was sent to Jack Bone's gang.

Mike was away that day, with a cold. It had been a bad night: a bomb had dropped on a house a few doors away from our own. Just before my mother's screaming woke me up, a whole dream of dread formed round her screams, and then my eyes sprang open to malevolent moonlight. Apparently from my mother's room came the explosion of the bomb and the sound of smashed glass, together with that great rush of air that was always as if some gaseous plant were springing, vast, out of the ground. Murmuring ludicrous consolations, I leapt out of bed faster than my body could really manage, and slipped to the floor ... We ran out into the street and stared with horror at the smoking hole where the house had been; and then found our neighbours, bland with shock, sitting paralysed in their garden shelter.

At the lunch break I lost myself in a dangerous slumbrousness. I stared up at the great white shapes of cloud above, and they became an immense, slow movement of abstracts: I lost my sense of what they really were; the clickings and cryings of the farm formed themselves into a beguiling music. I fell back through memories, back into childhood – was lying by the school cricket field, and then in a meadow where I'd played when very young...

I was woken by Tusk. I'd been asleep for an hour. I reminded him, he said briefly, of a rat, and if ever he found himself without a lavatory he'd be glad to use me as one. And meanwhile, I should get my bike and pedal rather a long way and surrender myself to that ogre, Jack Bone.

Jack turned out to be a remarkably tiny man, plump, with bowed legs and the face of a rather amiable, very ugly elderly lady. 'Ugh,' he said, when I gave him a purged version of Tusk's message: and handed me a spade. I joined the other extreme cases in the ditch – which seemed quite a commonplace one.

'New boy, Jack?' asked a tall youth who was digging next

to me. 'Ugh,' said Jack. 'They're giving you a nice big gang now, Jack.' 'Ugh,' said Jack; and then suddenly, in an accent which I later discovered to be Northumbrian and which enabled me to approach his startling vocabulary little by little, launched into an obscenely jocular comment on the War Ag's habit of sending all and sundry to join him. But it was plain that he was pleased. He flexed himself and blushed. 'Foreman Number One, eh?' said the tall youth with what seemed to me crudely obvious flattery. 'Ee, ma'be,' said Jack, and then turned to me and demanded my name. I told him my surname. 'Nay,' he said impatiently, brushing the awkward sound aside. 'Tha *name*!' 'Ted,' I said. 'Don' kill thasel', Ted,' said Jack, and bowled away.

It took me some time to digest the discovery that this punitive gang was a fraud. It took me less time to discover why. Jack's reputation wasn't entirely false. He was, basically, an immensely fierce little person, who'd got small and crushed and bowed because he'd once been a miner, and who'd made use of his telescoped condition to become a wrestler – of distinction, we gathered. Fierce he certainly was: yet, just as some people may be reduced to impotence by tickling, so Jack, his gang had found, was helplessly open to flattery.

And on the most absurd grounds. A day or so after I arrived he put on a pair of rimless spectacles and squatted by the ditch, reading a newspaper. It was known that he could barely write – everyone carefully avoided noticing that the tall youth signed our timesheets for him. He also couldn't read. We learned later that he'd picked up the spectacles in the hostel where he lodged. I think he believed that spectacles, if they could not cure the inability to read, at least made that strange skill less remote. And now, as he sat there studiously examining the front page, there was a chorus of admiration along the ditch. It was as if reading were some new and marvellous feat of acrobatics. 'Always keep abreast of the news, eh, Jack?' 'What's the latest, then, Jack?' Flexing himself, and blushing, Jack looked at us over his glasses, then turned the newspaper over and studied the back. 'All reet,' he said. 'Tha can come out o' the ditch now and tak' a bit o' rest.'

Mike Ferrini turned up a few days later. 'Sleeping in the ditch?' I asked, delighted to see him. 'No,' said Mike. 'They gave me a Christadelphian as a mate. He to'd me the poor would always be with us. Got the information from some book he'd been reading. The Bible, I think he called it. So I asked for a transfer.' 'And Tusk let you come?' Mike smiled. 'I didn't pedal here,' he said. 'My bike took fright at Tusk's language and freewheeled straight to Jack Bone's.'

It was a dull little farm, this first one on which we worked as Jack's men, driving a drain through a sad orchard. We hurried to direct the water into a pond of great moroseness, and then to be gone.

The next farm was bigger, airier. Spread over it, a pair here and a pair there in the brown ditches, and others chopping at hedges under trees still thickly leafed, we called to mind, I thought, the exiled duke's party in the forest of Arden. There were horses on this farm and one day we looked up to see Jack Bone high above us, staring over a hedge with a big brown horse's face between his legs, also gazing. 'You've a good seat, Jack,' said Mike Ferrini, hastily. 'Been riding long, then?' In a thick flood of words, bashful and obscene at once, Jack told us that he had indeed been a horseman all his life. He sat on the animal like a fat little rubber ball, and we were terrified that the horse would spoil things by canting to one side and letting Jack simply roll off. But the horse, too, seemed to have sensed Jack's weakness. It stayed obsequiously still.

There was, in the matter of Jack Bone, a problem left. How did he continue to convince the War Ag of his awfulness? The answer came the first time one of the official vans drew up in the farmyard. The dapper man from County Hall had barely got out before Jack was up and down the ditches, raging. We didn't, luckily, catch more than one word in ten. *They* were pretty horrible words. And while the official was there Jack had a rather odd shot at calling me by my surname.

We were breathless by the time the van had driven off. But the tall youth managed to say: 'Well, you know how to handle those fellows, Jack.' And Jack flexed his wrestler's knuckles and blushed. 'All reet,' he said. 'Tha can come out now and ha' a bit o' rest.'

And so long months began of hedging and ditching: from the middle of 1942 to near the end of 1943. We broke open the face of field after field; I was haunted by the smell of clay as I'd been haunted by the dust of threshing. And again, despite the boredom, the tightening frustration, the turmoil in my mind as I tried to feel full confidence in the stand we were taking – the phrase itself seemed excessive for our occupation of this green backwater while the flood poured past us – again, the quality of the material we were working in became beautiful to me. Once down through the dry stony first foot or so, in most places, there was clay – wet clay I found myself constantly moulding with my hands, leaving the sides of the ditches littered with little clay men, tablets scored with quotations or my name. It was good to be making channels for water. And the clay had such a range of colour as astonished me – from the darkest brown to the hue of pale straw. There was a day when we cut into a patch so intensely orange-coloured, so burning, that I looked up – though it was in the early morning – to see the sunset that had stained it.

I noted an effect of this endless manual labour: that now, when I saw a knot tied somewhere, anything heaped up, I thought of the men whose toil lay behind the knot or the heap. I became aware of the enormous boring daily labours on which the whole world rested. I thought solemnly that after years of middle-class schooling and then three years of petty journalism, this was a knowledge I needed to have. I hoped it was one I should not forget, if ever, for me, there came an end to it.

Among my new mates there was Bernard, a middle-aged conchie who believed that war was caused by the opposition of electrons: if man could learn to control the atom, then he would be able to control human behaviour. With no ironic prescience, we expressed mild astonishment. Bernard was gently and attractively unpersuasive. There was a young musician whose objection to war, and indeed to much of what surrounded him, seemed to be aesthetic. Unbearably graceful and wincing, he filled me, who aspired then to be apart and mysterious – I felt that to be truly intellectual one must be mysterious – with an odd guilt. I got on so well with the Franks and the Mikes, whose suspicion of the higher culture caused this young man such courteous distaste. I was reminded of a sentence in an editorial in *Horizon*: talking of intellectuals, it said, 'Most of us know that while we are always somewhat ridiculous, we are no more ridiculous than we were before the war.' Surely Vernon was ridiculous, and I, as a would-be intellectual, should be absurd exactly in his manner. I should be repelled, as he said he was, by the spectacle of Jack Bone: trotting about on his short, stout legs, in his ballooning overalls, the constantly changing weather of his moods making his rough sketch of a face uneasy. But I delighted in Jack. And if I wanted Mike Ferrini's company, as I did, I could not have Vernon's. Mike said: 'Why is his voice so languid? As if it's a great effort to talk at all. I always feel he expects me to fall on my knees and worship him for deigning to address me.' Well, if Mike was a philistine, then so was I. Vernon read Dostoyevsky at breaks: I read D. H. Lawrence. We smiled at each other uneasily, from the midst of our different tribes.

And there was Phil Perkins. Phil was broad of face, a perpetual joker: round of mind and body, and given to wearing a mackintosh hat that looked like a blackened cabbage. Phil had been sent on the land after a term of prison; he was constantly eating, to make up for the long hunger he'd experienced in Wormwood Scrubs. 'If it was food they gave you there, then I'm Lord Wavell.' He was also constantly meaning to read the ends and middles of books he'd read in a maimed state, in jail. 'Then I got this slim book, *Tom Jones*. Well, it was slim because of all the pages that had been torn out, for toilet paper. *Tom Jones* isn't about a hundred pages long, is it, Ted? It was the same with the Bible. You never saw such a short Bible. Someone had used the whole of Leviticus in the lav. One fell swoop, if that's the way to put it.'

By now I'd established myself as Mike's partner. There was something in Mike, his air of calm good sense, that gave him a special status in the eyes of foremen. Jack Bone was capricious in his likes and dislikes. For no very obvious reason, he would suddenly take against you. The mark of that would be his attempt, at some moment of apparently causeless rage, to use your surname. But Mike was immune; and, under his wing, I borrowed for a while his immunity.

'The bloody twats,' said Jack Bone. He applied the phrase,

108

every five minutes or so, to members of his gang; officials; flies, gnats and wasps; and a large range of inanimate objects. He grunted it out at critical moments, but with variations – it was like hearing someone read from an Anglo-Saxon dictionary, in a rage: as when he lumbered towards a group of us one day when a breakthrough had occurred higher up the ditch whose effect Jack had not clearly calculated: 'The bloody twats!' he cried, referring to those who'd made the disastrous cut: 'You bloody twats!' he groaned, referring to us who were staring at him in amazement. 'The bloody twats!' he called again, referring to the War Ag; and then 'The bloody twat!' perhaps at this point having in mind the gush of water that had just overtaken him. 'Look out, you bloody twats: there's a pond coming down! You bloody twats! why didn't you get out? All right, you bloody twats: you'd better dry yoursel'n.'

But the bloodiest twat of all was a ganger who was sent to join us for a day or so, in the vaguest of capacities: clearly a creature of Tusk's enemies. It was possible, from events of this kind that occurred from time to time, to figure out the progress of some conflict occurring between soft-liners and hard-liners in the War Ag. The spy, a curiously anonymous man, dogged Jack everywhere: and Jack treated him as a species of wasp or other irritant insect. He had little guile: 'What're yer followin' me for, you bloody twat!' he exclaimed, that first day, when the inexplicable ganger came to a halt beside him as Jack was staring down at Mike and me in a ditch. 'Ef y' *got* to be here, find some work o' yer own t'do, y'bloody twat!' 'But Jack ...' said the other ganger, uncomfortably sweet. 'Don't "Jack" me!' cried our foreman: and then, drawn to a vague verbal experiment: 'Go off an' "Jack" thasel!'

For the rest of the day we observed the two of them, here and there, Jack performing the most extraordinary manoeuvres for so stout a man who normally carried his body about with some caution, as if afraid that any rapidity of movement might cause it to explode. Jack in and out among the trees; Jack positively fleeing across a distant field; Jack dimly visible, peering from the doorway of a barn. The other ganger took advantage of one of these evasions to interview Mike and me. 'How's Bone as a ganger?' he asked, nervously casual. 'Any complaints?' We stared at him. 'Does he treat you right?' We scratched our heads and looked at each other. 'The Committee,' said this man, 'don't intend that conditions should be too strict.' 'Hmm,' said Mike. 'Too severe, that is,' said the ganger. I said: 'Hmm.' 'Too ... against the men, like.' Mike said, flatly: 'We're friends of Jack Bone's.' 'Ah,' said the man, and trotted away, sighing.

It was like that, in drainage. There was constant toppling of gangers, employment officers, equipment officers, the emergence of transient new powers. There were summonses to County Hall: mysterious disappearances. Simple Jack, baffledly aware of such goings-on, was kept by them in a state of constant exasperation: such intricate politics was not his style, at all. He spent more and more time with Mike and Phil Perkins and me, who'd become a trio of confessors for him. Not that Jack often made direct reference to the Machiavellianism of his employers. But he liked to come to rest beside us and snort: 'Bloody officials!' 'Bloody twats!' Phil would suggest. 'They're bloody twats a' right,' Jack would say, filled with astonishment at the justice of the phrase, as if it had been freshly minted. 'But you can handle them, Jack!' 'Ah! ... It's ten minutes afore break time. But you can get out now, if y'like.'

Meanwhile I learned more and more about Mike – and about Phil Perkins. Phil was a conchie, not for the more common religious reasons, but on what he ruefully called 'rational grounds'. Like Mike, he had a natural sense of the comedy of things, a gift for absurd humour. Thus we came across the field one morning after the first frost of the year: the dug-out earth of the pipe-line, which this day – the pipes having been laid – we must tumble back, was locked, frozen, to the ground. 'I told you,' said Phil, 'we shouldn't have left it out all night.'

Amused by my verbal innocence – which indeed, alas, went so much deeper than words – the other two would ply me with phrases for sexual activity: my role being to express incredulous amazement, and to pretend to make notes for some untoward dictionary.

'To go for a nibble?' Mike would gravely suggest: and Phil would rejoin: 'Ah yes – to have a kneetrembler.' 'Her dumplings,' Mike would murmur, with a great pretence of difficult scholarly recall, 'are ... boiling over!' Phil would clap a hand to his forehead: stroke an imaginary pedantic beard. 'Let's have a *railing-pudding*!'

Phil's sense of the comic was runaway, inventive. Mike was always more dry: his humour lay like a twist of the mouth over his great political earnestness. And yet even about the ways of his political world Mike had, as it were, a chagrined capacity for laughter. He told me once how, as a young ILPer, he'd been responsible for inviting one of his foremost heroes to come and speak. 'Set your blood racing,' he said. 'Ah, what a talker! What sense! What fire! What a mind! ... Then we gave him tea, afterwards. And what a shock I had! I saw this great man manoeuvring – manoeuvring, mark you – to get the best cake on a plate of penny buns! It was the first time I realized great men were ordinary men, too. But whenever I heard him after that, I could always see him twisting that plate round, ever so quickly and ... greedily – so that someone else should have a rotten cake and the best one would come to him!'

Under these self-teasing humours, Mike's heart bled for the world at war. He'd fall silent sometimes, sigh and say, 'Sorry! I've suddenly got the blue blind hump – thinking of what men are doing...' The war was trudging across the long aching plain of its infinitely weary strategies. 'I used to wonder,' Mike would say, 'how they endured four years of it last time! Four years! Way we're going, it'll be ten years, this round!' 'Like the Trojan War,' I murmured. 'Sorry,' said Mike, quickly defensive at references he didn't take. 'That's one I missed.'

At times, perhaps standing in his cape under a tree during a shower, looking like one man standing on top of another – sadly amused by himself, Mike would float dreams of comfort, freedom, fullness of life. 'I'll be a hermit, when it's all over. I'll find a cave and sit in it, herming. After the war I'll buy a secondhand panama hat and set sail for the south seas ... All my life has been spent in dirty cabinet-makers' shops under the arches, and now in Jack's dotty ditches. Longing for the weekend. And what's a weekend? The chain's longer by a few links, there's a slightly lighter ball at the end of it ... I'll build my own house on a deserted island and take my missus and sit and spit in the sea.'

In my earnest way, I'd persuaded him to read outside the pages of Dickens and the ILP weekly paper. It began when I lent him Arnold Bennett's *The Card*. The book filled him with a troubled enthusiasm for reading. 'Curse it!' he said. 'I must go to clink and get in six months with these *bloody* books.' 'To *The Card*,' he muttered one evening, as we rode home. 'If you see me with a long face in the morning, you'll know I've finished it.' And not long after that, he came to work with a copy of Burns in his pocket. 'Curse it – you've infected me with this bloody lark of yours! I was a decent, happy illiterate till I met you.'

But it was Burns for his radical image rather than Burns as a poet that had drawn Mike. He was obstinate in his distaste for poetry. It was 'long-winded', he insisted. We stood under a tree, one rainy day, quarrelling about this. 'I'm afraid you'll never convert me,' said Mike. 'Oh yes, I will,' I said. 'Give me long enough.' But I hadn't long enough – or persuasion enough . . .

We carried on a long argument under that tree, while the ditches and pipe-lines lay empty below us, along the slopes of a hill: and two fighters climbed among the uneasy clouds: and a curious rain creaked down, as if the weather had gone too long unoiled.

George was briefly home on foreign-service leave: he'd been sent to the West Indies, and thought he'd be at least a year away.

He'd fallen seriously in love – so seriously that he actually used the term – with an Irish girl, of well-to-do family. 'Middle-class house – middle-class manners . . . But they seemed . . . unusual enough to welcome a sharp-tongued bunting tosser as a sort of – suitor, I suppose – for their daughter.'

'They didn't mind your —?'

'Rudeness? It was very queer – but I think I was too much in love not to be nice.'

I gaped. George grinned, in a thin way, and said:

'Don't you know that you're making it possible for a man to go into the forces – or down the mines . . .? That's why I didn't become a conchie – because you can't really be a pacifist without withdrawing from society altogether . . .'

I understood that George was laying on a demonstration: he was showing that, disabled momentarily by love into muffling his guns, he was still heavily armed: I listened to the shot whistling over my head. And into it.

'I suppose you can keep your own hands clean,' he said.

'The war may be inevitable,' I ventured, amid the splash and whistle. 'But why should I contribute my small share of inevitability?'

'It's a point of view,' said George, like someone finishing off a bombardment with a pistol-shot. 'But not a logical one.'

We went to another concert. Someone played the more familiar Tschaikovsky piano concerto. 'Like chopping wood,' said George of the first movement. He slept through the second and third.

We said goodbye in tense moonshine: a searchlight flickered on and off, hunting jumpily through transparent cloud. 'We'll have to write letters,' said George. 'Keep on changing England – and I don't mean by knocking a few hedges down. It'll be rather nice to come back after a year or so.'

He looked up at the searchlight before he went. 'Like the young woman in question,' he said. 'She was always raking my skies for hostile aircraft. If you see what I mean.'

I felt that, wherever George was bound, he'd not yet sailed into the harbour of matrimony. Or rather that, if he married, the appropriate metaphor would have something to do with a fierce engagement and seizure on the high seas themselves.

2

For much of the autumn and winter of that first year of ditching we had a complete estate to work on – a tangle of trees and hedges, of gloomy little woods and neglected streams. It was a squelching, thorny maze when we first came to it, at a meeting of yellow lanes. You could smell the dead water, the dampness. Soon we were spread about those stagnant acres. Soon in several places were parked the great toolboxes, of which every gang had one. In the lid of each of these boxes was pasted, as a point of reference at moments of rebellion or infringement, those clauses of the Essential Works Order that a foreman might wish to quote – or, in the case of a non-reader like Jack Bone, to stab a thumb vaguely at. Three gangs at least were at work, uncomfortably side by side. Oddly, each took on a special character, usually coloured by that of its foreman; and even when this character was an unhappy one, it was jealousy cherished by the members of a gang. To be one of Jack's men, for example, was to have a sort of sturdy forthrightness, a faintly grumpy honesty much like his. We felt rather truculently tough, dirty, free. It was all, in a queer way, very like what happens with houses, in schools: and we of Jack's gang were in the cock house, no doubt of that.

Altogether, we were a swarming confusion of foremen, of visiting officials, of men marked by one ganger's livery or another's. Fires – and tempers – blazed in all directions. A small morose gang under a miserable man known, accurately or not, as Wally Worm, cut its way into a copse as melancholy as itself and was not seen again for weeks. Tusk came, filled with his own sense of ugly fun. It was a pity, he declared, to have so many fires, and not to burn a conchie or two. 'Wouldn't be missed,' he suggested to Jack Bone. Jack grunted, clearly unable to see that such incinerations would further the cause of practical agriculture. Jack's attitude to Tusk was that of someone on whose face a large, noisy fly had settled. He swatted at Tusk, irritably: pacing up and down and crying 'Ugh!' And when Tusk's van, which seemed to have taken on the characteristics of its driver, disappeared with coarsely cursing gears down the lane, Jack released us early. 'Go home, y' buggers!' he cried.

Mike Ferrini and I lost ourselves, for days on end, in the spiny entrails of hedges. We'd take it in turns to saw and cut and then elaborately extricate the severed wood, while the other looked after the fire. For Mike, so tall, working inside a hedge was often absurdly difficult: I'd stand over my fire and laugh as I looked towards the heaving, crashing, cursing tangle, at whose heart – as inside some iron maiden – Mike with infinite caution manoeuvred his over-long legs and arms. The thorns on some of the older bushes were inches long, and to avoid one was always to find another. We noticed with wry amusement that when we came out of a hedge, we continued for some minutes to move shrinkingly, ready to leap from a black spine and, in doing that, to leap back again from others into which we'd inevitably blunder.

There were lovely moments, in this work in hedges. There was one towards the end of a day when Mike cried 'Look!' and suddenly a whole group of small trees, green with moss, were standing in a thick green light: you felt that if you held a hand into this light, your flesh would be permanently painted with it. There were days when mists of rain came and went, and we'd stumble perhaps on some sombre alley of water long hidden among brambles. Everywhere the creak of falling timber, and the sea-like sound of tumbling leaves, voices, smoke. We'd never been so close to all the fumed colours of autumn; never felt such an intimacy with wood. Curiously, cutting our way through trees day after day, we felt alert to the whole nature of amputation. Limbs severed: in this spiky, tearing, smoky world of the saw and the billhook, we seemed to be working inside some model of the world at war.

I felt, during those days, something stirring in me that, thinking back to moments of a muddled excitement I'd experienced while doing sixth-form Latin, I called Virgilian: carefully keeping the adjective to myself. This sensuous, haunting sympathy with the white, sawn wood! A clogged stream spilling raggedly through a copse we were cleaning, with a weed growing in it that smelt like spearmint! The last moment of a day, when you touched the white bones of a fire with a fork and at the touch they turned into glowing spots, red as wine! And, as the first stage of our work on the estate came to an end, the spectacle of the naked banks where hedges had been, receiving the clean drop of one square, smooth field after another: and the trees that had been spared standing like exclamation marks, topped with their wild yellow heads! The immense scene, the tiny groups of workers, the pools of ashes! So often on the land I'd felt a fraud, a nuisance: rebuked by the land itself, which withheld its mysteries from my clumsy, half-hearted

presence. During that autumn I felt I'd almost been accepted – was that a possible word? – by the earth and its
fruits. I belonged, a little: with eyes that were never quite
free of sawdust, with stiff, scratched hands!

And yet it was tedious. God, yes! – side by side with the
extraordinary, rough beauty, there was the aching boredom
of being there, day after day, in that one atmosphere, our
very jokes becoming stale beyond endurance. There was a
wild morning when we were caught in a cloudburst: in a
thick black light, millions of leaves were hurled through the
air, clogging the telegraph wires that ran along a nearby
lane. Fragments of dead wood were blown across the fields
in their company. Within half an hour, the sky was absolutely blue: and this ravishing transition and exhilaratingly
swift reversal of weathers caused in me such a wild longing
for change, for the possibility and prospect of *motion* that
the war had brought to an end. I felt my curiosities and
desires, dammed up inside me, attempting to break through,
to seize upon the stuff of life and shape and re-shape it ...
'Analyse your annoyance', I heard a voice declare, early
one morning, on the wireless – it was the Radio Doctor,
perhaps, or some breakfast parson, giving advice to the
quick-tempered: but the awful smoothness of the phrase
created for me, all that day, a quite monstrous annoyance,
all the worse for being irresponsive to all analysis. There
came a day when, like burnt-out leaves lifted by the wind
from our fires, the birds assembled for departure: and I
caught a forlorn note in my voice as I called out to Mike:
'They're going away!' The birds, indifferent to our self-
tormenting world, had this simple power to vary their condition – to *go away*! It was hardly to be borne!

An odd effect of this boredom and restiveness that autumn made more intense was that Mike and I became fretful
about each other's mannerisms. He spent a long, black day
brooding over my incapacity to cure a fault in the dynamo
on my bicycle. Not till the last moment did he consent to
put it right himself: as he did in a matter of minutes. 'I'm
glad you're not my father,' I snapped at the end of a ser-
mon on self-reliance grunted at me from the middle of a
hedge, where Mike was wielding a billhook as if my neck
were under its blade. 'I'm glad I'm not,' Mike sniffed. 'If I
were, my lad, you'd be self-reliant in a brace of —'

He howled as a thorn drove into his hand.

'A brace of what?' I inquired coldly.

'I'm sorry,' said Mike, after he'd addressed the thorn, 'to use a phrase with which your lordship is not familiar; but what I was going to say' – here he addressed the thorn again – 'was that I'd have you capable of looking after yourself in a brace of *jiffs*.'

I had come to hate in Mike a habit he had, and that I'd only lately observed, and now was obsessively aware of: a habit of sniffing, which he used as a form of punctuation when speaking. I'd think: 'That sniff's a comma – *that*'s a semi-colon – and *that's* a full stop', and want to scream: or to say sharply, 'For Christ's sake, blow your nose, man!'

And then Mike would make one of his characteristic, wry comments, and I'd be deeply ashamed. As when, both of us limping towards the toolbox one evening after twelve hours in a particularly complex hedge, he said: 'You know – *we seem to have been here all day*!'

Jack was officially given an exercise book in which to note our misdemeanours: hopelessly riffling through its blank pages with a thick thumb, he cried: 'Tha knows what this is, then!'

'Yes, Jack,' said Mike, who was now our foreman's amanuensis in the matter of timesheets and other essential documents. 'But you're not,' he added delicately, 'going to ask me to write things down in it for you, are you?'

Jack looked hard at him, and Mike looked back with a similar hardness. I'm not sure that Jack was aware that he was looking into the eyes of a whole generation of radical obstinacy: in more solemn circumstances, this would have been the opening shot in an industrial struggle, and we'd have been out of the ditches and marching under banners. What Jack certainly saw was that an awful effeteness was being demanded of him – he was to peach on his men, to confess that Tusk had some disciplinary magic that he did not possess himself – and that, most humiliating, it was all to be by way of 'clerking', as Jack in general described such things – making the word rhyme (and more than rhyme) with 'shirking'. 'They'll be givin' me some bloody wench next to write down everything I say,' was how he summed up his qualms: and you could see that he half-believed it might happen. Then he threw the book into our toolbox, never to be seen again.

We had all become rather tetchy: partly because the nights had become sheer melodrama again. You were woken by tremendous bangs. It was like some huge rowdiness – as if hooligans had taken over the air. Odd, indeed, that feeling of having the darkness trespassed upon by hoodlums: the root of the objection that filled you was testy, umbrella-shaking. '*Disgraceful* behaviour!' The pure spectacle was sometimes breathtaking: those appalling angers turned into flares that hung in the sky, into the lemon rays of searchlights that bunched and spread and groped: into tiny globes, burning the colour of ginger, that flew light and low over houses: into gleaming explosive that ran about the darkness like quicksilver. When a bomb fell close at hand, it was like being clumped on the head. At times, hostile planes poured over, with a busy freedom that was horribly like that of a railway terminus at the rush hour. We waited for all that speedy mumbling to be split by the whistle of bombs. It seemed, often, so very unlikely that our deaths should be sought, in this way, in the domestic night. I'd look round the room, at the tiny details of its furnishings that might at any moment burst into burning dust. It seemed then that the nature of life was essentially sane and sweet – obviously a human being must wish to continue living, and to enjoy the continuance of life in others. How, even with that immensely magnified playground brawl going on above one's head, could one believe in the fact of this impersonal murderousness? It made as little sense as when, leaning on a spade, one stood during the day and watched tiny German reconnaissance aircraft being shot at in a clear and singing morning sky. What was that extraordinary chain of follies that led men, few of them in the least diabolic, to this lunatic pitch?

It was at moments like these that my daylight sense of the illogicality of being a pacifist fell away. In the end, it was all a madness impossible to take part in.

And again it was odd, and disturbing, that the powerful percussion, the shocking clatter and crack of gunfire was a stimulant, so that you felt depressed and let down when it ceased, when the crazy thunders moved away, to become whispering murders on the further edge of night.

Your feeling for life became so keen, so unbearably edged and bright! But often even that struggled with the simple passion for sleep – after twelve hours in the wind, sleep was so necessary, if one day was to be separated from the next, and your dreams were not to spill over into waking hours. When I was least tired, then my sleep gave way slowly to the barrage outside and the first bullying growls and claps. But at times of great exhaustion, sleep would split like a tense cord. I would lie, aware that time was whittled to a most precious economy, that I had none to spare. And I would hold sleep to me, the idea of it, until the flashes at the window, the killing roar of planes diving, the crack of guns, drove me downstairs simply for company ...

Jack Bone followed the progress of the war with studious incomprehension: he had sons caught up in it, in several of its theatres. He would halt beside us, in his supervisory tours of the estate, and say: 'See we got Baghdad, then!'

'Baghdad, Jack?'

It was Byelgorod, in fact, on that occasion. The Russian front was a special problem to Jack. He agonized over the absurdity of Russian place names. 'Bloody mouthfuls', he called them. The war swayed back and forth between one bloody mouthful and another. But Jack was comfortable about it now: for whatever these places were, so improbable as names, they had lately become places 'we' had 'got'.

Mike would try, not very urgently, to make Jack doubtful about that 'we'.

'Who's "we" then, Jack? Have you got Baghdad? Have I got it? Has Ted here got it?'

Jack would shake his rough white head, exasperated; but would half-grin, because he respected Mike as a practical person.

'You know, Mike!'

'I don't, Jack.'

'We's bloody us, an't it? It's us, the bloody allies, an't it?' Then, really anxious about Mike's slowness of apprehension: 'It's us that's fightin' the bloody Germans, an't it? An't that it?' And since he found it difficult to address his favourite phrase at Mike, he turned and barked it at me: 'Bloody twat!'

Some disciplinary dilemma arose in a gang to the north of

us, and Jack was sent to deal with it. For a while Joe Hicks became our foreman: a tiny man with red, mousy features and hapless eyes. He had virtually only two activities: drinking beer and belching. I have never known anyone who belched with more elaboration: the grace-notes and chromatic flourishes of his indigestion rang, for a whole wet spring, along our muddy gashes, through the thin little misty copses where we built our break-time fires.

At one time, Joe had been a regular soldier, garrisoned in India, and he looked back on those days wistfully. 'Gawd!' he would sigh, standing above us on the rim of a ditch. 'To think I've 'ad dinner with nabobs and the like. Gold dishes, that's what they eat off of. Honest, Mike! Honest, Ted! I've been nearer one of them rajah chaps than what I am to you.' He was very conscious of having declined. 'Yes, that was Joe Hicks once,' he'd say. And the tragedy of it all seized him with particular poignancy one day when, at the midday break, he remembered that it was his birthday. 'Cor,' he cried. 'Cor, Mike! Cor, Phil! Think of it! Sixty-one years ago they was smacking me little pink bottom and saying, "'E's a nice little feller!" Wonder what they'd say if they saw me now? "Dirty old bugger!" Eh, Ted? Eh, Mike?'

One midday he had himself driven in our lorry to a pub and didn't come back till two hours later. It was a curious ditch we were struggling with at the time. One of the War Ag's more splendid officials had arrived soon after we'd started and, having squatted impressively here and there in his immaculate jodhpurs, had announced that we were running the wrong way. We must correct the fault by going deeper. Later another official had arrived and decided that our original choice of slope had been right, and that we must revert to it by going deeper again. On the day of Joe's absence we were ten feet deep and most of what we were digging out was falling back into the ditch. Nearly everyone in the gang had reached a state in which all he wanted to do was hopelessly to shave away at some private spot in the canyon, seeing what thin slivers of prehistoric clay he could remove.

When at last Joe came back to us that day he adjourned immediately to a nearby coppice, more than usually filled with a sense of the decline of Joe Hicks, and fell asleep.

Towards the middle of the afternoon one of the canvas-topped committee vans drew up outside the field and two officials got out. What should we do? It did not seem right to leave even a foreman unhelped in such a situation: so Mike Ferrini and Phil Perkins ran across to wake Joe up.

'Come on, Joe,' they cried, shaking the snoring hero by the arm. 'Wake up! County Hall men!'

'Eh?' Joe mumbled testily. 'County-what blasted blighters? Nothing doing,' and he fell asleep again. They tugged him to his feet and drew him, hazily angry, across the field to the ditch. 'Be trouble 'bout this,' he was muttering when they got him there and pushed him down to a kneeling position at the edge. 'Look!' they insisted, pointing; and, forcing his eyes from the ground, Joe managed to make out the spruce, jodhpured figures approaching. Some dim sense of the crisis penetrated. 'All dam' right,' he hiccupped. 'You stick to your dam' ditching.'

'This,' the leading official was saying as they came up, 'has been a difficult job ... Ah, Hicks!' he called. 'And how's it going now?'

I cannot say we had ever liked this man. We hated the way he looked like an actor dressed up as a farmer. We hated especially his pork-pie hat. Joe himself had once said that he would like to make quite horrible use of that hat. In fact, however, no nabob, no rajah could ever have commanded more respect from Joe than normally he showed to officials of all kinds. For them he would have dug a ditch twenty feet deep. (And, indeed, later that winter he came near to doing so.)

But now, from his position close to the earth, he horribly screwed his head round and muttered: 'Exspecial.' 'Ah,' said the official. 'And the water?' 'Implossalbility,' snarled Joe. 'Running now?' 'Bloody ditch,' said Joe. 'Piss in it!' 'Well, well ...' said the official. His hand made a nervous tour of his pork-pie. 'Moresomeover ...' snarled Joe, and began to rise to his feet. Belches burst from him like bubbles – strings of tiny ones alternating with vast explosions, which seemed likely to blow his bones all over the field. 'Well,' said the official. 'That seems to be all right.' He turned, his confrère with him, and they picked their hasty and distasteful way back to their van. Joe collapsed and was borne back to his coppice, reverently, by the whole gang.

We waited for days for Joe to be sacked, demoted – at least summoned to County Hall. But when nothing happened we decided that the officials, too, must have lunched that day in a pub. They probably dismissed the whole outrageous occurrence as a figment of the local ale.

It was while we were under Joe that we saw our first prisoners of war.

Even when drunk, Joe was never so bold again. The atmosphere of the War Ag, increasingly that of some melodramatic Italian Renaissance court, caused Joe immense terror. To his belches he added volleys of small frightened farts, which the mere sight of a committee van could generate. Phil Perkins, head down and shovelling at the bottom of a deep ditch, once observed, on hearing this curious time-signal scurry past above: 'Ah, that'll be our wage packets!'

I'd not understood how much of bullying and fear there was in working relationships. George had said it was much the same at sea. I addressed lofty protests into the always receptive ear of my diary. 'Only when we learn to set store by the happiness of pulling together...' That had been at a time when Jack Bone had cast me out of his favour for a whole week. He'd yelled at Phil Perkins: 'Come away from...' His confused wrath had not allowed him even to make a shot at my surname. 'Come away from 'n. Spoils any he works with, the bugger!' Argument was impossible. Whenever there was a tremor throughout the vast structure of favours and disfavours that constituted the War Ag, then Jack Bone was touched by it and someone in his ditches must pay. It was me, for that black week. I nearly wept when it was over: an end as capricious as the beginning, when Jack wanted to get past me in a ditch and said, with gruff tenderness: 'Let me by, *Ted*.'

Those first prisoners of war were Italians. We were working on a hillside at the time. This was a charming corner of the county: a tomato-growing district, so that we looked down on glasshouses, in all directions. When the wintry sun came out from behind the clouds, you were first aware of it in terms of a sudden bombardment of sparklings and glitterings, as all that glass took fire at our feet.

The Italians came, halfway through an icy morning: an

invasion of song. They arrived, under guard, from the other side of the hill, so we were aware of them first as a line of dark figures on the skyline above: the whole procession wrapped in the thick, sad tones of *O Sole Mio*. I would not have believed, before this happened, that a body of Italians could have entered so infallibly chanting *O Sole Mio*. By the end of the day the most sympathetic of us grew restive about this air, which palls with very little repetition.

The first and prompt reaction came from Moke, a boy from London. 'Moke' can't have been his name, but it was what he offered. In a world of indiscriminately strong language, Moke raised indiscrimination to an art. He leaned heavily on one element in that language, but was remarkably versatile in making this element serve for all parts of speech, whatever. On one occasion he was expressing uncertainty as to the entertainment he would seek out on the evening to come. Should it be the cinema? He frowned over the problem, and canvassed opinions along the ditch. 'Sometimes,' he declared at last, 'I fink I fucking will, and sometimes I fink I fucking won't.'

'I fucking wouldn't,' Phil Perkins had suggested. But Moke was sensitive to parody. 'You fucker,' he'd commented, morosely...

Now, catching sight of the Italians, Moke cried: ''Ere they come! 'Ere come the runners! Fucking good runners they are! 'Ere they fucking come, the —'

'Have some sense,' said Phil Perkins.

'Fucking Eyeties,' Moke grumbled.

'Behave yourself,' said Phil.

But now Joe Hicks came scuttling down the ditch. ''Ere they come,' he piped. 'Bleeding Wops! Keep to the ditch! Keep to this end of the bleeding field!' He panted urgently, glaring up the field as the Italians, still chanting with the lustiest pathos, began to unload a trailer full of tools that had arrived at their tail. ''Ere they bloody are,' Joe groaned. 'Keep down. Keep to yer own end of the field. No going near 'em. I'll book the first bugger as talks to 'em.'

He scurried away from us up the hill; then turned and fled back again. 'We're not goin' near 'em,' he panted. 'We don't want to.'

'You think they're dangerous?' Phil asked.

'Only be borrowing fucking matches,' said Joe. 'And

fucking fags.'

Joe's disturbance was profound, all that day. He spent much time staring up at the Italians, breathing heavily. Now and then he hissed under his breath. And again and again he marched in their direction, never quite reaching them: to cast upon them, as we guessed, the glare of the ruling race.

I found myself staring up at them with what I realized was a quite foolish delight. It was odd to be so close to those green caps of theirs: suddenly a whole generation of newspaper photographs had come to life. I felt they must all come from Ignazio Silone's Fontamara: absurdly, for me, they were the Italians of anti-fascist literature. I saw them through a mist of literary and political excitement, for ... here were the sons of the men by whose side Ernest Hemingway had fought in 1917 ... here, too, were the reluctant conquerors of Abyssinia, Mussolini's grudging armies. Here, altogether, was the dismaying Europe of my boyhood, come at last to dig surely un-English ditches on a hilltop in the Home Counties: all the insanity of the thirties, those scenes in the Piazza Venezia, brought within arm's length. And the Italians seemed extraordinarily exotic, up there on the skyline – the chocolate brown of their tunics, dominoed with red, yellow or blue circles, matching their darkness of skin and hair.

They looked, I thought, stolen – like stolen men. They'd been stolen, by war, from their own world. There was another literary atmosphere, on the hilltop: they were like the changelings of folk tales.

To Joe's horror, as the day drew to an end, the ditch they were digging began to wind down the hill towards us. Plainly, it wasn't going to be possible to isolate ourselves. Joe seemed to feel better after he'd made contact with their bored guards. He came back reassured: British soldiers would not allow the obscure corruptions that Joe feared. There was not even going to be borrowing of matches or fags. And Joe's comfort grew greater day by day, even as our ditches converged. He began to pant less with panic. He strengthened himself further with mockery of the Italian language. 'Wallah wallah,' he called out, again and again, in victorious disgust.

'I beg your pardon?' Phil would say.

'Wallah wallah,' Joe'd repeat, exasperatedly. And then, when Phil looked politely blank: '*Them!* Fucking Eyeties! *Wallah wallah!* ... Oh Gawd! Don't yer catch on, mate? *Wallah wallah!* Their *lingo!*'

The first exchange of words between us and the Italians set back Joe's recovery. 'Get on with your fucking work!' he raged at the offending captive. The Italian looked Joe up and down, but largely down, with sparkling coolness. Then, very carefully, he replied: 'Fuck *you!*'

Joe clearly wished that he were back, armed, on the North-West Frontier. But he was comforted, I think, by the discovery that even more impressive Englishmen than himself were subject to Italian mockery. A War Ag official came to stare at their ditch, and felt it necessary to inform them that it was coming up. They must keep the bottom of the ditch lower. He gestured with his arms to this effect, and they mimicked his semaphorings with the happiest of grins. They took these gestures, indeed, as suggestive bases for the most curious obscenities, and also for caperings and dancings. The official turned to a guard, who grinned and yawned. 'I'm trying to make a serious point,' cried the official. The Italians began, as one guessed, to discuss his character in the triumphant immunity of their own tongue. Then they encircled him, ambiguously polite. One of them bowed and then declared, with an effect of the most fantastic courtesy: 'Boll-*ocks*, mister!'

We noticed they had only water to drink at their breaks.

'Well, that's all right,' said Joe. 'They're used to drinking water.'

Mike Ferrini said: 'He's like an old horse lifting its tail ... You know what's coming next.'

The allies were banging their way into Italy, and this seemed to bring home one of the worst desolations of war: that bleak narrowing of ordinary human sympathies that made enemies wherever it looked. In an odd sense, it was some gangs of landgirls who gave this its sharpest edge. They clearly felt that they were sexually on offer to 'our boys' and, in a very positive way, sexually withheld from the rest. When they were in the same field as Italian prisoners of war, they enjoyed, as groups, their awareness of the Italians' interest in them: and then set out to sharpen and thwart that interest. So they would posture, sing, stare boldly. They would call out encouraging remarks, and then, among themselves, and loudly, discuss their contempt for the prisoners. 'There go the men our men left home for,' they would chorus.

It was not at the formal enemy alone that this shrill dislike was directed. In their attitude to Americans, too, detestation played its part. There was huge hatred of the stranger – even of the allied stranger. Easy enough to see how this happened: how inflamed the instinct had become to close the ranks – to identify one's own in the narrowest possible way. But, with the girls, it was the use of sex to give an edge to this cruel reduction of sympathy that was so ugly. The fields seemed, at times, full of harpies.

Italians were prime targets. They were held to be cowardly; their language was unmanly in its musical nature; and Italy itself, of course, was a scrapheap of old churches. But the invasion of Italy brought about only the first release of a xenophobia that grew as Europe was flung slowly open. The girls took much of their language from the newsreels and the monstrous commentary on events provided by the popular newspapers. 'The Sicilians,' I heard in a brittle voice from cinema screen, 'now tell us they didn't like Mussolini. We didn't hear about that before!' 'Hamburg,' a headline shouted, 'has been Hamburged!' Such a coarsening of responses – so that everywhere the tragic evolution of war was commented on in the language of a gang fight in a school playground – was inevitable, I would tell myself: for this vast brawl, the crude pugnacities of brawling were called for. An indefensible over-refinement, to expect anything else. It might even be that human sensitiveness must protect itself by such a surrender to the most primitive kinds of partisanship. And yet ... much of the worst of it was given its expression, so infectious, by journalists and other commentators, who were certainly able to choose between one way of speaking and another. How could such an orgy of brutal over-simplification not shape, in many, attitudes that would last a lifetime? There was an awful sense that we were providing ourselves with political anti-education, and that the price, for us all, must be very heavy ...

There was a young Italian, as it happened, in our gang – Joe Mazzini, who at nights and at weekends followed his calling as a waiter in Soho, and made improbable and irate daily journeys from the West End to join us in our ditches. Joe was dazed by the requirement that he become a land worker. He'd been born in a Tuscan village, and rural life was not completely unfamiliar to him. But from an early age – in Milan before he came to London – he had worked as a waiter, and now only the world of restaurants made sense to him. He always wore a dark suit, white shirt and tie, looking like some highly unsuitable temporary visitor to the ditches; and somehow he managed to preserve a sort of dishevelled dapperness. The land laid no hold at all upon him. His impatience and distress he tried to weather by being enormously noisy. He would shout and sing, in a methodical way, though sometimes he'd merely raise his voice in a long-drawn-out semi-musical howl: and he would throw stones at anything that provided a reasonable – or, in the view of the rest of us, unreasonable – clang or crash. When drainage pipes were delivered on the site, Joe was in his melancholy, rowdy element: he would hurl one into the air and send another after it, so that they exploded together. He was also a great whistler: as a child in Tuscany, he told us, he'd made himself a master of local bird-song, and now the Home Counties were shaken by his shrill cadenzas and soaring arabesques. These performances were consummate but fairly intolerable.

'I don't believe, Joe,' Phil Perkins would murmur, 'that

Italy has birds like those. I mean, if it had, the people would have scarpered long ago.'

'In London,' was Joe's usual answer, 'I am a gentleman ... dat's true, I am a gentleman, *very*! But when I'm in dis places, I 'ave to shout or do somet'ing, to pass d'time away ...

'I am very *hangry*, all d'time! I ham a waiter, not —'

Then he would abandon the English language, as always he did after a grinning, earnest sentence or so, and sketch out the remainder of his apologia with shrugs and wide wavings of the arms: before pursing his lips for another terrifying recital of alleged North Italian bird-song.

We dug ditches of every kind, in every kind of setting. We dug pipelines: often the nastiest diggings of all. You'd start two spades wide, narrow enough, and when the cut was of any depth it was like working inside a corset of clay. The final dig was with a special, narrow curved spade called a half-round, which made a channel wide enough only to take the pipes. The loose clay left by this spade had to be removed with a scoop: you straddled the cut and dragged at the stray bits far below with this long-handled instrument – and, however, you did it, the strain was on your stomach, which in a day's work could seem to become the greater part of your being, the aching nucleus of your existence ...

But unadjustable ditches and impossible foremen – these remained (as 1943 wasted away) among our worst miseries. They came together for a while when we worked under a man called Spragg. Our ditch then was one along which no amount of tinkering or wholesale redigging would persuade water to run happily. We'd grown wearily familiar with the scene: and especially with a little wood close at hand, which was composed almost entirely of scores of old trees fantastically crippled. Here seemed to be, in a dim late autumn light, a writhing demon, here the essential shape of a mourner – the stilted branches hanging down like black tears falling, the trunk humped and racked with grief ... These trees were vividly green with rot; and around one of them it seemed that a conference of unnameable monsters was swarming, so numerously and curiously humped and curled that they appeared to be in continual, frantic motion: raising distorted arms into the air to support or oppose some hideous proposal.

Phil Perkins and I were working in a corner of this ditch, now a very deep corner indeed, arched over with trees stranded by our diggings and re-diggings. Out of one wall of the ditch jutted a big tree-root that was shaped exactly like a woman's leg, complete with a sentimentally charming knee. We found ourselves literally imploring the water, baffled by the contradictory sciences of half a dozen advisory officers, to disregard the now inscrutable errors in the runnel we'd dug for it, and to run, to lap down it regardless of human folly. Why could it not do what came so easily to water?

Into such a setting, Spragg entered aptly. He was compact of malice. Thin-faced, wildly bright of eye, he would sit day-long over a fire to the side of the ditch; and if we appealed to him for some word of advice, however inapposite, in respect of this perverse ditch, he would leap up, glittering, and attack some precariously high wall with scurrying and gasping little raps of the spade – in search, perhaps of an improbable pipe-line which would only have complicated our lives had it been found. He was often accompanied by a thin, dark dog, much like himself, and the other occasions when he would leave the fire came when this hungry creature scented prey. Then, chuckling with glee, Spragg would follow his pet – truly his *familiar*, the dog seemed – to return, perhaps, with the poor little corpse of a rabbit, its shabby fur wet where it had fled down the ditch from sharpnosed dog and dark-hearted man.

A warlock! He came to have, unaccountably, a deep attachment to the least interesting member of our gang, a Christadelphian, who made it his business daily to prepare Spragg's fire. The two of them, warlock and puritan, would stand over it while it took shape, and chuckle: Kitchen, the puritan, was a master's man, by nature, and he became welcome, during the working day, at Spragg's squatting side by the fire. There was ill-feeling about this, along the ditch: Phil would call, 'Learned to bark yet, Kitch?' An ILPer built a longish political speech on the example, in the course of which Kitchen was inflated into representing the entire petite bourgeoisie. Spragg, if I remember, was a *kulak*: and we should have recognized the historic moment for establishing workers' control in this corner of the county.

At the time I thought that was probably true. Any politically radical argument caused me very great over-excitement. For that reason, Fridays were almost unbearable to me: for that was the day of the over-wrought reading of periodicals – the *New Statesman*, especially. I was wholly at the mercy of the thrills and fervours that arose from those pages. It was like lowering myself into whirlpools. Here was the leader in the *New Statesman* – I'd plunge into it and be whipped round and round by the current of political high feeling: threatened with drowning by the welling flood of an idea, half understood. Then there were the literary pages, battering me with views of book after book. After two or three hours of that, I would be like someone thrown up by the sea and lying, bruised with exhilaration, on the shore of the empty island of my life. In time, I grew dismayed by the contrast between these experiences – ideas in all states of incompleteness marching through my head with banners, with bands, with such a tramping as belonged to triumph – and my own actual ineffectuality. It was quite terrible to feel so important, while reading – to borrow the apparent importance of others – and to end up, alone and powerless and deeply self-doubting, with oneself . . .

But the Christadelphian smiled smugly through the ILPer's crisp tirade.

Then, on a dull gusty day, enter an official. Two reliable men were required to provide a new gang of Jack Bone's with moral reinforcement. The War Ag had made its choice. Kitchen was one of the two selected.

The effect on Spragg was startling. 'Oh no!' he cried. He beat at the ground with a stick, gasping. *Not* his best man! And when the official stared at him, bleakly, Spragg slid into a flow of vicious words. Slid indeed! It was as though he'd stepped on to the treacherous surface of his strange, crazy ill-humour, and was skidding helplessly across it, calling out words that belonged to black magic. The official, the War Ag, would be most horribly consumed – devoured by the most hideous arts, over the exercise of which, Spragg raged, he had no control. 'I know what happens to people who cross me!' he howled. His eyes were shockingly like those of a man passing through some grave illness.

'Your flow of language,' said the official, briskly schoolmasterly, 'is inexcusable. I don't like it.' He ordered Kitchen into his van, and drove away: as he went, Spragg shook his fist elaborately after him, and then squatted again by his fire, muttering bitterly.

Later he talked to Phil and me: or in our direction. He'd have his revenge, he said: it would be a long time before he felt repaid for this humiliation. Ah! – all his life, men who had injured him had come to bad ends! There was a man he'd warned once – 'One day I'll get you!' ... A pure, almost amiable malice, in this report; there was a kind of fondness in the wild eyes ... His time had come. He'd worked and worked away until he was in possession of a fearful secret in respect of this enemy of his. He'd made it known that he had this awful knowledge, and meant to use it. And on the following day, the man had cut his throat!

Phil said very clearly at this point: 'You bastard!' But Spragg was not listening. There was this curious fondness in his eyes and voice, as he spoke of his foe: as if there was no one for whom he felt more of a twisted affection than some man who, having crossed him, had sealed his own violent doom.

We were dismayed when the precise instrument of punishment sent by the War Ag turned out to be Nutt: a minor official like some coarse fighting-cock, loud and helplessly incompetent, who left County Hall unhappily wearing jacket and tie but arrived on any site with his green hat drunkenly aslant and his shirt widely open over his furiously hairy chest. Nutt came stumbling over the field and delivered the War Ag's judgement: Spragg was suspended for a week.

There was another long violent speech of supernatural intensity. Nutt gave an ear uneasily, borne well beyond his small gift for continuous listening. When the rodomontade was at its height, he exclaimed:

'This bloody ditch still giving trouble?' His had been one of the first misdirections that had led us astray in our digging. Spragg, interrupted in his distribution of thunders, lightnings and snapped necks, cried:

'It'll be your grave, Nutt! It will be a grave for all of you!'

'I'd try another spit – you might find a pipe-line or something,' said Nutt ...

Nothing happened to Nutt: but then I believe any devil would have found it difficult to make a victim of a man so inattentive. And as Phil Perkins said, hell was a wiser establishment than the War Ag, and might well have hesitated to draw Nutt down into its orbit, however urgent the plea of its agent.

A day came when Jack Bone returned among us, with his gang. It was in another setting, for we'd botched up that unlucky ditch, at last, and faintly puzzled water had consented to run for long enough to convince our advisers that they now possessed a genuine ditch.

Our two gangs for a while worked side by side, laying pipes in the wake of a new machine that dug the pipe-lines for us. Between Jack and Spragg there was nothing so banal as hostility. Spragg insisted on seeing in the gruff ex-miner 'that foul-mouthed man', 'that man heading for a bad, bad end' ... The impression was given that fires were even now being stoked up for Jack's benefit. As for Jack, his distaste for Spragg barely needed expression in words. He simply fell against him, with bruising elbows and knees, whenever they met. There might be a mumbled: 'Bloody twat!' If anyone had desired a demonstration of the limitations of the black arts, I should have brought him to witness any confrontation between Jack Bone and Spragg. The malice of the one could clearly have no effect whatever on the scornful solidity of the other. At Doomsday, my money would be on Jack Bone as against any devil who attempted to lay hands on him. Whoever is dragged shrieking into the pit, Jack Bone could not conceivably be among them.

One rainy morning, Jack's supremacy was ludicrously illustrated. Spragg was rash enough to arrive with a punctured bicycle tyre. In the barn where we were sheltering, he began pantingly to tend to it. Enter Jack: a quick busy glint in his eye as he took in the spectacle. 'Tha's makin' hell's own weather o' that,' he grunted. His wrestler's elbows came into play and Spragg fell to one side, dropping the pump he was using. Jack snatched it up and gave two enormous lunges with it. The pump flew in half, very precisely. There was a squawk of dismay from Spragg. Jack threw the pump aside with an impatient cry. He then seized the wheel, tore off the tyre, and began to snatch out the inner tube with his immense hands. A second or so later the inner tube also was in halves. Jack then hurled the entire bicycle aside, with a rumble that roughly expressed his

opinion that it had been a trumpery thing. While Spragg
gasped and attempted to hurl annihilating beams from his
astonished eyes, Jack strode to the door of the barn: announced, 'Rain's stopped! Let's have 'ee, lads!': winked all
round in response to the applause his audience was too
astonished to offer: and vanished.

And long months yet of mud and water ...

Mornings when the air was crammed with bird-song:
when the flutings and sharp chatterings seemed more present than the landscape itself. So a hedge was defined by the
song that came from it, rather than by its twigs or leaves.
Trees were tall choruses that we walked between. And after
rain would come this other rain: scraps of melody, brisk
chips of sound.

Phil Perkins, always anxious to take his pleasures dry,
would murmur: 'I do wish those birds would get married
quietly!'

For a while, Phil and I were mates. It was a curious
feature of this monotonous life that one's luck in the matter
of a daily companion assumed an importance that at times
was half-lunatic. To shovel up for ten hours behind an un-
congenial mate was to have boredom multiplied. I dreaded
particularly being with one man who was as silent as the
grave. In his company, this phrase ceased to be a cliché, and
the ditch assumed a positively sinister character. Phil and I
had worked close to him a whole morning, once, and from
our companion had come nothing more by way of communication than an occasional, almost subliminal, groaning
hum. 'The Ditcher's Dirge?' Phil whispered: and over
lunch he said: 'This afternoon we'll change the subject!'

Phil and I came together at a time of huge winds. Day
after day I was blown to work, on my bicycle, as if I'd been
a sailing ship. Evening after evening I drove my way home,
achingly, in the face of air that had become a solid sheet
stretching across my path. We plied spade and shovel in a
world of scurrying leaves and scampering twigs. Phil alleged that when he changed on reaching home the room
was filled with gusts that had got themselves imprisoned in
his clothes. 'Great trouser-shaped breezes!' he groaned.

Phil prided himself on his practical character: like Mike
Ferrini, he felt a friendly scorn for my incapacity to make

or mend anything whatever, and added to it an impatience caused by my total lack of the skills of scrounging. This was his word for the daily collection of firewood, pretty leaves for his children, catkins for his wife. As we made our way home he'd stare at the empty carrier of my bicycle, his own heaped with finds, and groan...

Phil had a restless suspicion of those who wove subtle webs of argument – the well-educated, as he took them to be. He seized once on the word 'posit', in an editorial in *Peace News*. Why was it the mark of the well-educated that they used such words? Phil juggled with this unhappy specimen until indeed it seemed the most pretentious and unnecessary of verbal inventions. Didn't educated men go out of their way to collect such words, and then seek opportunities to use them?

Such questions were always directed at me in a way that caused me to wriggle: for Phil held me to be personally accountable for the manners of the educated. It was the same story as with Frank, my threshing mate, and Mike Ferrini. I was 'one of your cultured people'. Phil would express pity for the girl fated to be my wife. There'd never be coal in the hod – never a vegetable growing in the garden. 'She'll have to keep warm with some poem, or fill her belly with some of that chamber music,' he'd say, with such genuine solicitude for this imaginary lady that I'd have to lean on my shovel and laugh. 'I shan't go on, Ted – you're taking the mickey!'

I wished very often that I could make Phil understand that I was only a loose and terribly unconfident collection of fragments of this and that: a little literature, a little music, insecure schoolboy scraps of two or three languages. No plausible representative of the intellectual classes, at all! But every now and then our daylong talk would tumble into this curious gulf between us – the product of dissimilar educational experiences. I'd got through the 'scholarship' to the grammar school: Phil hadn't even sat for it. That was the gulf. It led to dialogues such as one sparked off by Phil's attack on the nude in art. He'd not have painting from the nude on his walls, ever!

'Why on earth not, Phil?'

'Look here, Ted! I remember how I used to *pore* over such pictures myself when I was a lad. Now, suppose some

134

boy came to visit us, and he saw paintings like that on our living-room wall! Wouldn't he look at them, out of the corner of his eye, and wonder if my wife was like that under her clothes?'

'Oh Phil!' It was hopeless! I was always meaning not to be appalled, not to be vehement at such moments: but here I was, rapping the ground with my shovel and spluttering:

'What the devil, Phil! What a *contorted* reason for not hanging a picture on your wall! Good Lord! But the human body is a beautiful thing, and it's perfectly proper for the artist to celebrate it and for us to enjoy his doing so. A painting of the nude isn't —'

And so on, Phil's round face red with obstinate conviction. My own pale, with the same cause. Brandishing of spade or shovel. Perhaps a warning bark from our current foreman!

And Phil saying, in the end, as he always did: 'Oh, you *cultured people*! You'd talk yourself into anything! You'd *posit* anything, you barmy *positers*!'

George was back from the West Indies. The world was a different place to him now, he said: England being no longer its centre, but a place like any other to be hunted for on a chart.

He didn't look forward to returning to the naval depot. It was not just that it was cut off from the world by barbed wire – that you could defy. But it was a horrid world of its own, built a century ago in brick. A dismal shed through which you entered ... and beyond that, an enormous drill shed like some major railway terminus. The discipline was rigid. At sea, things were different. There you didn't stand to attention: you shambled. 'I like prostituting discipline,' said George wistfully.

I told him that in a few days I should have been on the land for three years. 'How many more, I wonder?'

'Three at least.'

'Yes. I'm very tired of it.'

'I'd like to get out too,' said George. 'But supposing we did? In civilian life, we'd be even more miserable. I guess the only thing to say is that, while the war lasts, our years are bound to be wasted, anyway ...

'I know a sailor who can peel potatoes with a cigarette in

his mouth. But then he's a chap who could keep his eyes open through anything. I keep shutting my eyes, I find. I suppose I'm a coward, rather. Don't you think so?'

That hadn't struck me, I murmured.

'But you probably think I'm selfish,' said George, 'grumbling about a little boredom.'

We walked into the country. For me, lately, there'd been a galloping sequence of stupid days. The laceration of laughter at what had ceased to amuse. The only pleasures had been little, slightly mad ones: pretending a ditch was some great enterprise: or releasing the deep cold water from a pond, seeing it gush thickly down the gully made for it. The drowned grasses twisting faintly ...

Now George and I were drawn by the simple, powerful song of a thrush. The bird was standing on a low branch of a tree: its attitude was absurdly that of a professional singer giving a concert. Its bold happiness ('No parentheses or conditional clauses in that,' said George) made us pleasantly sad ...

'It's a pity,' I said, 'that your connection with the sea is fundamentally insane – as mine is with the land.'

'Yes,' said George. 'And yet wheat always has been grown, and people always have crossed the sea. For all the latterday madness, I suppose we're learning ancient skills'.

I thought I was learning nothing much, alas. Heavens, George would by now have been an authority on agriculture and its processes. What blockage was it that prevented me from learning anything much about anything at all?

I was so often amazed by the knowledge and practical skill possessed by my mates. They knew how to waterproof a cape, how best to cook crab apples, how to felt a roof.

They could turn odds and scraps to all sorts of uses. I was the only one among us daft enough not to have any habit of collecting this or that. 'Scrounging', in Phil Perkins' phrase.

With us we had briefly a strange boy, a seventeen-year-old with a passion for collecting violent objects – fragments of bombs, bayonets, cap badges. Daily he brought specimens from his collection to show us: once it was a range of knuckledusters – although 'range' suggests a variety they did not possess. We found it difficult to recognize the difference between one abominable set and another, and he became impatient, for there *were* differences, he held, and they were of solemn moment to any historian of this type of armament. A very large sheathknife always hung from his belt: and his jacket was turned almost to solid tin by the patriotic badges pinned to it. Phil Perkins felt there must be a future for the lad, as curator of some as yet unestablished gangster museum.

It was to him that Joe Hicks turned, with suspicion, one morning when he discovered that a pair of large cartwheels that had been lying in a ditch had disappeared. Joe, back with us for a while as ganger, had hovered over these cartwheels for some days, unable to imagine a use for them, but equally unable to believe that it was good sense not to make oneself their owner. 'Well, yer might always be glad of a pair o' dirty great wheels like that,' he would mutter uneasily: and kick leaves and dirt over them, to hide them from a thieving world until he'd decided what to do about objects so bothersomely and imprecisely tempting.

'They've gone! They've bloody gone!' he yelped that morning: and turned at once to the boy, as a known collector of strange things. 'You 'ad 'em, lad?' he demanded.

The boy looked hurt. Certainly not! He jangled a little, in his carapace of badges, as he expressed his indignation at such an ill-aimed accusation. 'What would I want with two old wheels?'

'What would you want with them?' cried Phil Perkins. 'Why, boy – use your loaf! With a pair of wheels like that, you'd have had the makings of a field-gun!' ...

This collector of brutal gadgets was a gentle boy: and there was really no violence in Fred Creak, who drove our van, busied himself miscellaneously in our ditches, was my closest rival in a wet-weather game we played for which a knowledge of book titles and authors' names was valuable – Fred had once had a job replacing books on the shelves in a large public library. An amiable, smiling fellow who during the thirties had been one of Oswald Mosley's fascist bullies.

He told us how he was recruited and paid small sums to take part in marches and demonstrations.

'Well,' he said, 'it was like overtime money ... Anyway, I gave it up for a bit when I met this woman. Did I tell you about her? Well over forty, she was. Ran a hairdresser's.

137

Pots of money. Bit long in the tooth, o'course. But Gawd
... she fancied me. Thought she'd eat me, Ted. These big
teeth. Biting, an' all that. Wanted to get married. She'd set
me up in a garage, she said. That was when she got passionate, like.'

He grinned foolishly. 'My dad said: "Hang up your hat
there, boy! You're in there, lad! It's your big chance!" But
my mum was against it. Soft, my mum. Though she always
gets her way. Said it was disgusting. Old enough to be my
grannie. Well ...

'I was a fool, Ted. Why should you marry *nothing*, after
all?'

He was filled with a fidgety wistfulness. 'When I think
what a fool I was.

'Of course, I felt awkward, at times. When she laid on a
dinner – *that* used to crease me up. Candles on the table. All
these knives and forks ... And then she'd take me out. I
never understood the menus. "What will you have, Frederick?" She always called me "Frederick". Well, I never
knew. Nothing I could get my tongue round.

'I dunno why I let mum make me ditch her. Just think,
Ted. I'd never have done a stroke of work again.

'That's when I went back into Mosley's lot. Well, for the
loot, y'see.'

Fred had a fresh, impudent face: and he had – what to
me was an astonishing faculty – a flair for seeing lovers
'hard at it', in his phrase, in every hedge, every bus stop and
shop doorway in his village. He would give almost daily
accounts of such visions. 'I could see his brown arse going
up and down! Funny, it looked!' I began to think I had a
special restricted kind of eyesight.

Fred's younger brother also worked with us: Jimmy,
eighteen, thin and nondescript and puzzled. Jimmy frowned
at the world, under pale eyebrows: and, when it addressed
him, grinned unhappily and shuffled his feet.

Creak père had decided that Jimmy must establish conscientious objection to service in the forces. He filled in the
relevant forms for his son. Fred showed us these shortly
after his brother had appeared before a tribunal, shuffled his
feet miserably, and found himself unable to utter more than
a fatal word or so. The tribunal had struck him off the
register. Mr Creak's preliminary statement on behalf of his

son began: 'I beg...' and ended, 'I will toil from morning to night for the benefit of others.'

'Toil?' asked Phil Perkins, peering over Fred's shoulder.

'Well,' said Fred, appreciating the joke. 'You got to be cunning.'

Alas, among his exercises in cunning, Creak père had alleged that Jimmy was a constant, indeed a frantically pious, worshipper at the parish church: one of Jimmy's few tangled responses to questions put by the tribunal was so revelatory of his ignorance of churches, times of services and even the precise location within the week of the sabbath day, that the case had floundered instantly. But Mr Creak, we gathered, had not given up. When the tribunal impatiently attempted to cut him short, he was still adducing urgent reasons why Jimmy should be accepted as a convinced pacifist. He was in the end pushed out of the room by an attendant, Fred confessed, while crying: 'The boy's scared stiff of air raids! He's not very intellectual!'

'Your dad's a card!' observed Phil.

'But my *mum*!' Fred cried, in his perpetually renewed anguish and regret. 'My mum's soft! The old cow's soft through and through!'

Fred's story gave a little warmth to a day near the end of 1943 that was unbearably cold – with a green east wind, that made the tears start in our eyes. The greenness turned blue, and then became a greeny blackness, from which at last the snow began to slant: thin, to begin with, a drift of dots. Phil and I set off home together. The clouds, so black and heavy it seemed they must fall from the sky, had drawn away from the horizon and suddenly the sun was there, setting, a great and unlikely fire. The light became quite extraordinary – it laid a dazzle over the clouds, against which you could see the snow falling, a universal wind-blown chalky smoke. And we cycled in ecstasy! 'Look! Look!' The most amazing colours shone in the trees: each intensified beyond belief. We skimmed down a hill past a radio station: the four wireless masts were giant skeletons of shining green. The sun burned brighter still in a spreading pool of its own light. Brown leaves threw back this light as the base of a breathtaking pattern at the peak of which tall slim trees, bent towards the roadway, gleamed silver. Both of us exclaimed with delight at the spectacle of one tree, the highest of all, that was wreathed from head to foot in ivy: it had turned into a pillar of translucent green.

We seemed to be gliding through a world so beautiful that it could hardly be ours. I've never forgotten that moment – and the fairly apocalyptic quality of it. Perhaps I have never seen light so marvellously rare, or colours so heightened – or so revealed, as it seemed, in their very essence. Perhaps it was that, at this point in history, any unusual experience of natural beauty took some of its impact from bombs falling, continents torn, the daily multitudes of murder and grief. But, whatever the cause, for that moment we were drugged with a loveliness that spared nothing – that turned our very bicycles into gleaming frames on which we sailed along a blue-grey brilliance that could hardly be mere macadam.

And then, suddenly, the snow ceased to be smoke: as if at the touch of a switch in some immense piece of stage machinery, the sun fell away, the wind dropped, and the snow became floating planets and then such a driving mass that the whole air was snow. It settled – a swiftly broadening film and then within seconds a thick blanket. 'Oh bugger the beauty!' Phil cried, as we crouched over our handlebars to keep our eyes clear. In no time we had thick white coats. Softly heavy it lay upon us – so pleasingly on our laps! It was as if silence rather than snow was falling from the air. With crowns of ice on our brows, we whispered through whiteness – through a world from which all that wilder light had vanished, leaving a single staring radiance in which everything had the quality of an engraving cut in steel.

A few days later, my career in drainage came to an end. Jack Bone, unlikely messenger, appeared as we were collected round the evening toolbox. He was in one of his angry moods – they'd told him to call in, he said, bloody twats, because he'd be passing on his way home, which wasn't really true, bloody twats, but you couldn't say no, and they knew it, bloody ... The point was that – he dug me in the ribs – '*You* – wake up!' – I was to report to a certain Women's Land Army hostel in the morning. What for? What do I think it was for, twat? Not for what I had in mind! Oh, I could take that look off my face! A handyman, that's what they wanted. A handyman, God help them!

Part Four

1

It was an old house, set in a large, unkempt garden. Nutt was the official who, in moonlight on my first morning, showed me the garden. When I was not wanted in the house, he said, I could come out here. He swelled with hasty schemes. 'That old monkey puzzle tree...' he said. Then, not explaining what he thought I could do with that – cut it down, trim it, hang myself from its branches – he went on: 'These flower beds...' There was this possible vegetable patch: these perhaps prunable fruit trees ... Nutt was noted for the hurried vagueness of his suggestions. He wore a perpetual frown, as though made hideously anxious by what he was saying: at the same time, he clearly was not his own keenest audience. It was dangerous ever to act on one of his proposals – he forgot it the moment it was uttered. He could fairly have argued that he'd simply not heard himself.

Now, sweating with aimless haste, he took me to a shed at the back of the house: flung open a door. 'Electric plant,' he gasped. 'Keep it going. D'y'understand? Nothing to it.' Swimming in oil, the thing was connected to tanks of water, a row of immense batteries. There was a towering flywheel, and a switchboard thick with dials and switches. It was everything I'd refrained from understanding, on principle, since we split into arts and science at school. 'Kid's stuff,' Nutt panted.

He hurried me into the house to meet the warden. She was a middle-aged woman, giving out an aura of early-morning sadness: drawing on a cigarette as if it had been an oxygen mask. 'The new chap about the place,' Nutt cried. 'Good morning, Mr Nutt,' the warden murmured – but he was gone. 'That man,' she said, 'has the manners of a...' She hid for a moment in an immense exhalation of smoke. Then she asked: 'Are you a handyman about the house?'

'I'm – well, really, I've never thought of myself as ...'

She reinforced her smokescreen, and sighed. 'Oh well,

you'll get along, I expect. Anyway, it's better than drainage.'

Was it, I wondered, as she took me down to see the boiler. Clear out the ashes this way: pour in the coke that way. Watch the pressure. And here were the coal and coke scuttles. I could put a washer on a tap, of course?

I left her and stood in the pale garden, suddenly wistful for the familiar labours of the ditch and its companionable boredom. A landgirl joined me, briefly, on her way to fetch her bike.

'What's your name, love?'

I told her.

'Because whenever we see you we shall call it out at you. Bye bye, love.'

I watched the thin moon sinking. A few birds were stalking up and down in corners of the garden, seeming as aimless as Nutt. Over there, girls' shirts hung on a line, stiff with frost. I tried to imagine myself into the role of a handyman.

So unhandy was I that for long periods during my early days at the hostel I simply stood, in some crook of the garden out of sight of the house, thinking of what I might do and dismissing each thought as impracticable. Large areas of the garden had been ploughed, ready to be turned into vegetable beds. The thick strips of earth lay half-tumbled over, locked into place by sprouting grass. The idea of working from this to the condition known as tilth made me feel faint. I could tidy up that scrap heap, perhaps – but would it be worth it? I could light a bonfire – but what little impression *that* would make on the total task represented by the wilderness Nutt had placed in my care!

Finding myself one morning in the plumb centre of the garden, reading a book, I resolved that I must in future confine myself to volumes of smaller format. It was absurd to stand in that spot reading anything as large as Harold Laski's *Parliamentary Government*.

My first deliberately small book was W. H. Hudson's *Adventures among Birds*. I began, uncertainly, to listen for bird-song. I became obsessively aware of these creatures: the air was suddenly crowded with them. I thought how true it was that the noises of our civilization had deafened us to those little, exquisite songs and calls. The warden found me, late one afternoon, peering into a hedge.

'Are you being handy?' she asked. She held the upper part of her body, as always, wrapped in her arms. I felt, with no experience behind the feeling, that she was perhaps like some mistress at a girls' public school. She had a detached, dry, middle-class attitude to the girls in her care. They appalled and amused her, with their constant singing of popular songs, their talk of boys. She didn't like the way the world was going, at all. She tried to hold herself aloof from it, with a fastidiousness that broke down now and then, when she was touched or warmed by something a girl said or did.

'I've been listening to birds,' I said. 'After reading W. H. Hudson.'

Poor Miss French! She'd been cast, I think, as one of those gentlewomen, of modest private means, who live in country cottages, smoke immensely, tend their gardens. Wartime had nudged her into this service, and she was half-inclined to think of the hostel as an over-large, awkward substitute for her cottage. The girls adored her, rather angrily. They were touched by her fastidiousness, by her way with flowers – the hostel was always full of them – by the wry intelligence she brought to their untidy problems. They came to her to have their emotions set, for a moment, in some neat pattern: or simply to have contact with her tasteful, alien daintiness. And at times this adoration was crossed by anger because they saw that, to her, they were foreign specimens, half-exciting, half-deplorable. Their easy softness of heart, their equally loose furies, their general quality of being emotionally unhooked and unbuttoned – these things were capable of causing Miss French disdain, or a sort of uneasy scorn: and the girls knew it, and were confused. I felt oddly drawn to her myself for such queer reasons as that her hair was thinning – you could see her scalp through it; or because at times, though still neat of figure, she had a sort of heaviness, which seemed to be not so much a matter of flesh as of her awareness of ageing. I felt strangely tender because she had sometimes to sleep in the afternoon. And there was now and then a kind of queenliness about her by which it was impossible to be offended. She would ask me to cut some flowering twigs for her, and then wouldn't stay to help, as usually she did, or to point out the twigs she favoured; instead, silently, she would return to the house, hugging herself. And with just this queenliness she would withdraw, at times, from some youthful scene in the hostel, some giggling rowdiness. She would suddenly have gone, to the small private room where the twigs stood in tall vases.

Poor Miss French! Burdened now with this unhandy handyman! It made it no easier that he read W. H. Hudson; or was a comfort to her when something particularly coarse had occurred. She would appear beside me, as she'd done now, in the garden or one of the sheds or down in the cellars, and would say: 'My dear fellow, we do speak the same language, don't we? That Nutt! How can any one man be so thick and still have time left to be such a boor!' Or it might be one of the girls, who'd been cheerfully indelicate or stupid.

I'd say, perhaps: 'But Nutt's wonderful, isn't he? Half the time I think he rushes about as he does because he can't for the life of him remember what he's doing, and he's afraid if he stands still someone'll challenge him.' And Miss French would laugh and caress her elbows and say: 'You cheer me up.' A compliment that filled me with the deepest gloom. What was I doing, skulking in a corner of this garden, cheering up this chain-smoking High Tory?

Because Miss French was very conservative indeed. I was young enough to be startled when I entered the hostel kitchen and heard her say, of the departing laundryman: 'That man's a *red-hot socialist*, y'know.' It was the banality of the phrase that astonished me, as much as anything. And on another occasion I'd overheard her saying, to no other confidant than Nutt himself: 'I sometimes wonder if it's worth going on, Mr Nutt, when these conscientious objectors...'

So when we met in the garden, often glad of the encounter, she must have been as appalled by her gladness as I was by mine. Red-hot socialist and treacherous conchie chatted with disgracefully class-conscious bourgeoise, and both were comforted by it.

Comfort I needed. The loneliness, and something irresolvably silly about the job, filled me with self-disgust. The surest escape from that was through books. Books had al-

ways offered another life, led alongside the trapped existence in ditches, now in the hostel garden. But escape was
perhaps not the word for what came from them. It was
curious, often, the flavour of reading, in wartime. I would
read, say, Jane Austen, and it was like reading of life on
another planet. All those choices of action! *That* was peace
– to have ahead of one a hundred possibilities of change!
War was the dwindling of possibilities to single, unvariable
destinies. There were times when, reading in one of the
hostel sheds at some break – or when I could no longer
endure some solitary task I'd given myself – I would find a
sentence, sometimes even a single word, leaping at me out
of a page: vibrant with an offer of freedom that was at
painful odds with the caged quality of wartime life. It was
now a sentence from *War and Peace*: 'Mere existence had
always been too little for him: he had always wanted
more.' Then it came from Dostoyevsky: 'Though he had
great hopes, and great – too great – expectations from life,
he could not have given any definite account of his hopes,
his expectations, or even his desires.' It was strange – such
sentences seemed to be written elsewhere than in this
world: in some scarcely imaginable universe where people
set out on long journeys, exchanged one occupation for
another, went on picnics and spent whole summers by the
sea.

'Sometimes,' George wrote from somewhere in the Atlantic, 'I wish I had a shore job. I have these base thoughts at
times, believe it or not.' 'Be encouraged,' I replied. 'There
are moments when I shrink from my garden.' I thought I
had never made a glummer joke.

There were good days – made, usually, by kinds of
weather. Thus, in a February that thought itself to be April,
there was morning after morning of the softest, mildest sunlight: and every now and then, rain would slant across the
scene, the most delicate rain possible, leaving barely a trace
of itself. Later there was a day of quite amazing wind, in
which every loose thing was shattered: yet, while the world
was full of falls and fractures, the tiniest white blossoms
held easily to their stems. When the wind died at last, it
seemed impossible that mere air could have been so violent.
I was called in to have tea with Miss French, that day, in
her room among the tall vases, and out of her fine china:

while she took aspirins for a headache as if they had been items of *haute cuisine*.

I was never at ease with the electric plant. It would die on me: and I would stand in that dim shed and wonder how a machine that I gathered was a relatively simple one, based on a now ancient principle – familiar to most if not to me – could have the nerve to fail, as if it were some highly experimental late invention. I would solicit the aid of visiting tradesmen. It was the baker who first prompted me to do this. I was standing at the door of the shed, one morning, quite wild because all my oilings, turnings of wheels and snapping on and off of switches had led nowhere. The engine had grumbled a little, and an item of brass – which I'd taken to be decorative – had spun once or twice and fallen off. I foresaw that such merriment as was planned among the girls for that evening would have to take place in a glimmer quickly followed by total darkness. Only a few days before I had allowed the boiler to race up to such a temperature that the whole house had shaken with the violence in its piping, and we'd had to turn on all the taps and fill the hostel with burning steam. I couldn't afford another such *débâcle*.

The baker appeared and said: 'You don't look very happy, mate.'

'It's this machine,' I stammered. 'So perverse. I think some radical malaise...' When I was embarrassed, I seemed doomed to choose unsuitable words. The baker looked at me sharply, put down his basket and entered the shed.

'Plugs?' he asked.

'Ah well,' I said. 'Now, the plugs —'

'Tried drying 'em, of course?'

'Ah, well – now —'

He had one in his hand. 'No visible imperfection —' I gabbled.

'Wet,' said the baker. 'Soaked.'

'Ah yes.'

He dried the plugs one by one. Then he replaced them, set the big wheel going, and the machine began complacently to hum.

'Infinite possibilities of derangement,' I ventured.

'Always try the obvious things first,' said the baker, severely.

In time I had a small team of unofficial mechanics, who could be relied upon to drop their baskets or abandon the delivery of coal or laundry to tinker, always successfully, with this sullen machine. I saw that it drew them as I was myself drawn to a crossword puzzle. Once, when something not quite elementary was wrong, I had three of them together in the shed, while the whole district waited for loaves and clean sheets, and I stammered my grateful literary phrases at them. 'A real termagant! Hideously temperamental!'

Slowly I built up an acquaintance with the common faults that afflict such machines. But there seemed no end to them. When I'd mastered the disorders of the petrol tank, the trouble shifted to the carburettor: I'd only to understand that for a breakdown to occur in the magneto, of whose very existence I'd been unaware. Mostly what went wrong seemed to come from the very ABC of the combustion engine. I began to think that this invention had an ABC stretching from A to Z, and then beginning again.

I became obsessed. I tried to keep the plant in order by a kind of statistical witchcraft: I made graphs of its performance, of its consumption of oil and petrol, hoping that by being systematic myself I could shame the machine into regularity. My aides became increasingly contemptuous. Miss French said that my predecessor, without having any actual love for the machine, had not allowed it to create this wellnigh perpetual condition of crisis. My only sympathizer was the laundryman. He was an aesthete among engineers. 'That's a crude affair,' he had said, early on. 'I don't wonder you have trouble with it.' He poured scorn on its various components. I contributed elegant rephrasings of his grunts and groans. 'The man who designed this magneto ought to be shot.' 'Ah – most ill-devised!'

My morale was raised a little by some small success I was having with the garden. I had made a neatness, here and there. About this, too, I became obsessive. I broke the earth up to a super-tilth. I gave my new-gained beds the straightest of edges. I was deeply dismayed one morning when a gang of girls, unable for some reason to go out to work, were sent to help me. They came with united, sidelong humming of 'Have you ever seen a dream walking?' The popularity of this tune seemed rather recent, and not impossibly to have something to do with my presence in the hostel. I thought the apologetic manner in which I made my way about the grounds or through the rooms might be a cause of it, together with my shy habit of address. Certainly a girl had said to me recently: 'Don't speak to yourself, mister.' That morning, as they fell with musical violence upon my latest vegetable patch, I was buttonholed by Jane Riddle. Though it was never really buttonholing, with Jane. She was one of the hostel's few intellectuals – a reader of poetry, among other things. She had taken to me in a rather confusing way: at least, with my small romantic expertise, I found it a puzzle. She addressed me habitually as 'Poor darling.' 'Oh you poor darling!' she would cry, finding me on a cold day at the end of the garden. 'You must be frozen.' I could never decide if her teasing were affectionate or simply feline. 'Still sleeping upright? Poor darling!' 'She loves me – she loves me not,' I'd sometimes ponder, hiding in the shed with nothing better to fill my thoughts. She'd also so place herself – a smallish girl – that her hair tickled my face. I'd stand there, awkwardly, with this mass of pleasantly-smelling female hair brushing my cheek, and would attempt to judge her intent in subjecting me to such erotic trials, or to decide indeed whether she had any intent at all. Perhaps girls quite often brushed men's faces with their hair, and it had no meaning whatever? But it was bringing about this juxtaposition of her hair and someone else's face that, with her, resembled a kind of buttonholing.

'Poor darling,' she said, that morning. 'With us around, you can't slide into a shed and read your book! Poor old thing! And look what Frightful Flo is doing to your lovely vegetable patch!'

Florrie, poor 'Frightful Flo', was the hostel butt: a fat, red-faced, floundering child, who took constant alarm from the smallest causes, and was said to wake her room-mates every night, declaring that she'd seen a man at the window, or could hear one under the bed. But this information I'd had largely from the enigmatic Jane Riddle: and after all, I'd heard Jane herself described as 'a silly bitch'. But then again, the little minority of book-readers and listeners to classical music were all held to be 'silly bitches'. To *them*, the others tended to be 'poor things'.

But it was certainly true that Frightful Flo was doing horrible things to my vegetable patch. Within half an hour those girls, Jane Riddle among them, had brought my pride in the garden very low indeed.

I would cycle to the small nearby town to buy seeds. Miss French would finance me for these expeditions in a manner wonderfully suggestive of the lady from the big house briefing a rather favoured under-gardener. 'My dear boy,' she would say, 'I think we might have a little parsley. Would that be reckless? It's pretty, as well as useful.' She would pour sixpenses out of her purse. 'Parsnips, of course. *Not* turnips. I will *not* have turnips. We have enough utility things.' She would hold back a sixpence, and then offer it as if it were a special coin, one with some mark of distinction about it. 'And that's for some marigold seed! Say nothing to anyone! Say nothing especially to Nutt! But I've lived a whole year without marigolds and that's a year too many!'

On one of these expeditions I was struck by something marvellous at a crossroads, without being able to say what it was. I got off my bike and stared around. Then I saw that this beautiful item in the scene, of which I'd been subliminally aware, was a signpost. For three years there had been no signposts anywhere. Until I saw that one, boldly announcing place-names with its four fingers, I had not understood how much I had missed them. And it was one of those rare events during those years, this replacing of the signposts, that seemed to promise that the pieces would be put together again, at last. I sat under it, for a while, and imagined lights in the streets.

The parsnip seeds surprised me. I'd always thought that seeds must without exception be round and hard, designed to be inserted easily into the ground. These were like confetti, and clung to one another as confetti does. I had, in fact, a fundamental scepticism about all seeds whatever. I *knew* that vegetables or flowers would spring from them, but I did not really *believe* this. I had not yet lived the knowledge of a seed's growth. So I scattered them in the hostel garden, and buried them there, as if doing so were a kind of supersititon.

I made myself a rake out of wood and nails. I dug trenches for peas. I collected the green splashings of cows from a field next to the garden. The soil, after I'd dug or raked it, turned pale and greyly dry under the sun; I liked that. I studied the early flowers as I had never done before: amazed to observe a shadow of deep orange inside the outer petals of a crocus. I dreamed of growing remarkable flowers for Miss French's delight: I imagined her saying, 'Of course, it *is* absurd to think of you as a handyman ... I'll arrange these in a vase and then you must come and drink some tea with me, in my room, and we'll pretend it's peacetime, and we've not met in this false way.'

I began to think of myself as a spreader of civilization, in the form of horticulture. Even my vegetable beds should be in flawless taste, and free from all vulgarity: their utility should be aristocratic.

There was a day of early spring, when I dropped pea seeds into the drills I had drawn: the soil was dry and fine and warm under the sun, which heightened the pale green of the peas as they tumbled down. The sun seemed to hold me in its arms. Certain phrases made their way, slightly ashamed, around my head: 'One wants,' for example, 'to lay one's cheek against the warm young cheek of the day.' There'd be about that none of the uncertainty that brooded over Jane Riddle's wanton hair ... On a nearby apple tree, as I worked, a tree all joints and claws, shadows sketched a second tree. I had more peas than my drill would take, and extended it another yard. In doing so, I dug out a root, and the muscle of it, the bulge of its fibrous biceps, seemed somehow a general promise of vigour to come. I thought how ridiculous it was to be seeing a future of possible sexual pleasure – for surely that was it? – in a root dug from the ground, and how ridiculous indeed it was to be sowing peas in this hostel garden, in the middle of the greatest war the world had known. But then – were there other than absurd frames for human activity, nowadays? 'Whatever we do,' George had said, on one of his leaves, 'it's bound to be rather idiotic – until it's over ... A long apprenticeship to bugger all.'

But I had no idea, then, that my trim, clean husbandry must within weeks be under attack from weeds. As a gardener I had never plied a hoe, nor known that it must be plied. The sudden mats of unsolicited green, which so soon became beds of stinging nettles, took me by surprise. I stood by helplessly while the weeds increased even in my most carefully dug beds, obliterating the tiny legitimate plants. I began to sneak away from the garden, to hide from it.

And the electric plant became increasingly perverse. One day my most loyal aide, the laundryman, elected to blame its latest silence on the oiler. This was a tin can, roughly adapted. 'Try a new one,' he urged, before hurrying off to complete his round. I had difficulty in removing the tin, but managed it in the end, with the help of a hatchet. I was sure this was not the proper tool. But it did its work, with limited damage to the surrounding machinery. Then I began to fashion a replacement.

Alas, my nervous excitement was such that I felt bound to provide Miss French with a running commentary. 'I've stripped down the faulty part,' I announced with trembling grandeur, at lunch time. 'This afternoon I must improvise a new oiler.' Miss French sighed. 'I'm glad you are happy,' she said. She provided herself with a cloud of cigarette smoke, to make faces under, and out of it inquired: 'Did you never go to the Science Museum when you were a boy?'

At the end of the day I reported: 'The operation on the machine is almost completed. Everything now depends on what happens tomorrow, when I try to set it going.'

'We have electric light for tonight?' Miss French inquired sadly.

'Ah – plenty in reserve.' I hesitated. 'So long as you don't all read in bed till the small hours.'

'Sometimes,' said Miss French, 'I think you have a less than realistic idea of the way of life of a Women's Land Army hostel.'

The machine took kindly to its new oiler the next morning, and the shed shook again to its erratic vibrations. I was drawn back to it a little later by its obvious silence. I dried the plugs, dismantled the carburettor, examined the magneto and fell into despair.

The milkman enrolled himself among my aides. He gazed keenly at the plant – put himself, as it seemed to me, into psychic rapport with it – and at once declared the fault to be a blockage in the petrol pipe. He blew through the pipe and the machine, with a mocking chirrup, started instantly.

I gave up.

When it rained, the girls would return from the fields and fill the hostel, and normally they'd be in a state of shatteringly high spirits. I dreaded these occasions, for they'd often come in search of me. 'Miss French says we've got to help you saw some logs.' There'd be hours of myself at one end of the crosscut, and a succession of girls at the other. Their twittering talk crawled over me like ants.

'Are you courting, love?'

'Courting? Hmm – not exactly.'

'What d'you mean, love – not exactly? Hey, he says he's not exactly courting! What sort of courting's that, love? Don't think I'd care for it, myself.'

'You're a sentimental chap, though. Anyone can see that.'

'The sort that gives you flowers.'

For some reason, enormous laughter at that. I noted that the giving of flowers was mysteriously comic.

'I don't think I've ever given a girl flowers.'

'Hear that, girls? Never given a girl flowers. What have you given her then, love?'

Wilder laughter still. I noted that flowers were not the most comic of gifts.

The mixed mockery and sentimentality of their chatter dazed me. Sometimes they sang popular songs, stressing particular lines, so that I was lost in a hopeless attempt to make sense of a dozen contradictory insinuations and innuendoes. They would tumble against me; or my current mate on the crosscut would make her eyes swim with longing until, amid a general tittering, my face flamed. At other times they would be purely good-natured: or I'd be ignored in the discussion of some satisfying scandal.

They came in once, a dozen of them crying: 'Buggery! Buggery! Buggery! Buggery!'

I gave them a formal smile of welcome, as if this cry had been an unusual substitute for 'Good afternoon!' One of them said: 'We've got ever so interested in buggery. You're always reading. Have you got a book about it?'

I shook my head, not having the faintest idea how to pursue such a line of talk. Whereupon they turned together, the whole dozen, and left the shed and began to march round the garden, providing the entire world with the information (set to music) that I hadn't got a book about buggery. The laundryman was at the back door, and on his next visit he went out of his way to have a word with me.

'What's all this about you and buggery?' he inquired.

I reflected gloomily that I'd thought I'd plumbed the depths of reputation, long since, in becoming a conchie; but that plainly one could sink very much further yet.

An institution full of girls was an unnerving place. It was as if the whole house was subject to moods – to me, quite inexplicable. The very banging of doors formed a kind of language – at times it was sullen, at other times high-spirited. And there were days when those doors seemed to shut on whispers, hysterical outbursts and sobbings. So often something shrill and bitter seemed to be happening somewhere on the edge of what could actually be seen or heard. The very cellars, where I blundered about on heaps of coke, murmured to themselves, some mornings.

Nutt contributed his own angers, at times. He stormed into the hostel once, hat over one eye, and cried: 'They want a good hiding, some of them!' Miss French said, in the most reasonable of tones: 'We must appoint you chief executioner, Mr Nutt.' Nutt's eyes became blank at this: the warden's ease with words gave him great trouble. Any spoken statement of the least sophistication always stopped Nutt in his tracks: at such a moment, always, there was a stutter in his machinery at this unexpected consequence of a speech of his own. Then the motor would roar again – as it did now. 'Never had a good hiding in their lives,' he bellowed. And Miss French turned to me. 'You and Mr Nutt together, perhaps,' she murmured.

The girls had invented a hostel ghost. It was widely believed in, and was held to be that of a farmer disappointed in love, who'd hanged himself in the cellar. There were times when Miss French encouraged talk of the ghost. 'Someone has seen him again?' 'Not *seen* him,' a girl would say. '*Heard* him! You listen, miss, in the night! All that bumping under the house.' 'The boiler,' I'd intervene, 'is a great bumper.' 'Shame!' Miss French would cry. '*Must* you be so rational?' And a girl would point out that it stood to reason that such an old house, out in the country, would be haunted. Frightful Flo once observed: 'You've only got to read the Bible...' '*You* read the Bible, Florence?' Miss

155

French inquired gaily. '*I* don't,' said Florrie. 'But you've only got to . . .'

I was looking dully through the window of a bike shed one day, more than usually unable to decide between unwelcome tasks, when a heavily-bearded sailor crossed the lawn. The beard was unfamiliar – it was like one of those that children draw, a scribble of thick loops. But the eyes were George's. So was the tongue.

'This is a national tragedy,' said George. 'They told me where to find you. You can imagine my disbelief.'

I took him on a tour of the premises. 'Worse and worse,' he said. 'I sometimes defend you, to old schoolmates of ours met here and there. What shall I do now?'

Contact with George had always been like stepping on to another plane of existence. At school, when he was writing straightforward and stinging social criticism, I was labouring for hours over my poetic prose. I remembered a phrase that had made his eyes narrow with distaste: 'Day was uncrumpling its flower and urging five-storey stamens at the sky.' There had always been a comic tension between his very masculine precision and directness and my thickly inexact, emotional quality. He was brisker than ever now, more busy-minded, restless with comment on the way of the war, on economics, marriage.

As it happened, it was economics he was reading, interspersed with John Donne, Shakespeare. 'The more I read, the more left-wing I become. Not that there's really any science of economics. Do you think so? It's basically a religious question.' He stared down at my cabbage patch and shook his head sadly. 'We're living in a very queer age, you know. Bits and pieces of all sorts of influences – Christianity, for example. And the Christian idea of the home. We've nothing to replace that with, yet. For the communist it's easy. The home's a bourgeois relic. But it isn't as simple as that for us – is it?'

He glared impatiently at an apple tree.

'And marriage. I'm far from sure about marriage. Are you? I'm afraid of it, really. I'm always having these mental spring-cleans. Throwing out the old furniture. Wouldn't I be likely to throw out a wife along with the rest?'

I struggled, appalled, with my sentimental images of marriage, but George swept on.

'I've just been reading *Romeo and Juliet*. Isn't that the worst of Shakespeare? Romeo was such a fool! ... Really, when you think how few people you can remain interested in for more than a few days! ... I suppose this job of yours must leave you with plenty of time for romantic dalliance?'

It wasn't only his dread of marriage – related, I gathered, to the sharpening of his interest in some half a dozen directions – that filled George during that leave with a sort of vivacious depression. As we wandered through London ('Not Oxford Street again! We always seem to be walking down this bloody street!') he expressed gloom about the political state of things. Cripps had been expelled from the Cabinet: there had been the long shadiness of the Darlan affair. A revival, this last, said George, of the atmosphere of the Congress of Vienna: a pointer to a new Treaty of Versailles. 'I really begin to wonder why I am fighting.'

I was startled, having believed that George's decision to fight must be based on grounds other than a hope of some political transformation, carried out during the war by the existing parties. 'But surely,' I said, 'it was obvious all along that this war in itself would only confirm the present system?'

He agreed glumly. We were fighting fascism, and in the process were building up a counter-fascism of big business, hand in hand with an acquiescent trade unionism.

We thought Hyde Park greatly improved by the loss of its railings. It was haunted for me (though I said nothing of this to George) by the ghosts of the sheep that had once, with such a curious absence of excitement, watched Jean Hopkins and me as we lay on that grass and embraced. 'You know,' said George, as we trod among dozing couples, 'we are so near to socialism in our economic organization! If the monopolies were publicly owned, we'd be there! That's what interests me now. But can we make the jump? Must we go back to the beginning? Must it be the long knives and the Red Sundays...?'

At Speakers' Corner we stood watching, rather than listening to, a painfully thin anarchist who flapped flimsy hands as he spoke. 'At least he's physically consistent with his beliefs,' said George. 'Have you noticed how fat I'm becoming? ... You know, even if socialism were established here, the United States would seize the colonies and we'd be reduced to trying to live by making matches ... What the devil's to be done, I don't know. I suppose one can bleat about it. I suppose one can even join a society and persuade others to bleat about it.'

I caught myself wondering at the paradox that George's vehement despairs were, to me, a form of invigoration. It was like being mentally birched – in the sauna-bath sense of birching, of course. I glowed with furtive well-being when he growled: 'Has it struck you that we might as well resign ourselves to being an American colony?'

We went to a concert, sitting among the girls with long rolls of hair making them one-eyed, Polish officers with shaven polls, fawn-faced doughboys. George explained his latest test for excellence in music: you swallowed a tot of rum and found yourself sleeping through anything that was not worth hearing.

A pianist played Liszt and Chopin. George was critical: 'She shouldn't have worn that violet frock.' He'd rather it had been an orchestra. 'I come so rarely to concerts that I like to be inspired, not to be mildly interested.' He sighed when the pianist was followed by a soprano: but gave her some marks for singing in Russian. 'A soprano should always sing in a foreign language. Then you don't have to trouble to catch the words.'

In the interval he talked about the Navy. He'd tried to write about it, but no magazine in wartime would accept an article stating that the Navy was rotten from top to bottom.

'As it is, you know. But I'd rather be for'ard than aft. At least they're men, for'ard. If there's smut, it's virile smut. And the men are able to talk about themselves very amusingly – without affectation. Aft, the conversation is ... like an Old Boys' Club. Either you'd get yourself thoroughly disliked, or you'd be very miserable.

'I can't bear being ashore, you know. I can't bear anything except the Med and the Russian convoys. I'd like to be on a Russian convoy. Or a Free French ship. Restlessness. Desire for excitement ... It's unhealthy, I suppose. Do you think so?'

I shrugged my handyman's shoulders, helplessly.

'All round me I see people aspiring to be what they are

158

not – well, specifically I see men aspiring to be *officers*! Ugh! It makes me cling to myself. At bottom, I want to hang on to being myself. A sort of guttersnipe. The only decent thing to be.'

George smiled into the single eye of a pretty girl standing at his elbow, and lowered his voice. 'Talking of bottoms, do you know there are men on board us who have a fox hunt tattooed across their backsides. I don't suppose you've run across anything like that on the land?'

I admitted ruefully that I had no reason to believe that my colleagues' backsides were anything but blank.

'Redcoats in full tilt across each cheek, and the fox just going to earth.'

'Are you thinking of having one?'

George smiled again at the girl, who seemed unaware of these amiable events occurring under his beard. 'Nice for my wife – if I drift into having one.'

'There's nothing respectable you could stamp over it, is there?'

'No. The very location is bawdy.'

'Really, they should have borne in mind that they might one day wish to be respectably nude.'

George digested the phrase, for his own purposes. 'Respectably nude,' he murmured, and smiled reassuringly at the girl, who had certainly heard him.

At the end of the concert he sighed deeply.

'Yes,' I said. 'I'm sorry. I should have looked for something more ... dramatic. I'm afraid it was rather a programme of rarities for the well-fed musical ear.'

George shrugged, smiled, and turned in the direction of Victoria Station, the naval barracks, the violent sea.

'Truffles,' he said.

Suddenly, Miss French was going. She had found a hostel more deeply in the countryside than ours. 'You understand what I'm after, don't you? It has an established garden. Oh, don't look so guilty. You didn't stand a chance with this one.' She commissioned me to make a last gathering of twigs and leaves. When the van came for her furniture, I hid away, astonished by my heartache. Had I some sort of illness that caused the sufferer to fall in love wherever it was entirely inappropriate for him to do so?

I was sought out by Jane Riddle. 'Poor darling! Miss F's having trouble with her bed! She's seething! You'd better dash!' I dashed: and then flew about in a state of wild distress, Miss French having inquired why I'd bothered to arrive in her bedroom without some bed-dismantling tool. I managed to remember where I'd left the hostel hammer, and returned for the warden's last tenderness:

'You knock it *up*, my dear chap! *Up!*'

After the van and the car bearing Miss French had gone, Jane sought me once more. 'A command, poor darling! A command from Our Lady! I am to strangle you with my bare hands.... But I think you've had enough. Poor darling! ...'

Miss French was succeeded by an entire family. Miss Phipps was the new titular warden, but she was surrounded by a brood of deputies: all, most of the time, at sulky war with one another. They came, raged, and went: the permanent members being Miss Phipps herself, and her old mother, and a sharp young aunt, and a stray cousin, aged seventeen, who possessed a hush-hush baby. The obscure source of this baby was a cause of much delicate hesitation and rephrasing in their talk. It may also have been at the roots of their very strongest shared opinion, which related to the male natives of the United States. 'I met a man who's been to America,' the central Miss Phipps told me within five minutes of our first meeting, 'and he said he wouldn't let a daughter of his go within a dozen yards of an American. They're filthy.'

'Filthy?'

'Leap on you,' said Miss Phipps. She seemed to feel that I was as much in need of warning as any tender fool of a girl. She even added: 'You want to watch them!'

If the Phippses were at war, it was with the USA and with the Women's Land Army. They smelt Miss French in the atmosphere of the hostel, and didn't like it. Miss Phipps, given to bustling into the garden to share some shocked opinion with me, once did this in order to exclaim: 'Wardens ... they're stuck-up cats, some of them.' The slight air of the superior girls' school which Miss French had made a characteristic of the hostel was quickly sneered away by her successors. They disliked the girls, whose presence made life so exhausting. 'This isn't a guest house,' Miss Phipps would groan. 'It's Army life. That's what it really is. They've no right to expect.' She never specified what they had no right to expect. They were not justified, clearly, in entertaining anticipations of any kind.

Though the Phippses never abandoned the front against America, it was on their second front – in the war against the girls – that they were most passionately engaged. I cannot imagine the grounds on which they were chosen as a suitable family for a wardenship, since at no point whatever could they have disguised their smouldering hostility to any group of young women. There were times when it seemed that what they held against such groups was their potential willingness to become fodder for Yankee lusts. 'All they think of ... *men*,' Miss Phipps would grumble, scrubbing away at some surface – table or windowsill – as if it were fouled in some unspeakable way.

In the light of this attitude to men, it was disconcerting that they took so readily to me. I think, alas, it was my grammar-school voice. They thought me polite and socially commendable. It was not easy to imagine my leaping on girls. They laid out the whole range of their bigotry before me, gaily. As when they once talked of a captured German general. 'He ought to be crucified,' said Miss Phipps, in the equable tone of a woman who was saying that the hearth ought to be swept. 'He ought to be tied to a tree and whipped,' amended old Mrs Phipps: as one might say – Ah yes, but the hearth needs polishing too. And as they said such things, they smiled comfortably at their resident conchie and offered him another slice of cake.

Over one morning tea-break, imagining that it might give a little fantastic amusement, I mentioned a wild report I'd seen of a German plan to empty the Mediterranean by evaporation.

There was no laughter. Instead Miss Phipps sighed: 'Oh!' and a curious half-smile appeared on her face. Then she said: 'I don't think Our Heavenly Father would allow that. After all, He walked on the waters, didn't He?'

I thought it was a stroke of deadpan humour, and that I'd altogether underestimated Miss Phipps; but she repeated gravely, amid nods from her relatives: 'I don't think Our Heavenly Father would allow that ... not when the Mediterranean is so important to us.'

The devil, she went on to point out, had already reigned for four years, had he not? And was that not one year longer than was laid down? Staring into my amazed eyes, she murmured: 'There is a red devil and a green devil, isn't there? I wonder who the red devil is?'

I felt the ground give way under me. Was one nowhere safe from this lunatic mumbo-jumbo?

In fact the Phippses rose to these apocalyptic heights very rarely. If, when they really put their minds to it, they saw the war as a game played by devils of various hues, their everyday opinion was that at the roots of war lay virtually any vexation they might run against. 'That's why we have wars' was a phrase they all used, and often. The girls had not wiped their boots when they entered the hostel. 'That's why we have wars.' The price of potatoes had risen by a halfpenny. 'That's why we have wars.'

I found the phrase very contagious. When the power plant failed to start, I was glad to have a new piece of abuse to hurl at the silent engine. 'This,' I would say, hopelessly flooding its chambers with petrol, 'is why we have wars.'

I could be in a silly job, I concluded after six months as a handyman, only because I was silly.

The RAF bombed two great dams in the Ruhr. Reporting that 4,000 people had been drowned, and 120,000 made homeless, the *Evening Standard* described the event as 'majestic'. I wondered what the German adjective had been for the bombing of Coventry, and even as I thought such things felt the old uneasiness. Irony came so pat! I remembered Phil Perkins making much of a newspaper story about an exchange – in North Africa, was it? – of captured nurses. German doctors had talked warmly and at length with their British colleagues. Phil had pointed out how idiotic this made all our belligerency. Of course. Yet – what was the relevance? The fact that most human beings could find occasion to be amiable to one another was probably quite unrelated to the political disease of war ...

And yet, again ... It *was* deeply callous to describe an act resulting in much death and great misery as 'majestic'. And the thought of individual enemies exchanging friendly words did make the general obligations of enmity more than usually intolerable ... I would wake up, some mornings, with a curious concrete image of my mental state. I would see myself as split: the larger part wanted so badly to continue in its ways, with confidence – but there was this smaller part, exposed by the candour of sleep, so small and shaken and miserable that it brought the other to a standstill: as if it were a hopeless inadequate engine for some monstrous dynamo.

A girl spoke in the kitchen one day of having seen the king at a Home Guard parade. 'He passed by only a few yards away. It *was* nice!' To the warden's old mother, who spoke seldom, this seemed to be a cue for which she'd been long waiting. 'You haven't any Reds here, have you?' she asked. The girl said: 'Oh, we don't talk about such things.' 'Oh, shut up, mum!' said Miss Phipps. 'It's lunch time, and we don't want to talk politics.' Old Mrs Phipps said, comfortably: 'All right. But those Reds – always causing trouble!'

She was silent for a moment – then she burst out: 'I told that soldier I told you about, the one I met on the train, I told him, "Anyway, the war's thinned the population," and he said, "Well, there's something in that." '

'*Mum!*' cried Miss Phipps.

The end of being a handyman came for me, as the beginning had, in the form of panted instructions from Nutt. 'Report ... Monday morning ... the Quarry,' he gasped. The Quarry was the War Ag's main transport depot, in the county town: fifteen miles from where I was living. 'How am I to get there?' I asked. Nutt suddenly made a joke. 'It depends where you're starting from, don't it?' he ventured. At once he fell into total mental collapse, and my hope of a practical answer vanished.

There'd been a sudden fit of severity at County Hall. It had been observed that a number of conchies had infiltrated into jobs of notable comfort and even dignity. They were working in the engineering departments, in accounts: and one or two were occupying positions of indefensible softness in Women's Land Army and other hostels. They were all to be sent at once to the very bottom of every possible ladder.

'You know it wasn't our doing?' said Miss Phipps. Her old mother, who was all for skinning German generals alive and had indicated her view that anyone prepared to dispose of Reds by lingering torture was a contemptible milksop, said she would miss me, filled my pockets with apples, and was standing with the hostel baby at the gate when I passed through it for the last time.

Part Five

1

The Quarry, as I found at the end of a long cycle-ride, was so named because the depot was built on the site of an old sand-pit. It was a yellow bowl in which stood garage buildings, workshops, a litter of lorries and vans, stacks of drainage pipes. I found myself in a curious gang that included Oliver and our unhappy Italian friend from Soho, Joe Mazzini. The whisper was that we were there to tidy the yard. But no one officially approached us in this or any other matter. In the office important men were to be seen moving about agitatedly. Oliver, who'd been at the Quarry for a week already, said there'd been an attempt, early on, to establish contact with this official group. 'One of us asked what we were actually there for. The man looked furious and drove off in a van and hasn't been seen since.'

Joe Mazzini's sense of outrage at having been torn away from his Soho restaurant was sharpened by the daylong idleness. To shouting and throwing things (he'd discovered a heap of scrap iron into which he methodically hurled bricks) he'd added a new mark of his irritation: he would rock vans. It might seem nothing much – rocking vans; but Joe would set them swaying, one after another, with such angry vigour that they would all vibrate together and form, with their hideous squealing, a single huge unmusical instrument. In my early days at the Quarry I found it odd that the official attention should be quite uncaught by anything so extraordinary – to the eye as to the ear – as half a dozen vans being set rocking by a crazily bored young man wearing a very smart black suit. But the disorder in which the Quarry operated soon blunted any observer's feeling for the unusual.

Then one morning Oliver disappeared. He was back among us a couple of hours later, looking very pleased. He'd been out with one of the lorry drivers, he said, as a mate. As it happened, it was a girl driver. Her name was Mollie Nunn. We'd noticed her about the place, perhaps – a nice, plain girl, given to blushing? They'd taken a load of empty sacks to a mill. Oliver was minded to apply formally for a position as lorry driver's mate. If possible, he'd like to be permanently attached, in this capacity, to Mollie Nunn.

'Have you any Biblical justification for all this?' I asked him coldly.

'Certainly,' said Oliver, who seemed uncommonly elated. ' "Rejoice, O young man, in thy youth." Ecclesiastes, chapter 11, verse 9.'

I was the next to be given a respite from our puzzled idleness. I was taken out by a driver with no resemblance to Mollie Nunn, carting a load quite unlike the one she'd been carrying when Oliver was her mate. Briggs was a man who might have been called taciturn, except that his silence was so condemnatory of people and things, and so supported by little glares and groans, that he seemed fairly to be flowing with acid comment. His regular mate being ill, he called me to his service with a beckoning frown; and we drove in the bitterest silence to pick up five tons of oats from a farm. Then followed an awful period when, for him, Briggs was talkative. These breaches in his silence, most of one syllable, were caused by my untrained way with sacks. In general, having had them lowered on to my back in a barn, I fell flat beneath them before I'd reached the lorry. It was clearly not for this that sour Briggs had picked me out of the mob at the Quarry.

In my last years on the land, I became as good as the next man at carrying sacks. Hundredweights – of potatoes, for example – I learned to shift so fast and with so little strain that, talking away to a companion, I'd be surprised to find I'd emptied a five-ton lorry. Corn was heavier – usually one and a half hundredweights for oats and barley – though the convention was to sack wheat in two-hundredweight sacks or even larger. I fell down, that first nightmare morning, under the smaller weight of oats. I had time to crumple and sag. My first sacks of wheat, a week or so later, simply felled me. There was a horrid sensation as of a sack having gone straight through me and out at the front. Then I was a heap of bones and jelly on the ground.

In time I learned the knack – but not from Briggs, nor from the farmhand who grumblingly helped me to carry those oats. The trick was to put the sack on exactly the right spot high up on your back – but not too high up, or you'd snap your neck. Find this exactly right spot, and you could carry a two-hundredweight sack with a smile, and go on carrying such sacks all day. Later in my career as a lorry driver's mate I'd watch men much larger than myself, much stronger, but without experience, offer their backs confidently to a sack and go down at once, astonished, flattened. Beyond a certain point, strength had nothing to do with it at all . . .

I got back to the Quarry, sore and dismal, to find that Joe Mazzini had been out with another driver to pick up three heifers from a railway station. Joe was deeply peeved at having been obliged, a skilled waiter with urban refinements, to travel in a box lorry with cattle suffering, as it seemed to him, from spectacular indigestion. Joe turned his groping way with the English language to great effect in his failure to describe the thunders and stenches with which the lorry (he claimed) was filled. But he obviously felt as much pleased as piqued. Something had happened, at last. And he had a story to amaze the West End of London with.

Oliver had been out with Mollie Nunn. 'We seem,' I said, 'to have found jobs for ourselves.' I felt that his nod, and the smile that accompanied it, had behind them more than pleasure in employment; and I resolved to displace him, as soon as possible, as Mollie Nunn's mate. It could not be consistent with his religious dreariness to be so professionally attached to a young woman, and to display such pleasure as a consequence.

And so we became, by no apparent design, lorry drivers' mates at the Quarry: this was to be my last occupation on the land, from mid-1944 to mid-1946. It was marvellously different from drainage, which had tied us to single places. There was, as it seemed at first, the excitement of not knowing what the day would offer – in terms of load, destination, driver. Sometimes it would involve, horribly, a visit to one of the War Ag's stores, in the stables of an 18th-century house a mile or so out of the town. The setting was romantic. A hollow square of buildings, still handsome, entered under a gateway that was heavy with blurred angels and urns and topped with a belfry of bright green copper. Around us, parkland. As we drove in, I was Lord Edward —, a mysterious figure performing the first action in a novel set in the year 17—, or I was the Scarlet Pimpernel, disguised as a drayman's mate, entering the courtyard of a certain prison in Paris. The child in me, only a few years outgrown, longed to play in that setting – perfect property for so many swashbuckling boyish fantasies ... The reality was chemical fertilizer. The War Ag had stored in Beechall Park the main bulk of its superphosphate and sulphate of ammonia: and all of it, in Beechall Park's romantic damp, had gone rock hard. You tugged at a sack and it was like trying to be on friendly terms with a tombstone. One of these on your back – perhaps two hundredweight of it – caused agony even if you managed to keep it still, so it didn't slip down your back and take your flesh with it.

Many loads were abrasive. Drainage pipes, for example. In time I came to know these objects with a strange, haunting intimacy. I would hurl and catch them throughout long stretches of the night, asleep. They were corrugated, six inches in diameter, four inches, three inches. Some were a sort of saffron-yellow in colour, shot through with wandering smears of brown. Some were vividly pink. They were thrown from the lorry to us on the ground: usually in twos, but sometimes in larger numbers: then, as often as not, they flew in all directions, smashing against the stack we'd made. For hour after hour, when a convoy of lorries carried loads to a site, there'd be the click and clank of these pipes as we laid them in place. In those early days, I received them ineptly – on the tips of my fingers, woundingly on the thick of my palm. Blood mixed with the pale clay dust on my hands. And all round us grew the honeycomb heaps.

We'd be mates, sadly, to Briggs, who hated all things; or gaily to one of the conchie drivers. These were, in many respects, the aristocrats of our curious breed. They'd had the skill of driving, to begin with. They'd added to this a determination not to be tied to drainage. What they'd looked for was a job that gave scope for private enterprise. Sometimes, indeed, in the strict sense of this term. There was Reggie Gordon, for example, who seemed to me yet another man who'd become a conchie out of a kind of cussedness – a strong resistance to being pushed around by anybody. It had simply not been possible for Reggie to remain long in a gang; and he'd been one of the first to fight his way out and into the freer world of the War Ag's transport division. Reggie's father was a decorator's merchant, and had a small shop in the London suburbs. Reggie had busy ideas for its development, once the war was over. Meanwhile, he worked in it on Saturday afternoons, and brooded over its affairs while driving his lorry. He sold paints, wallpaper, paintbrushes to people in the Quarry, at special prices. Officials of the War Ag were among his customers. It was clear that, in some curious way, this activity won him respect even among those who were formally most opposed to the conchie. His busy, practical charm and readiness for business were qualities that overlaid, and at times made quite invisible, the queer disgrace of his pacifism. He was candidly ambitious, and that made sense, too. There was a Saturday when the Transport Officer wanted us all to work overtime: there was corn that could not be left out over the weekend.

'I'm sorry,' said Reggie, crisply. 'As you know, I have my own affairs to look after. I was ready to work last weekend, but you didn't ask me. This weekend I can't manage.' And he smiled – a beautiful, deliberately sad smile. Reggie had the features and complexion of some ideal 1920-ish tennis player – and the ash-blond moustache to set them off. Quite impossible to think of him in a ditch, enduring Jack Bone's erratic angers!

Had it been Oliver or me, the Transport Officer's answer would have been biting and noisy. But to Reggie he said:

'You're a brute, Gordon! You're a brute, you know! I've affairs of my own, too, which I'd like to look after. But this comes first.'

'Not with me,' said Reggie, pleasantly. 'I'm sorry, but it just can't be managed.'

And that, astonishingly, was that. The Transport Officer went off to be angry somewhere else. It was Reggie's calm appeal to the general philosophy that a man had a right, at any time, to pursue affairs of business – it was this that neutralized the officials, and made them unable to play their usual game.

Sitting beside Reggie – or his friend, Ralph Tarbox, who had similar qualities – I felt a muff: shy, gauche, ignorant of the world, socially incompetent. Worst of all, I felt terribly unentertaining. When Reggie met Ralph Tarbox, or another friend of his own kind and vintage, then the gentle dullness of our association, his and mine, was suddenly torn open by the shells and rockets of the most delicious jokings and teasings.

They were all great storytellers, and every day yielded its anecdotes: comic accounts of War Ag eccentricities, complete with perfect passages of mimicry. They had sets of facial tricks, very funny, and a whole apparatus of jokes that could be used over and over again, with slight and telling variations. I'd feel, at times, helplessly miserable in their company, because I could contribute nothing at this level; and helplessly happy, too, because they had the gaiety of true comedians, and their conversation was a circus ring in which the words and ideas ran about and fell down like clowns. It was uncomfortable, being a prey to opposing emotions of equal force.

At times I'd feel such an idiot – standing and watching life, it seemed to me, in this matter of their comic spontaneity as in this whole matter of the war – watching life like some baffled observer from another planet. I was sure, by now, that I *was* a complete idiot: someone who, among other things, had left familiar gaps in the essential argument of his pacifism unbridged ... had been content with the gimcrack landscape of his habitual thinking, if it wasn't more vague feeling than thinking.

And then I'd have an odd good day, with Reggie Gordon or Ralph Tarbox. Perhaps the gift of clowning, in their style, would for once seem less essential to companionship than I'd thought. Or we'd jolt and clatter through brilliantly green, unfamiliar lanes, and I'd trail a hand out of the lorry window as if trailing it in water. And perhaps we'd have threshed linseed to carry, big slippery sacks filled with those greasy chocolate-coloured grains: sacks that fell and slipped all over the lorry like a regiment of spineless men. Trying to move one of these evasive sacks could bring us to a giggling standstill.

Or we'd lain, perhaps, in a lunch break, on the edge of a field delicious with the scent of blossoming beans.

Meanwhile, I was very busy, beginning to yearn for Mollie Nunn. Mollie was no one's driver, permanently, and I'd soon been out with her as often as Oliver.

She was one of the drivers of longest standing at the

Quarry: a shy girl of attractive plainness. She was always known as 'Miss Nunn', and was much admired for her sweetness and modesty. She drove a high van for which I found myself feeling an absurd affection, as if it had become a part of Mollie herself. Seeing it standing empty in the yard, I would experience a tenderness perhaps rarely felt for a five-hundredweight Ford van. Especially for one with a perpetually leaking radiator. 'See Miss Nunn is filled up,' was one of the commonest cries in the Quarry. And the most unlikely men would stroll over with water, when they heard it.

Mollie was a great blusher, and had a voice of uncontrollably high pitch. Sometimes her voice threatened to sharpen to a mere wordless squeak and she would blush and begin again whatever she had been saying. It would not have been an original remark. Mollie talked in clichés: but she gave to these a curious innocence that was at times a very fair substitute for freshness. She also expressed her own understanding of the obviousness of almost everything she said by using incessantly the phrase: *'Of course ...'* It might be that one had rushed up with water, for her ever-thirsty van. After blushing, Mollie would squeak: 'Of course, if you didn't put water in it, it would boil, wouldn't it?'

Most people would grin gently and nod. I was in some danger of simply staring at her, with mute adoration caused by this very obviousness of hers. It had such a warmth about it – as though she were anxious to acknowledge, and always with a mild but most friendly surprise, the extraordinary inevitability and familiarity of almost everything that happened.

'Nasty wet day, Mollie.'

'Of course, if it didn't rain, the crops wouldn't grow.' And she might add, in a squeak of real inquiry: 'Would they?'

'Of course, we often do have rain at this time of the year, don't we?'

'Common enough, Mollie.'

'Of course, we'd rather it didn't rain. But then, of course, we're not farmers, are we?'

'No, Mollie. We're not ...'

She was worried by a certain easy tendency she had to

171

tears. Almost anything could make her weep. These tears, she told me, were rarely meaningful: they simply came, if in a situation there was the very slightest and sometimes barely recognizable element of sadness. Mollie shedding her not in the least unhappy tears was a common sight. 'Bother it,' she'd say, brushing the facile drops away. She was most annoyed that she was driven to weep at all partings, whatever. 'But I don't even like him,' she grumbled, dabbing wrathfully at her eyes as an extremely unattractive temporary driver left the Quarry for the last time.

I loved Mollie for her plainness, her sweetness, her absurd flapping run as she hurried late to the canteen. I loved her for the modestly coloured scarves she wore about her head, for the neatness of that head and of the bun-coloured plait she tethered across its crown. I loved her for her jeans and her jerseys. I caught myself, at times, in a most unholy state of complacency because I had elected to yearn in this way for a girl so unbeautiful and so unwitty. But there were moments when my adoration was put under great strain: as when in the canteen another girl driver was speaking of letters she'd received from her boy friend fighting in Italy.

'Of course, Italy's very dirty,' said Mollie. 'And very hot. And it's full of old churches, of course, isn't it?'

She looked at me for confirmation, and I responded with what must have been a sort of tender scowl.

'Of course,' she said, 'that's what we think about Italy, isn't it? I mean, the Italians don't like England, do they? And the English don't like Italy. It's what you're used to, isn't it?'

I don't think she can have read the tortured expression on my face. But she then shed tears.

One of our favourite drivers, using the word in a special way, was Bob Doyle, a man whose loud thick-lipped speech made him sound permanently drunk. Big and clumsy, he lurched from side to side as he walked; and drove a lorry with a kind of violence, as if he knew the skill was really beyond him. His driving expressed his nature, perfectly. He pumped at the accelerator, so that we were always plunging absurdly forward, and then dropping to a snail's pace. His huge, vague hand would feel for the gear lever, always too late: sometimes he would miss it altogether: he would wrench it, finally, from one position to another, like a man trying to pull an obstinate post out of the ground. There were always these enormous hiccups of gear-changing. He had his special lorry, L 72, a clapped-out Albion, and the Quarry garage spent much guile on keeping him out of the cab of any other. 'Christ!' the garage foreman would shout, as Bob Doyle came into the yard, in the wildly leaping, shrieking, hiccoughing Albion. 'I don't know how it holds together.'

A trip with Bob was terrifying. It wasn't merely this altogether inexact way he had of driving – as if he'd never more than half-understood what it was all about. It was also that he'd devote much of his time at the wheel to fantasy. He was not really with us, at all. He was not in England. Usually he was in Canada, where he claimed to have lived before the war. It was a curious Canada that he spoke of. He'd been a sheriff there, with a six-shooter. 'That's the place – Canada,' he'd say. 'Cattle. I had – I don't know how many *head* of cattle – on my *ranch*.' He would stress any term that he felt was expressive of that great world where he'd been a rancher, fantastically prosperous. It was a man's world there. None of your French letters, for example. A Canadian would as soon think of using a French letter as he would of sucking a toffee with the paper on. Bob was curiously insistent on the Canadian's contempt for French letters. It was the detail on which he hung his entire picture of the Dominion. Canada was also a land where you simply weren't allowed to drive at less than fifty miles an hour. In your *truck*. He *packed* a *six-shooter* in his belt, but he always had several spares in his *truck*. Well, a *sheriff* never knew . . .

I think Bob Doyle was the most perfectly insincere man I've ever met. I mean that his whole character was compounded of a sort of clumsy, oddly touching absence of candour and principle. If, in his talk, he left Canada, it was usually to give wildly implausible accounts of conversations he'd had – often on the telephone – with the senior officials of the War Ag. Faced with one of these men, Bob was almost childishly anxious to please. But it was otherwise, one gathered, on the phone.

The pacifists among us he treated with his usual absent-minded amiability. But many of these telephone conversations on which he reported – happily enough, in our presence or even to our faces – were concerned with his detestation of the conchie.

'I swore at him – yes, I *swore* at him! "Fuck that," I said. "I'm not working under a fucking conchie," I said. "He's got his way of looking at things," I said, "but if he comes here, I'll plough him into the ground. You keep him away," I said, "or I'll kill the poor sod. You ask anyone who knew me in Canada. They've seen me hit a few people, over there." "Well," he said: "I've never met such an outspoken man as you, Bob." I said: "Well, I've always been like it. You have to take me as I am. And I didn't leave my *ranch* and come and help with the war effort to work under a fucking conchie. And that's straight." He said: "I admire you, Bob, for that." '

Although real live conchies somehow escaped Bob's admirable outspokenness, he did once startle Oliver and me – as he groped unhopefully for the gear lever and missed it – by confessing: 'I'm not a conchie myself – and *I don't mind who knows it.*'

We digested this most superb of Bob's dabs in the direction of candour, and then Oliver said, in a choked voice:

'That's remarkably honest of you, Bob.'

Bob missed the point as if it had been a gear lever. 'That's the sort of man I am, Oliver,' he said absently. 'Take me or leave me.'

His way with any awkwardness was to become even more than usually inattentive. Talk of any pretension at all – anything with the faintest smack of the intellectual about it – brought on one of these instant trances. If a comment was essential, he would take the most blurred line possible, smothering anything vaguely bordering on an opinion: 'I don't know, Ted – I should say you are wrong, but I don't know, so I shan't argue with you: I don't know, and I don't argue when I don't know.' Then the usual grand offer: 'Take me or leave me.'

One day he took me to his home, in one of the nearby villages. The tiny house – kitchen, living room, everywhere one looked – was full of curious boxes, packing cases, sacks of corn, fertilizers, potatoes, drums of oil. It was possible to conclude only that Bob was some sort of agricultural fence – a surely absent-minded receiver of stolen corn, machinery, petrol ... anything that placed itself within his clumsy reach. He waved at these things as we weaved our way among them. 'Odds and sods,' he said vaguely. 'I'm a great one for odds and sods.' There was a large woman somewhere in the house who was perhaps his wife and whom he passed without speaking or indeed anything that amounted to recognition. There were also several children, whose heads he smacked as we met them, leaving behind him a trail of roars and snivellings. 'The old bugger!' I heard one of them wailing, as we pressed on.

Out in the village street again, we met the vicar. At this encounter Bob became phenomenally abstracted. To a man with such an instinct for avoiding serious exchanges, the vicar must have been a perpetual threat. And yet one saw, as we stood briefly together, that Bob met this threat by actually, almost literally, *not seeing* the man.

'Ah Bob,' said the vicar. 'How's the family?'

'Hmm, hmm,' said Bob.

'The wife?'

'Ah.'

'And the children?'

'Hmm.'

And we parted. '*Your* vicar?' I asked.

'What?' said Bob. 'Who?'

I didn't press the question.

One reason why we liked Bob Doyle, in the odd way in which we did like him, was that he was too lazy to be effectively cruel, as some of the Quarry's workmen were.

This cruelty – a product, clearly, of the narrowness and monotony of their work – lay often in the way in which they regarded lack of skill or strength as gross defects of character. It was so with my early struggles with sacks of corn; it was so again with my rather longer apprenticeship in the art of starting a lorry on the handle. I would bear down and turn and the engine would fire and kick my hand into the lacerating honeycomb of the radiator. I had grown used to injured hands, but the wounds were now often deep and complex, and were constantly renewed. In my first winter at the Quarry, we carted clinker as material for making roadways across a great marsh, where sugar beet was being harvested: and my hands were covered, all the time, with scores of fine purple cuts that made washing, or contact with rough cloth, or even the touch of cold air, an agony. It was nothing much, at such a time, to have damaged hands: but then I'd not known, until I'd gone on the land, that there was work that caused such damage. I'd simply not known that most of the world's population, at all times, had lived with sore, scarred hands . . .

Because the scorn for any lack of skill or sinew was so vicious, I'd persuade Reggie Gordon or Ralph Tarbox to let me practise using a starting handle, again and again, until I had the trick. I'd no desire to be like one poor fellow in the Quarry – not a conchie, but someone who'd been thrust by order into land work – who was everyone's butt, in a hideous way. 'Paralytic', they called him, and they made sure this sickly man was to the fore in every gang unloading a pipe lorry. He shrank in terror from those stinging tubes, hurtling towards him: caught them, when he managed it, in a fumbling fright, his breath noisy. He'd try to escape by fussily straightening some far corner of the stack of pipes. 'Blimey,' they'd cry. 'Better bring some bricks, next time, for the poor sod to play with.' 'Don't you be rude!' the unhappy man would cry. And sometimes half a dozen would throw pipes at him, together, at such a moment – 'Catch 'em, *dad*!' – and he'd turn and run.

They were oppressive months, on the whole, those first I spent at the Quarry. The old county town itself had barely grown since the 18th century: heavy wartime traffic, our own included, had to thrust itself ill-temperedly through a tight tangle of streets. We were a centre of American preparation for the invasion of Europe. Immense lorries were always on the move, driven as if they were sports cars. I grew to have an unreasonable hatred for the long numbers on their doors. They came and went from a great weapon park just outside the town: hundreds of acres of mud on which stood, rank upon rank, silent monsters – a wilderness of huge rubber tyres. The silent countlessness of them, the endless repetition of similar machines, had a curious effect on any observer. A single human being moving among them would have helped: but they seemed to stand outside the human scene, altogether.

American military police roared past us as we went about our work: themselves gleaming machines, their motorcycles turned into fantasies by the high white knee-guards and body-shields behind which the merely human gadget crouched.

Once, we picked up a little group of our own soldiers, who didn't seem entirely clear where they wanted to go. They sprawled in the back of the lorry, grumbling and cursing in northern voices, and there was about them a quality as of beings who had been so long separated from normal life, with its elements of choice and decision, that to be abroad was a cause of acute sullen alarm. I remember the bad-tempered figures sprawled in their coarse khaki among the tarpaulins and empty sacks, and the recurrent cry: 'Where's the fucking village? Where's the fucking village then, mate?' 'We're going into town. Is that where you want to go?' I asked early on, sitting among them: we'd been on a big corn-shifting job, and the cab was full of driver's mates. But they stared at me. 'The fucking village – that's what we want, mate.' 'We're going into the town.' They stared uneasily, and then fell once more to their grunting quarrels. Again and again one would raise his head and cry: 'Where's the fucking village, then?' On the outskirts of the town they all leapt up in a storm of alarm, and beat furiously on the sides of the lorry and kicked at the floor and the back of the cab. Reggie Gordon, who was driving, drew up in a panic. 'Here, mate!' they cried. 'Bloody murder! This is it!' And then they were over the sides and scuttling down the road.

But the war did this to so many of us – found monstrously limiting roles for us, which in their lunatic special quality cut us off from our fellows: so that we lost much of our capacity to live outside these particular contexts. Those soldiers were extreme examples, only: and the dark grumbling sullenness with which they boarded and then left us sharpened this feeling we had, that they were moles blinking in accidental daylight. Some kind of soldierly panic was operating in them, that dark afternoon.

And it was generally true that soldiers, of whatever kind, formed a special race, moving among us but not of us. This seemed particularly true of the Americans billeted in the town. Not far from the Quarry, a group of them had taken over a whole terrace of houses, built just as the war broke out but never normally occupied. The curiously fawn faces of American soldiers appeared at every window: the terrace was at times like the setting for some exotic play, so unconnected with the town did it seem. And I remember, one late summer evening, seeing a little group of Americans tending the garden in front of the houses. Some were digging, methodically, silently, others were planting seeds. It seemed grotesquely poignant that, at this halfway point in their journey to the hell of invasion, in a rundown English county town, they should be trying to make a garden out of the sour patch, strewn with builder's rubble, of their most awfully temporary home.

'The trouble with Churchill,' said George, 'is that he's fat. That's a very serious disadvantage for a politician. It will go against him, when this is over.'

It seemed that George's twin problems, whether to marry and (if the answer were 'Yes') whom to marry, had been further sharpened by an encounter in the Outer Hebrides. As usual, he referred to this mumblingly enigmatically. 'I met a Scots girl,' he said. 'Very reasonable.'

I said nothing, wondering how George would have described Helen of Troy. I imagined him on his return from Ilium: 'I met an African girl. Presentable.'

'Yes, Jill was very tolerable,' said George. 'The sort of girl who, if she couldn't waltz, would make it up as she went along. Resourceful.'

I listened solemnly, trying to identify the virtue George was describing. I had to admit that I was baffled. I had never danced in my life, and couldn't begin to estimate the importance of being able to invent a step. In any case, remembering experiences with my old friend in the school gymnasium, I suspected that Jill might have been adjusting herself to some quite manic irregularity of motion on his part, which George would have no doubt was waltzing.

'She would have suited you,' he said.

Alas, I knew what this meant. Jill must be the fifth or sixth of his girls of whom he had, so to speak, made me a gift. I was certain now that this indicated the death of George's own interest. He was using me as a book to press his faded flowers in!

His ship had been sunk under him (he revealed in a dry parenthesis), and he was anxious that he shouldn't be swallowed up in the crew of a cruiser or something of that size. 'What I'd like really would be a Free French ship – where I wouldn't be answerable to the captain for little points of discipline. And I could polish up my French – and maybe see a little action. Eh?'

He was thinking (this was how he put it) of being married after the war: there was someone else he'd not perhaps mentioned previously, whom he'd met in the West Indies, and whose name happened to be Jeanne – well, as he saw it, and not to bore me with romantic detail which must vex a fellow of my stern calibre, if you married an intelligent woman you were free from the danger of marrying an unintelligent one. That was the strength of it. Jeanne was very intelligent indeed. He'd been thinking about the little cabin they might live in, *if* he did marry her and *if* they decided to live in England. *Plain* furniture! Oh, that damned stuff we'd been brought up among!

'I shouldn't be above using a sugarbox if I couldn't get a decent cupboard,' said George.

What should he do after the war? Local government, in which he'd worked before being called up, was a devil! It had paid him throughout his service in the Navy, it offered a good job and a pension! But how awful if, after all this, we opted for comfort.

'Holidays at the seaside!' said George, making a long face.

But he was not equipped for anything else. 'I'm not fit to be anything – except a political agitator – and they don't pay you for that.'

He was worrying away, still, at his decision to fight. 'It was touch and go whether I joined in or no. But the more I see of it, the more I feel that though the war's such an ugly and sprawling thing, it was necessary. Seeing America has shown me how terrible the effect would have been had Hitlerism triumphed. America would have gone fascist immediately.'

As he spoke, I realized that underneath all I thought had always lain the confidence that the triumph of Hitlerism would be prevented. If in George a pacifist was gnawing away at him, inside me – all the war long – had fidgeted a hopeless belligerent. But how (I thought as I wrung from him a few laconic details about the sinking of his ship)

179

could I compare the muddled silliness and ignobility of my days with the stern and perilous adventures of my friend? Alongside George's wartime life, my own was a matter of mere dreams and drabness.

'Once or twice, you know,' said George, 'I've half-heartedly told Jeanne she was beautiful. I'm not very good at that sort of thing. You ought to advise me. What honeyed things do *you* say when you want to heighten the colour in a land-girl's cheeks?'

Far from being the offhand Lothario of George's teases, I was still observing, with wonderment and disbelief, the easy sexual manners of my mates. When a landgirl, in the sun, removed her sweater, Ralph Tarbox pawed the ground like a stallion and neighed brilliantly. I wondered why I could not do these simple things. It was true that I had no gift for the impersonation of horses: but why were similar natural gaieties and candid insinuations, which must bring much relief, altogether outside my skill? It was not possible to begin imagining what my own performance in such fields might turn out to be, if ever I made the venture. So self-conscious, so bashfully vague – I shuddered at the very thought of them.

For a week or so I found myself attached as mate to the only perfect egotist I have ever known. Terry was so wrapped up in himself that any situation which required that he take even vaguely detached interest in someone else was plainly a pain to him. He followed his own affairs with an undistractible nose: and the boredom of being with him was itself a physical ache. He talked of his hobbies, of his excellences; spoke with compassionate indulgence of a few picturesque faults he found in himself; and referred with methodical unkindness to his wife, whose crime was clearly that she was a separate human being with demands of her own. Indeed, he spoke of the poor woman as if she had been some weight tied to him – he was wailingly oppressed by her existence. One of those endearing faults of his had been to take to himself this boring burden. 'She expects me home early tonight,' he'd say. 'She can wait. She can't have everything she wants.'

Terry denied himself nothing by way of sexual pleasure. We were sent once to cart potatoes being riddled in a field by a team of landgirls. Terry introduced himself into their midst with cries of confident greed. So far as I could make out, glancing shyly at events from under my eyelids, his confidence was justified. He laid siege to the young women with a shrill set of familiar insults – many of which were sly proposals as to the arrangement of their anatomies and the quality and quantity of their underwear, in respect of which he plainly expected to be put right by the most direct of disproofs. He filled their pockets with potatoes and with a dead rat or so, in order to have the opportunity of emptying them again. Very soon such a shouting and snickering arose, and such tumblings and fumblings, as I had no gift whatever for participating in: glumly, I paid my attention to the task of filling sacks with potatoes and lifting them on to the lorry.

By lunch time I'd lost all touch with them: of Terry it might be said that he had gained full touch with them. His was not the cold sexual avarice I'd observed in another, temporary driver, who had moved among the girls, acquiring them by placing a freezingly mandatory hand on their thighs. I think the frigid and horribly successful collector's skill employed by this driver was the grimmest concupiscence I'd ever encountered ... Terry's greed contained as little interest in its objects as human individuals: but at least it was accompanied by squeakings and shouts of coarse delight. As it was now, during that lunch break, in tall grass at the edge of the field: limbs flew at giggling angles out of the grass as, woefully alone, I sat in the lee of the lorry and wondered at my separateness.

At last I could bear it no longer. I could not imagine how we should meet again, when the break was over: how I should simply encounter this ribald group as they returned to the riddling and the sacking. Some communication must be established. So I edged myself, very slowly, very uncertainly, across to the tall grass that danced with the antics it contained. I was within speaking distance, though with no idea what I might say, when I heard a female voice cry:

'Hey – here comes *creeping Jesus*!'

I fled.

And then, to a town that seemed empty because suddenly the fawn American faces and olive-green uniforms had gone, came the news of the invasion of Europe.

Everything else seemed smaller than ever. We spent wretched days, that Wednesday and the days that followed, in a field, sacking potatoes. June had become ominously cold: low clouds raced before the wind.

Never had war been so intimately reported. There were breathless clipped descriptions on the radio of the first landings: men spoke from bombed destroyers, or dazed from landing by parachute, at night, in a mine-sown, hostile land. It was like hearing speech from the world of some immensely magnified Grimms' fairy tale. That was the nature of it: it belonged to the world of nursery terrors. But from this there was no waking to find it a bad dream.

There didn't seem room, or air, for moral judgement. I found I was angry with Reggie Gordon for arguing that here was yet another proof of the rottenness of man. Sterilization, he said (with his charming smile), was the only solution of our troubles. It suddenly struck me that life could not possibly be regarded as consisting solely in the solution of our troubles. Some of these troubles led to such spectacular human action that one could only – as now – hold one's breath. Hold one's breath and hurl prayers against the dark, windy, unfortunate weather.

2

One of the Quarry office's most intricate problems at the time was presented to it by the existence of Leonard Noon. He was, in every sort of profound sense, an outcast. In his case, the phrase about a square peg in a round hole was laughably inadequate. The labour force at the Quarry was full of pegs merely square. The War Ag knew how to hammer these down, most of the time, into their ill-fitting holes. But it would not be easy to name the shape of peg that might suggest Leonard's unsuitability and crazy awkwardness – and his unhammerability.

He was usually to be found hanging about among the stacks of pipes. Drivers took him as a mate only when there was no alternative whatever. Few of the girls would ever agree to have him in their cabs. 'He's daft,' they'd cry. 'He's ... sinister, like. Gives you the hump. A day with that Noon and you want to go and hang yourself.'

There was certainly a sinister quality about him – which he carefully cultivated. He was a dusty creature – there seemed to be a film all over his skin, and he wore the greying remains of what had once been a dark suit made for a much larger man. Quantities of string drew in the vast waist of his trousers, which were shortened by being given several tiers of turn-ups. His hair was always cropped close to his head. He had green teeth, usually visible because his common expression was a snarl, coupled with a glare. The only other touch of colour about him was in the lapels of his jacket, which formed a gallery of badges. Dominant among these were the badges of most of the political parties – including the Communist Party – a Peace Pledge Union badge, relics of several Poppy Days and Primrose Days, and a large badge which made the unlikely assertion that Leonard Noon was an Ovaltiney.

'Keeps people away,' he'd explain in one of his moments of glaring expansiveness. 'Something there to put anyone off. Never meet some new sod but he sees one of these badges he don't like and says "Piss off!"'

It was, he wished you to believe, his chief aim in life: to push other people to the point where they required him to piss off. There were times when, in despair, quite impressive delegations would come from County Hall with precisely this intention, with respect to the whole matter of his service with the War Ag. Their problem was to define the unsatisfactory nature of that service. He had never refused to do a job. He was always on hand. He never came late, and never left early. And indeed, one of the attitudes that Leonard struck was to claim that he alone was an ideal servant of the Committee. The rest of us, from County Hall downwards, were consumed with indolence, softness, corruption. 'You want discipline, the whole bleeding lot,' he'd mutter. 'I'd have you under military law. You'd jump to it, if I was in charge. Slack, decadent buggers, the lot of you!'

No obvious fault to be found, then. He had simply been so successful in that chief aim of his that no one would willingly work in his company. And when he did find his way into the cab of a lorry, or was admitted to a pipe-stacking gang, he was perfectly capable of reducing his fellow-workers to a state of suicidal gloom.

Delegations would come, then, as if hoping that the sight of Leonard would remind them of some definable inadequacy for which he might be sacked. The most high-powered of them arrived when for some days he'd been at work, in a corner of the yard, on the construction of a cottage. That is what he called it: a shack built out of odds and ends, planks, broken pipes, old bricks. 'Agricultural Cottage', said a notice pinned to a pole at the entrance. 'All modern discomforts. Apply to L. Noon, Agent.' As an afterthought he'd prefixed the word 'Agent' with the word 'Double'.

It was the Chief Labour Officer himself who, making a hopeless effort not to look foolish, bent down to peer into this weird building and glowered at Leonard, squatting in a dark corner within. 'Oh, look here, Noon!' he cried. 'This is the limit!'

One of the two members of his department he'd brought with him barked: 'D'you call this work, Noon?' And the other added: 'This kind of nonsense is not what you're paid for, Noon' – attempting to infuse his voice with the tone of a man confident that his opponent had gone too far.

Leonard did not bother to rise from his squatting position. 'Gentlemen!' he began – and from the quality of that voice rasping through the motley walls of his cottage we knew that the green teeth were bared to the roots. 'We don't have to go through all that again, do we? You know the bloody size of it. You can't be quite that stupid, can you, gentlemen? I'm on the job. I'm ready for anything. It's not my fault if these soft-hearted parasites here are afraid to work with the only disciplinarian and patriot on your bleeding pay roll.'

The Chief Labour Officer, scarlet with bending and vexation together, straightened up. In this position he could no longer see Noon at all: but he barked across the remarkable roof of the cottage, 'Your language is quite insufferable! Your—'

'Extraordinary attitude,' suggested one of his juniors.

'Quite! And your—'

'General unsuitability,' ventured the other.

'Absolutely! Make you ... completely unemployable.'

'Write it down,' came Leonard Noon's voice from within the cottage, 'in a form that will stand up in front of the National Service Officer.'

'Not the point!' cried the Chief Labour Officer.

'Deliberate attempt to make yourself unacceptable to your mates, cried one of his juniors: adding, in a tone of shrill surprise, as though he'd not been aware that he knew the word: '*Pariah!*'

'Sailors facing untold dangers to bring you food,' said the other, sounding like a gramophone record across which some accident has sent the needle leaping from the beginning straight to the end.

From the cottage, a scornful snort.

The three officials looked at each other helplessly. Their leader caught himself bending down in search of Noon's green snarl, thought better of it, drew himself up and shouted over the roof: 'Our decision will be communicated to you within the next day or so.'

Listening to the hollow laughter that came magnified from the cottage as our baffled masters made their way back to their van, I wondered whether Leonard might not have constructed his curious home as a sounding box for just such an occasion as this.

He had his – well, the word is not 'friends'. There were some among his enemies whose company at times he was bitterly willing to endure. I was one of them. At our first meeting, stimulated by his oddity, I'd thrust questions at him, challenged his wilder statement. He'd narrowed his eyes at me, at last. 'If you don't stop your clever—!' he'd hissed. But I'd detected a grim amiability in that hiss. As we'd parted on that first occasion, he'd detained me, as it were. He'd prevented my going, that is, with a gesture of the curved hand that commanded me to stay, for a second longer, in the presence. There was so often about what he did a touch of the dusty Caesar. 'You're one of the fucking intelligentsia, I take it,' he'd uttered: then reversed his hand to send me on my way.

Thereafter he gleamed when I came near him. 'Leonard,' I'd call, in my brash, interested way. 'You keep it up, marvellously! This pretence of not needing anyone! What's behind it, then?' I'd be given a full view of his teeth. 'Why this ... nihilism?'

Unmistakable delight, then, while he hissed and pretended to grow rigid with scorn.

'You'd all like to know, wouldn't you? "What makes Leonard Noon tick?" ... *Nihilism!*' He'd taste the word, hold it in his green mouth. Nothing, as I'd soon discovered, pleased him more than to be offered some account of himself that was expressed in some such terms as this. 'You think I'm a *nihilist*, then?'

'Not necessarily, Leonard. It's just a word that comes to mind. A suggestion.'

'Ha!'

'Or this pretence of fascism, Leonard.'

'*Pretence of fascism!* Ha!'

'Why do you parody Hitler?'

He'd have to walk away from me, to conceal his delight. Returning: 'You'd like to know, wouldn't you! That's the type you are, isn't it – the nosy type? Nosy intelligentsia?'

'No. Ordinary curiosity, Leonard.'

'*Ordinary curiosity!* Ha!'

The girls tapped their heads when his name was mentioned. I even had a tender difference of opinion with Mollie about Leonard's character. 'He's touched, isn't he?' 'Oh Mollie...' 'I mean, he isn't right in the head.' 'He's *unhappy*, Mollie. If everything went wrong for you, you'd be likely to turn into a Leonard. Without being at all mad.' 'What – me?' I stared at that simple plain worried face. 'No – I guess you'd have to find something else to turn into, Mollie.' I thought then how oddly protected against derangement Mollie was, with her built-in persistent mild expectation of disaster.

One idle day – no communication having come from County Hall – Leonard commandeered my services; he had tired of his cottage, and had now embarked on a colossal scheme for clearing the yard. He had worked out an elaborate plan for this: as he told anyone whose attention he could catch, he had his *methods*. 'That's what you're all short on. *Methods!*' He refused to leave the work, even when it rained. In the absence of a guard, the scheme might so easily be sabotaged. 'You'd be surprised if I told you ... who might be interested in *that*. In mucking up any work I do. The *names* would surprise you.'

Mad? I made myself his slave, that day, with some irritation. Nobody else would humour him in this supine way. My gloom increased as he gave me inanely precise instructions as to the disposal of minutely differentiated types of rubbish into special and widely separated heaps; when he gave me detailed orders as to the use of a wheelbarrow. My spirits sank as he passed from one of his attitudes to another. 'The one thing you mustn't be nowadays – for Christ's sake, don't mix bits of pipe with bits of brick! – you mustn't be pro-British – you can be anything else – pro-German, pro-Russian, pro-Spanish ... but you mustn't be pro-British ... Over here with the barrow! Look sharp!' 'Now, look here, Leonard —' 'If people knew what I thought of them, they'd go off and swallow poison.' 'Oh come off it, Leonard —' 'There's a bloody art in using a wheelbarrow! Think about what you're doing! ... I'm fed up with this bloody job! I'm sick to death of the lot of them.' 'Look, Leonard – we're all fed up with the job!' 'You don't do anything about it, do you! That's the difference! You—' 'If you've found some small loop hole through which to escape—' 'Not on that fucking pile – on this one!'

But then he began – glaring furiously, to counter any impression that he might need to let such confidences trickle out – to talk about himself. A Londoner, he'd had 'no home worth the name' ('What was wrong, Leonard?' 'That's all I'm going to say. I'm not filling in the details'), and had left school at fourteen. 'I should have been a clerical worker but I was pushed into a factory.' ('You were drawn to office work, Leonard?' 'Don't ask bleeding questions. Just listen! And it's not an excuse to lean against that bloody wheelbarrow.')

Somehow he'd drifted into the peacetime Army – and had come into conflict with it. No, he wouldn't tell me why: surely I knew by now that he was a secretive fellow. (Green smile at that, quickly turned to a glare. He needed so desperately to create his own legend: and was so pleased when, as in this way, he stumbled against its existence).

He'd been sentenced to the glasshouse, at Aldershot. It was the first of several sentences. He would allow me a strictly edited glimpse of his experiences there. On arrival at the military prison, you had to run into it. Everywhere, you had to *run*. Inside, you stripped and then stood, legs apart, arms folded behind you, staring for a quarter of an hour at a board displaying the rules and regulations. There were very many of these. Thereafter, you'd be expected to know them all.

The warders – always to be addressed as 'staff' – were physically powerful men with no hope of promotion elsewhere within the Army. You might not speak to them – 'except when they spoke to you, and then you'd got to speak fucking fast'. Equipment had to be cleaned and polished every few hours. 'Takes only two hours for it to get dirty,' the 'staff' would taunt.

'They'd find out how you could be hurt, and then bang away at that,' said Leonard. 'They'd find out where your nerves were raw ... And the jobs they'd give you! The dirtiest they could find! The most useless! Scrubbing your floor with brick-dust. You'd do it, till it was clean, till it couldn't be cleaner, and then ... a "staff" would walk all over it. Round and round. All over it. Then – "It's dirty! Do it again!"'

'They gave you a half-holiday. Oh yes! That was Saturday. You'd sit in your cell, cleaning your equipment – with your door open – four inches. *Exactly* four inches. They'd come and measure.

'I grew a moustache. I thought I'd grow a moustache – so I could think something was happening. It was fucking awful. I don't get much hair on my face. One morning parade – sergeant-major stops in front of me. "So – growing a 'stache! My cat could lick that off!" Then he grabs a hair, and rips it out. I had to take the sting of it – I had to take it without moving a muscle. If I'd moved – if I'd twitched, even – it would have meant a fist in my face ...

'And when a staff spoke to you, he'd always *glare* at you. They never spoke without glaring.' Leonard smiled, his dark bitter smile. 'That's why I glare! If you live with them long enough, you pick up their ways. I picked up all sorts of habits in the glasshouse. I can sit for hours, without moving, just staring into space. That's what I do here in the evenings – I just go into the park and stare at the castle – till the park shuts...'

And somewhere at this point in his monologue, Leonard forgot about his yard-clearing scheme: he leaned against a heap of drainage pipes and stared ahead of him, but with little flickers of observation at me: he was clearly enjoying my cries of dismay, my startled face.

'You have probably decided,' he said, 'that this is a pretty grim picture. But I wouldn't mind going back again. I wouldn't squawk if I was back in the glasshouse, at this moment. I expect you think I'm mad. You all think I'm mad! I like that! I can't do without it! I can't do without people thinking I'm mad. *I don't want people to like me!* – All right – it's a kink.' That sudden touch of complacency in his voice. 'Everybody tells me I have a kink...

'But I wouldn't care if I was back in prison. You see, when I'm threatened with something, I consider it – and then I say, according to how my consideration has worked out – do you understand me? – then I say, "I don't mind that" or "I don't want that". But once I've sampled it, then it's... lost its sting. It can't touch me any more.

'You see, it's like someone taking poison, in small doses. In the end, he can't be poisoned. That's me. That's how I work.'

Then he leapt away from the stack of pipes and shouted: 'Come on, fuck it! I've promised myself we'll have this bit done by six o'clock. Not a moment before. Not a moment after. Get that barrow moving. I'm not having any sloppiness here.'

At six o'clock, having checked the hour with the office clock and the bell of a nearby church, Leonard held that the stint he'd had in mind for us was precisely completed. He supervised tetchily my wheeling of the barrow to its exact place of rest for the night. He gave me my dismissal. But as I moved away, he called after me, making his voice more than usually venomous and hostile:

'We'll resume our little talk later,' he rapped out. 'I'll be watching you for a day or so, to make sure you're not gossiping about my affairs. If I'm satisfied, we'll resume this talk... some time next week.'

If Leonard was a heavyweight victim of our parsimony in

189

the matter of education, Puffing Billy was in all respects a flyweight. Short, dusty, with the smallest of simian faces, and sleepy eyes, Billy was animated, though that is hardly the word, by a curious, sad sense of being put down by almost everybody. He was, he claimed, a mechanic of potential genius, untrained, of course (or huntrained – for Billy was uncertain about aitches, and drew upon them nervously, hopefully). Sid Roach, manager of the War Ag's repair shops, knew this, of course – knew of Billy's amazing, if dormant, skills. 'He knows!' Billy would say. 'He's heard me – harguing!' Other officials, he believed, kept him down because they were jealous of his power of 'hargument'. 'They know!' Billy would cough, through streams of smoke.

In fact, there were two Billies who haunted the Quarry. One was a slow, agreeable, rather absent-minded workman – as it were, the Quarry's staple hand. Any team engaged on any task whatever always seemed to have Billy in it. The poor visibility within which he operated, caused by the smoke that forever wreathed his tiny head, made him a fairly unproductive colleague. Drainage pipes thrown in his red-eyed direction fell, as often as not, to the ground. 'Wasn't ready,' Billy would murmur. 'That's Billy,' someone would explain to the pipe company's lorry driver. 'You have to watch for the right moment to throw something at Billy.' And Billy would blink and grin and mutter: 'You can chuck 'em at me when you like, but there's a risk hattached to it.'

The second Billy was the put-upon one: the Billy aware of a great conspiracy to suppress his genius. This Billy would always work a conversation round to the theme of the vast unfairness of the educational system. Given half a chance, Billy believed, his fantastic skills would have emerged. He would push our talk along until it arrived at some such generalization: then 'Take me, for hinstance...' he'd mumble, even for a second removing the damp stub of cigarette from his mouth. 'Sid Roach knows! He's just a haverage mechanic, but still he's got a hinstinct and – Have you hever wondered why he keeps me hout of the garage?'

Having none of Leonard Noon's vehemence and violence, Billy had come to terms with himself as one of the Quarry's favourite jokes. A wistful grin would form on his face when one of his speeches was cut short by, perhaps, an affectionate jab to the ribs from Reggie Gordon's fist. 'Off your soapbox, Billy, before you set it on fire!' It was easy to think of Billy as a comic victim of delusions. But once, when he and I were eating in the British Restaurant, he showed me, in his gentle, sad way, what real despair lay under the grinnings, the smoke, the absurd speeches.

It was always a bad day when you had to go to the British Restaurant. Maybe the little café round the corner served nothing much better in the way of food: but you felt Mrs Bolton's variations on the theme of spam and chips were by some indefinable advantage of individuality and privacy an improvement on the anonymous offerings of the British Restaurant. Eating in the British Restaurant was awfully like being fed by the Government – positively by the Minister of Food himself. And there was a long period when the local BR seemed to be cooking everything in ammonia. You swallowed and all was almost well for a moment – just an elusive strangeness about the taste – and then suddenly this acridity was released, and little clouds of it formed in your passages and rose until they filled your mouth. It didn't always happen, and rarely throughout a whole dish: and I used to think that perhaps I was tasting my sad, sour wartime mind. Perhaps my mind got into my stomach and my throat, in the British Restaurant: and that certainly would be the place in which such a misery would be visited upon you.

That day, when I sat there with Puffing Billy, the ammonia was very strong and continuous: and Billy said, 'I'm sorry, but hall I hever taste is hash. Cigarette hash.' Then he said: 'I smoke because I'm so unhappy.' It was a perfectly quiet and flat remark, with no self-pity in it; and Billy even smiled, as if to demonstrate his unhappiness. Then he told me how lonely he was, in the village where he'd always lived, and how attached – but in a puzzled sort of way – he'd been to the all-age school he'd attended: and how he'd worked in a local garage and been fired – 'He said he just wanted someone who could use a spanner – he didn't want a bloody professor.' Billy had brought his unsuitably grand notion of mechanics to bear on the work of the garage, and it had held things up insufferably. 'They say you got to walk before you run,' said Billy. 'But I think I don't know how to walk. Do you know what I mean? I think I'm one of those poor buggers who can honly run or nothing.'

He pushed my plate away for me as I leaned back weakly, ammonia pouring out of that factory in my head and filling my mouth. 'Some people don't have a chance, really,' said Billy. 'Take me, for hinstance . . .'

Or take me, I might have said by way of echo: who in certain senses, having been given my chance, had suffered from a grotesque rush of education to the brain . . .

For some weeks, about this time, our job was to take loads of wheat to the London docks. Most days I was mate to Jim Mead, who was a Jehovah's Witness.

The contrast between Jim's gloomy faith and his own sturdy cheerfulness never ceased to astonish me. He was tall, with a jutting chin and a face that was always ready for laughter. And amusement flushed his face with blood: he wept with it: when he was not driving he would stamp with his feet as though his laughing blood might otherwise burst out of him. I was sometimes half-afraid to amuse him, since his enjoyment seemed so dangerous.

But I couldn't help entertaining Jim Mead, simply by what I was. He'd been himself, before the war, a journey-man tailor employed in a large factory, and was full of amazing stories about the duplicity of his employers. 'Oh the cunning rats!' he'd cry, and tell of some occasion when the cloth promised for a suit had been replaced by a cheap and plausible substitute: when disastrous short cuts had been taken in some matter of stitching: when cloth cut for one purpose, abandoned, had been artfully made to serve a pur-pose entirely different. 'You can't help admiring them – the sharks!' he'd cry; and the tears would burst from his blue eyes. And you'd wait for him to recover, anxiously, while he beat his feet on the floor, and grappled with the severe anguish of his amusement.

I caused him laughter in the first place because of my vocabulary. He was quick to seize on my habit of saying 'Quite!' He'd get it in first, often, and then turn red and weep. I was also, he made me aware, given to murmuring 'Extraordinary!' It was certainly an ejaculation out of place, where it was more common to cry 'Bugger me!' But indeed it was the whole range of my language that put Jim in peril of his life. He confronted me with it once when we were unloading in Bermondsey. 'You'd never fink,' one of the dockers had grunted, gloomily, 'that this fucking lorry could carry so much fucking corn.' 'Oh quite,' I cried, wheeling another sack to the tailboard. 'It's unexpectedly capacious!' Jim, tugging at the next sack and making it ready for the barrow, fell flat on the floor. Dreadful paroxysms shook his body. 'Oh Gawd!' he cried, and beat at the wood beneath him with feet and fists. 'Oh Gawd's truth!'

When he had partly recovered, and was lying back exhausted against the sacks, he said: 'Thank God they never hear what you say. I mean, they might hear, but I don't expect they believe it! ... Look man, adapt yourself to your situation! Talk English to the English! Talk Cockney to the Cockney! And while you're at it, try to look like a bleeding lorry driver's bleeding mate! You march up and down the back of a lorry like some *ber-leeding* admiral on the bridge! Try —' But here he fell victim once more to his perilous laughter, and I felt bound to beat him about the back. 'Unexpectedly capacious!' he carolled, and stared unseeingly through his tears at the docker waiting patiently for the next sack.

'Sort of fit, eh?' the docker asked, with mild curiosity.

But I had my revenge a few days later, when we were unloaded by seven warehousemen of profoundly inactive inclination. Small, pinched men with sharp teeth, they existed in an atmosphere of private jesting, which left little room for work. They taunted one another on a narrow range of topics. Wives, and women generally. Money, and miserliness in particular. 'He wouldn't give yer a penny for a shit!' 'He wouldn't shit, mate! He's not giving anyfing away to the fucking Council!'

Jim was in his cab, dozing. I loaded each sack on to my barrow and wheeled it to the tailboard: grinning but – with Jim's lecture in mind – carefully not speaking. But there was no call for speech, from me. Slowly I would load the barrow. Slowly I would push it across the floor of the lorry. Below me, this wild pattern of quips and taunts. Slowly, out of it, a pair of arms would rise: a sack would be hesitantly groped for: and, very slowly, it would be borne away. It seemed we'd be there for hours. I listened, grinned, wheeled: and Jim slept. And then, suddenly, I became a topic for the warehousemen.

'Good little bloke, that,' said one of them.

'Keeps us going,' said another.

'Most of the bloody mates leaves it to us,' a third explained.

They all inspected me, then: and the first said, 'Hi, matey – you ain't always done this work, 'ave yer?'

I was as careful as I could be. 'No,' I said. 'No. In fact, I haven't.'

'What was yer before then, lad?'

'Ah. Well ...' This was awkward. 'I used to be a newspaper reporter.' I stifled the word 'actually'.

'By God – was you!' Seven amazed faces. 'By cripes! That was a real job – weren't it?'

I tried a shrug.

' 'Ow'd yer come to be doing this, then, matey?'

'Well —'

'Yer need to be ejjicated for that, don't yer?'

'Well – ah – a bit, I suppose ...'

'That's what I mean! Yer got to 'ave a 'eadpiece!'

Amazement stared back at great embarrassment.

'Yer see,' said one to another. 'That's the point. Yet got to 'ave a 'eadpiece for that. For newspapers. Stands to reason.'

When Jim woke, a few minutes later, and came unhopefully to inspect our progress, he found himself famous, as the driver whose mate had a headpiece. 'Used to be on the papers, that little ol' boy of yours! Writing!' Jim's huge blue eyes filled with tears, instantly. 'Brains!' one of the warehousemen proposed. Whereupon Jim rushed back into his cab – drawn to do so, I imagine, by the notion that the confined space there would help him to deal with one of his most hazardous attacks of laughter.

And behind all that sense of fun lay the bleak landscape of his beliefs. I grew to associate that with the outskirts of London that we drove through to the docks. Along the arterials, those dismal accretions of houses, the dense rows of semi-detacheds, a bedlam of brick in which there was nothing at all to please the eye or raise the spirits. The disregard of all pattern was nightmarish in its extremity. In those raw suburbs, you were nowhere, nowhere. Each suburb had its name, but this was merely formal. The sense of place had long since been brutally stamped out.

And it was something of this sort – a refusal of grace, of all gaiety – that I found in Jim Mead's faith as a Jehovah's Witness. It was such a speculator's suburb of belief. What drew to it such a vivid, amusable person as Jim Mead? Why did laughter desert him as he made his special use of the word 'religion'? 'Religion' was the Jehovah's Witnesses' word for the deeply wicked racket that was the nature of every system of belief but their own. The worst thing Jim could say of anyone was that he was a 'religionist'. I would protest against this, on merely philological grounds. What could one say of a faith that so abused words? Jim's eyes would be tearless as he tried to slip his thoughts, like sly pamphlets, into my head.

Bible study. That was another of their phrases. And Jim was a student, all right. He was professorial about the strange, madly reasoned conclusions drawn from a network of Biblical texts. And as I listened, it seemed to me that perhaps it was partly this *studiousness*, this need to master a fantasy of curious reasoning, that drew someone like Him to this faith. It was again, surely, a matter of a dissatisfied intelligence – an intelligence that had been underfed, educationally and in other ways – seeking out some apparent grandeur of learning, of argument . . .

And from the deserts of outer London we'd pass to the ruined mazes of Hackney, Clapton, Hoxton. Older deserts: black, not pink. Sweet smells from warehouses: of oranges and lemons, and the greasepaint smell of coriander seed. The only kindly things in these diabolical boroughs, I thought, were the parish churches: and many of these were shells . . .

'Take the Archbishop of Canterbury . . .' Jim Mead would say: laughter remote now from his insistent blue eyes.

A little revolution occurred in the Quarry office, and we had a new transport officer. To the drivers' alarm, the new intendant was Fish, who'd been the War Ag's driving instructor, and so had a quite undesirable knowledge of the drivers' private practices as to unscheduled visits to cafés and circuitous re-routings which made such visits possible.

The cafés were punctuation marks in our daily rounds, and had assumed quite absurd importance. Visits to them smacked most desirably of truancy. I had no natural heart for the thick dark tea in which they trafficked, or the fried food they offered that usually had the smell and taste of infinitely antique cooking fat. But in the monotony of things, a visit achieved to any café was an excitement, a small triumph over rules and regulations. So the worst was expected from Fish's promotion.

But he was a modest, shy man, who wore a mackintosh in all weathers, and walked with his hands buried in his trousers' pockets, the tails of his raincoat swimming behind him. The air all this gave him of purposefulness, of being unready to put up with nonsense of any kind, turned out to be his sole contribution to the rigour of work at the Quarry. Face to face with an erring driver or mate, he would flush, frown, make the tail of his mackintosh rise and fall, as if it were uttering some inaudible speech full of remonstrance and strictness: and then march on. If ever he were driven to speech, his awkwardness would often cause him to miss the target of some disciplinary phrase. As when once he came looking for some of us, who'd hidden ourselves at a time when no specific employment had been offered for a day or so: he found us playing a word game behind a barricade of drainage pipes and, tossing his coat tails phenomenally high, growled:

'Looking for you mates is like looking for a mouse in a mousetrap!'

Whereupon he wheeled and marched off, leaving us staring: but richer by an idea he'd given us for yet another word game.

He made it difficult for me, though, to escape a fate that was dreaded by several of us, and by Oliver and me preeminently. The paper work of the Quarry office, the making of invoices and inventories and timesheets and reports, was in the contented hands of two pacifists to whom this work was reassuringly like their peacetime labours. They were natural clerks. We had a quirkish contempt for them. If we had to work on the land, let it at least be landwork – let it be in the open air, and marked by the variety that was offered, at the Quarry, by the constant change from loads of corn to fencing stakes, drainage pipes, potatoes, sugar beet. Ach! we had no wish to sit all day in that dim little office, clerking! Jim Knowles, the chief of the two clerks, had had his eye on Oliver and me for some time. We were so plainly literate. There was an office boy hidden in each of us. Someone was needed to take command of the stockroom: the whole of the War Ag's armoury of tools was there. Counting tools in and out, ordering new ones, branding them with the War Ag's initials – this was a strain on Jim's time and energy. Wouldn't we care —?

Oliver practised characteristic kinds of evasion whenever this suggestion was made. He'd laugh distractedly, and take Jim into his arms in a hug that had a warning savagery about it. Jim would disengage himself, looking very white. 'Ha ha ha!' Oliver would howl. The technique was much like that he used when confronted with an unbeliever. No one, watching him, could quite say what was going on: he knew only that for a moment Oliver had been transformed into a fiendishly snickering dervish, and seemed vaguely intent on crushing the other man's ribs. And while the situation was still at this mysterious stage, and amazement was being felt by all concerned, Oliver would have disappeared.

'He doesn't seem very keen,' was Jim Knowles's interpretation of all this.

I had none of Oliver's curious gift for refusing an unwelcome invitation without specifically stating that he was doing so – or, indeed, entering into any discussion at all. In my dreadful amiability, I would nod, murmur, even say, 'Yes, you must find it very difficult...' But until Fish's ennoblement, I was able to escape simply by avoiding the neighbourhood of the office until Jim Knowles had lost heart. But one of Fish's first acts in his new role was to approach me, circle round me with coat tails rising and falling most eloquently, flush and mumble:

'Jim Knowles would like you up in the stockroom. Think it a good idea. Give him a hand. Good chap.' And he fled, those coat tails expressive of vast apology.

So for some days I sat up in the dark stockroom, among the slashers, bagging-hooks, spades, shovels, billhooks, mattocks, hoes ... I counted them. I listed them. Gloomily, I built them up into piles: the hafts of new axes made charming heaps, curved whiteness opposed to the blue bloom of the unused heads. I listened unhappily to the noise of lorries leaving and returning. I branded tools, and drew as much pleasure as I could from the smell of burning wood.

Oliver pinned a notice to the door, which said: 'Private. Please knock.' In my dismay, I quarrelled with him about this. We had known each other too long, in these frustrating conditions. Oliver took the opportunity to refer back to an occasion when, he alleged, I had claimed that I was sometimes hailed for my resemblance to the actor, Leslie Howard. He wished, he said, to make it clear that the features of this handsome man had been most authoritatively held to be duplicated in his, Oliver's, features. The notion that *I* was like Howard was laughable nonsense. At this point I did what I think I had never actually done before with anyone: I laughed in Oliver's face. I had, as I did it, a very strong sense of realizing a hitherto casual cliché: I advanced my face towards his and laughed, loudly and coarsely. Oliver than reached out, seized my nose and tweaked it. We parted in horror. What animosities secreted in our long companionship had leaped into grostesque life, in this monstrous quarrel and these disgraceful actions!

I knew, in my brief career as overlord of the stockroom, only one felicity. This was when Mollie Nunn came to collect a miscellany of tools to be taken out to some newly formed gang. I ran up and down the stairs from the stockroom with this suddenly precious assignment, and Mollie cried:

'Ted, you must be used to these stairs now!'

'Yes, Mollie.'

'Of course, you're always having to go up and down them.'

'That's so, Mollie.'

'You go up and down like ... like a *gazelle*!'

Deliriously delighted, I came bounding down and proffered my love thirty-six billhooks, eighteen slashers and a dozen spades...

A few days later I crept into Bob Doyle's lorry as he took it farting and hiccoughing towards the gate: and no further effort was made to convert me into an agricultural clerk with a bias towards branding.

It may have been in revenge for this, though, that shortly afterwards Fish withdrew the van that had been bringing Oliver and me fifteen miles from our home to the Quarry and taking us back in the evenings. 'You'll have to find your own way here,' he said, in collaboration with his coat tails.

'Economy. Hope you can do it, though. Good workers.'

We could have joined some ditching gang close to our homes. But we'd grown used now to work at the Quarry: when we looked back on those days in drainage, we seemed to have moved upwards, from a purely serf-like role to the status of serfs who were granted some kind of mobility. We couldn't bear to return to the world of foremen, to the ditches and hedges and bonfires and the long days fixed in single places.

So we cycled. Thirty miles of cycling a day, on top of the work we did, was exhausting. The road was winding, hilly. There seemed to be more windy days than not, when we'd feel we were butting our heads against some giant's waistcoat.

But we cycled.

It was while we were on our way to the Quarry, one morning, that an unfamiliar throbbing note came from the sky above us. The sky had so long been dangerous, but this was not the sound of any of the recognizable dangers. It had an automatic, persistent quality that was wholly puzzling. Then suddenly it stopped; and we looked at each other, wondering. The sky seemed quite clear, yet somehow crowded with an ominous silence. Then there came a gigantic crack and rumble, followed by a bright-green flash – so abrupt, so inexplicable, that for one startled second I half-expected my head to fly off. On the horizon, smoke rose. Then came real silence.

That evening, the newspapers published the first story about 'pilotless planes'.

George, who was back on the Atlantic run, said he was disgusted by the craven attitude of people towards the flying bomb. We'd been to a left-wing theatre in London, on one of his leaves, and the audience was thin. 'You'd think *they* were made of sterner stuff,' said George. He couldn't understand such shrinking from people who'd stood up so well to the blitz. Well, perhaps there *was* an explanation – one he could illustrate from his own experience. The first time he went to sea he'd been too busy for seasickness. On the second occasion it had been different: then he'd found time to be ill.

'A nervous echo, perhaps,' George concluded bleakly, 'of

the blitz.'

When, later, the flying bomb was succeeded by the rocket, which made no announcement at all of its arrival, I was struck by the phlegmatic way it was accepted. Or rather, I wondered at the gulf between the reality, the calm with which most people went about their business, and the fiction that a writer of science fantasy might have made of the plight of southern England: a whole region, a great city, on which fell a rain of massive explosive that gave no warning of its approach. Wouldn't such a writer imagine universal hysteria – all ordinary life swept away by the tide of dread? Perhaps science fiction had never taken enough note of the human capacity to remain absorbed in local commonplace even in circumstances of pure Grand Guignol...

Perhaps there had just been too much ...

One night I followed a searchlight that was trained down through suburban streets till its curiously lovely violet light fell on a wide, tinkling path of destruction, where a rocket had fallen. Across torn fragments of walls lay flapping webs of lath, and within those fragments rose great heaps of pink rubble, over which men were climbing: it was not their movement alone, but the natural constant small subsidence of this desiccated ruin, that provided the scene with its endless tinkling, a sort of abominable shrugging noise as the rubble shifted and settled. The scene had an awful beauty, there in the night: I'd stopped and stared at it, at the way the light bloomed in the torn branches of a tree, at that pink pyre crawled over by frantically searching men ...

It was curious how some kinds of violence and horror became domesticated. Once, that summer of the invasion, a convoy of us – we'd been moving machinery in preparation for the harvest – were told by a farmhand of a Flying Fortress that had fallen not far away, after a collision with a Dakota transport. Our informant made much of stories of fragments of flesh being found on the scene. The accident had evidently already become a macabre rural legend. And in our decision to visit the spot, in its eagerness, there seemed to be an edge of unpleasant curiosity.

The plane had fallen in a meadow. All round the fields brimmed over with corn, with only the tops of old, dark haystacks visible above the golden sea. In many places the thick silky gold was higher than the hedges. In the midst of that swishing life, the only coherent remnant of the Fortress was its colossal tail, standing upright, incongruously painted in colours of frivolous brightness. The wing had buried itself in the ground and burned, leaving a perfect black image of itself, with here and there a fragment of silvery alloy. The engines had entered the ground with crushing force, and the tips of the airscrews grew from the earth like large silver leaves. Everywhere was strewn the litter of a fantastic technical cleverness – gaily painted shreds of instruments, of what in those days seemed a wonderfully light metal: stamped with the code-numbers and letterings of a complex system of production. Fire – not the steady fire that feeds on wood, but an explosively quick, chemical flare – had swept through the shell. Everything about those scraps, lying in a meadow near London on a gentle day in 1944, spoke of a violence dreadful to imagine – in which bodies would have been torn to fragments like the feathery metals, or crushed into the earth. I thought of the men who'd been in her, fragile men who'd played games, heard music, written and received letters, had names and hopes, and suddenly, at ten minutes to four on a Saturday afternoon, had fallen to this appalling annihilation in the anonymity of a machine.

Bob Doyle said: 'The silly buggers should have looked where they were going.'

The end of the war came close, receded ... Having beaten in the door, the allied armies rummaged in the great black cupboard of Europe – that's how it felt. Was I mistaken, I wondered, in sensing, in the reaction of my fellow-countrymen to the ecstatic utterances of liberated continentals, a coldness, an antipathy even? There seemed to be a deeply unimaginative mood behind which lay the thought: 'They must have been a poor lot to be conquered, anyway.' It was our famous insularity, of course: our not knowing what it was to be at our neighbour's mercy. It was what was behind Fish's red-faced fury when he read a legend chalked along the Quarry's most prominent wall by an Italian prisoner of war. 'SONO STUFFO DI QUESTA GUERRA', this read. 'Let 'em wait till they get home,' Fish quivered, 'and write their dirty jokes on their own dirty lavatories! The sooner this war's over and they're back in Eyetie-land, the better! I'm fed up with it!'

I was fed up with myself. There was an autumn day when a thick grey mist of cloud came down, blotted out all horizons, made ghastly landscapes. The light, as we drove from store to farm with loads of fertilizer, became yellow and difficult; then the sky vanished and there was so much rain, coming down in powerful, abundant shafts, that there seemed room on earth for nothing else. Water, too much of it to escape, brimmed every faint hollow in the ground. The very air became rain. And in this incomparable cover, we knew, the flying bombs would be pouring into England. Indeed, as we stood in a farmyard, there were explosions all round us. What was happening in London?

I was dismayed not so much by the way my mind split, at moments like this, as by my reluctance to face the fact of the split. I was with Reggie Gordon and Oliver, that day. They took the plain pacifist stand. Men were not made to endure such outrages. Men should say so! – should rise up against such violation! The cry 'We can take it!' came from people 'living in villages 14,000 miles the other side of Northampton'. That was Reggie's phrase. But I could still hear George's voice: 'Why should people be jittery? They ougnt't to be, ought they? Not if they look at it from a rational military point of view.'

Reggie's attitude was the honest one of a man who was (presumably) prepared to have the war lost. I couldn't help thinking that he'd not reflected fully on the consequences of defeat. Those consequences would surely be more terrible even than flying bombs ...

And when I reached that point in this tormented, panicky thinking of mine – but it was not so much thinking as a sluggish flow of half-ideas mixed up with confused emotions – at this point I would feel: I cannot any longer stand aside. If I believe the war would be better won, then I must act accordingly.

I dreamed of joining a relief unit. But I never performed any precise action that might make this possible. When it came to the point, I felt I was making too much of a fuss about the opinions and conduct of an unimportant human being.

And for four years already I'd been sustained, like so many, largely by animal vigour, a purely physical flame that one day lit for the next, one week for the next ... It was not easy to break that sequence.

Such a strange time it was! The end of it was shambling towards us – there were flashes of light in the darkness. Or perhaps not flashes, nothing so sharp and certain. More like the street lights that had now been restored in a dimmed form. As I cycled through the edge of my home town, there were sheets of gauze draped in the dark air, gathered at the pinched yellow points of the lamps – so that a sad series of curtains hung before and above me; and behind these, cautiously red and golden, crawled the lights of car and cycle ... It was this kind of uneasy break in the long blackness that this strange period offered – this last year of the war in Europe ...

But now that the shooting was coming to an end, now that the unsealing of European cities had begun, and the length and desperate continuity of the war could be felt – now I began to ask myself what I had done during those years.

I had not shared the characteristic experience of my fellows – instead, I'd spent the time in ... *cowardly useless-ness*, said this stern commentator I carried around with me. I believed that Nazism had to be opposed – yet I drew back from the method of it: from the great slaughter of masses by masses, from the surrender of individual judgement that seemed to be involved.

And how far, I wondered, had I been motivated simply by the dread of being killed, or maimed? Why could I not avoid a feeling of shame around which I could not marshal my arguments, or be clear of my feelings?

Wasn't it true that through five years of universal agony I had hidden away in a despicable refuge? Had I even been a good pacifist? I had shuffled, hummed and hawed, put off all painful decision, and now it was nearly over, and I was ashamed of myself ...

Was that true?

George disappeared into the Pacific. In an airgraph, he wrote: 'You seem a long way off and so does England and everything English. We are sailing near the equator: everything steams, everything crawls with greenstuff, lice, Yanks.' It was interesting, but he would like now to get on with other things. 'My brain is in a state of serious decline.

203

You must have been aware of that during our recent meetings. I would like a period of very severe and exacting study ... But we mustn't moan – there's a lot left.'

So many jobs. Wheat to be poured into barges: millions of drainage pipes, fencing stakes. Gentle, sometimes eccentric little loads, in Mollie Nunn's van: once an inexplicable tea service, to be carried to a hostel on the northern edge of the county. It was a bright day, and the perching ranks of white insulators on the telegraph poles became odd flowers in a landscape all flowers ... Mollie wondered if, one day, I might write a book about the War Ag and its ways, and perhaps (an elderly lady, she said without real conviction) she'd read it, and find herself there. 'As a funny character,' she shrilled, 'perhaps as a very funny character,' and her voice climbed to new heights of adorable falsetto.

'The funniest of them all,' I promised.

Corn to the docks. Through Silvertown, among sharp smells of sulphur that threatened to burn away our noses: everything about us eaten into ragged shapes by the acid air ... And early one morning we climbed Ludgate Hill, in an Albion whose engine made a noise like someone blowing his nose, and suddenly, behind the heavy dark outlines of buildings broken by war, there – cool grey, so beautifully inked on the air, grave and so different from its neighbours that one wanted to laugh or cry ... there stood St Paul's. The broken city streets were as heavy as lead, but the great dome floated above them lighter than the air itself ...

Winter. Carting clinker. The icy oblongs of glasshouses. Winter on the land, I thought, had always been the same: out there in the middle of the dark, solid week, you felt stunned. A day when fir trees thrust out thick fists of snow, and of other trees the snow had made each drooping group of branches a gigantic many-fingered open hand. Driving between the sparkling, interlaced trees gave me a childish feeling of being honoured. Here and there lay those serpents of barbed wire that had been part of the defences against invasion: normally hideous in their harsh rustiness, these had now become glittering coils executed in thick crystal solely for enchantment's sake.

One day, I was sure, Mollie and I would be sent to fetch a grand piano. Oh, well, it was ... it was the gift of a rich old musicologist, and was to be taken ... was to be taken to a

Land Army hostel. We would stop in a lane somewhere and Mollie would say: 'Can you play?' and I would say, 'Well, yes, before I did irreparable harm to this middle finger of mine – but for you' ... 'Well, yes, I can, a little' ... 'Well, yes, Mollie – though I've promised Pouishnoff, who gave me some lessons' ... The upshot was that I'd play – it would have to be a piece that was something of a compromise between my tastes and Mollie's probable ones – a Hungarian Rhapsody, perhaps – and Mollie would murmur ...

Sometimes I would wake up from these awkwardly persistent daydreams and realize that the register of Mollie's voice did not allow of murmuring: and that she'd probably say:

'Of course, some people like that sort of music, don't they? I mean, we all have different tastes, don't we?'

I wished I could have an experimental supplementary existence in which I might ask Mollie to marry me ...

An Italian prisoner of war, choosing French as his medium, informed Fish that he liked European women in the following order: espagnoles, arabes, françaises, italiennes, anglaises. 'Les anglaises,' he said, in a tone of temperate dissatisfaction, 'sont trop froides.' Fish, who'd not understood a word, said he'd have had the man charged under military law, had it been worth the effort.

Oliver and I were sent briefly to help in a mill in a nearby town, and met Frank again – with whom, behind the threshing machine, I'd exchanged lessons in mathematics and French. I could have guessed Frank was there, from an examination of the woodwork of the place. The mill was full of dark cramped spaces, intersected at a great variety of angles by chutes rustling with grain. Everywhere a twilit geometry of chutes and belts – with, suddenly in the obscurity, the white square of a hoist-door: the outer world fiercely white, to eyes grown accustomed to this darkness in which swam many kinds of dust. Generally, the dust was hot and needly and black: but here and there, where meal was being mixed, odorous white clouds of it arose, slowly drifting across the hot, dim interior to become part of the general needliness, and to add itself to many other smells: of fishmeal, balancer meals, nameless powders crushed from corn and other crops. The place shook, always, with the thunders of small machines, of wheat draining through a hopper: it was clamant with the noises of these operations, the squeaking of sackbarrows.

And much of the woodwork of the mill was scribbled over with French exercises, algebraic equations, bars of music. A young flautist, a conchie, was working there, and Frank had set up with him another academe like the one we'd established at the rear of the threshing machine. Frank was as diffusely inquisitive as ever, and the flautist was teaching him his instrument.

'Furious with me,' said Frank. 'Wants me to learn – studies – *études* – ah! And I play *The Red Flag*...

'*The Red Fag* on a flute, Ted! I'll play it to you when we have time.'

But time was not easily come by in the mill. It went slowly, in a monotony of sack-tying, barrow-wheeling, stacking, handle-turning. But it was early spring, and there wasn't a moment of unemployment. Dusky sacks popped through the hoist-doors like sequences of pantomime devils. We stored them, tight regiments, in difficult corners. It was all sweat, dust, noise: blackness of mouth and tongue and nostrils. 'A few more days and the old mill will burst,' said the foreman, apprehensively. In those feverish weeks, I had only two moments when I was free to look about me and listen, to shake off the curious feeling that the true inhabitants of this shrieking and bursting place were the ranks of dark, eared sacks. One moment came when I was sent into one of the deep bins, to keep the grain flowing through a square hole in the floor. An electric light bulb was slung over the edge of the bin, and I sat on the wheat, under the glare of the bulb, and watched the silent movement of the grain, the eddies it made as it drew nearer to the hole in the bottom. I sat, in that rustling silence, and watched the fortunes of single grains. I was reminded, as the huge sea of wheat swirled about and under me, of the twirling of potter's clay. I imagined shipwrecks with the sucking down of each mast-like length of straw. Oh, the astonished peace of simply squatting there, observing the curiosities of this eddying motion of millions of identical microscopic fruits...

And then, at a strange moment of inactivity, I met Frank amid streamers and pools of sunshine that lay on the suffocating floor of this dark place. Frank said, out of the thought then in his head:

'You know, I don't feel my age, Ted. I feel really *childish*! Yet, if I look back, I can see I've had no opportunities at all, really. Think! I was reckoned to be worth two bob on the dole ... Y'know, once this job would have been paradise to me! Once I'd have looked on my employers here as little tin gods!'

Frank's employers, the owners of the mill, had to go without such admiration, I gathered. One had told Frank: 'Oh, you talk like a member of parliament...!' Odd, I reflected: this was the second time that this grave charge had been levelled against him!

'When the work dies down,' said Frank, 'we'll have a good time again. I can teach *you* a few things now, Ted.'

But as suddenly as we were sent to the mill, we were snatched away from it again – stepping into silence, it seemed, for the first day or two back at the Quarry, away from the mill's dusty madness through which, from all direction, had come the thick steady whispers of grain jigging through the chutes ...

And then, in Europe, it was as the end of the harvesting of a field had been in Cold Clapton: the cutter and binder bearing down on the last strip of standing corn, and all round us the men of the farm and the village, with their shotguns and their hungry dogs. The sails combed down the last of the corn and the cutter took it with a heavy rustle, and the field was suddenly a squeaking and exploding terror, a barking menace, as the rats and the rabbits lost their last hiding place.

And Germany surrendered.

On VE night I walked with Oliver through my home town. The night before there'd been a spectacular thunderstorm, and now it was a mild and tender evening. The pubs had flung open their doors, and light spilled into the streets. In fact, a new town had been added to the old one: a town composed purely of artificial light. After all those years when a light uncovered at night had been a cause of guilt and alarm, it was an extraordinary thing to wallow in it, to spill it and broadcast it, to give it full freedom.

The church was floodlit, the light coming from lamps set

in the ground; and it was in the churchyard that I saw what seemed to me the least ambiguous of all that night's celebrations. Children had discovered that, running between the lamps and the church wall, they cast immense shadows. More and more children were drawn to the scene: there were a score at a time treating that electric brightness as if it had been water to dive in at midsummer. They plunged and splashed in the unforbidden light and laughed wildly at the shadows that rose like black spume from their leapings and gesturings. It was a curiously forceful measure of those five years of war in Europe – that here were children for whom this was their very first experience of light used freely and without fear, in public, at night.

There was a carnival air. It was a carnival of anti-repression. Especially of the repression of light. Even our utterly ordinary council offices, under arc lamps, had the warm boldness of some stage-setting: and, with an eye sharpened by five blindfold years, one was conscious of unsuspected colours in the brickwork – exotic mauves and purples and firework greens.

But best of all – the new leaves hanging, bubbles of clean colour, in the light of the street lamps ...

People had possessed the streets, were strolling up and down, arm in arm. Here and there they formed thick singing crowds.

'It *is* rather remarkable,' I said to Oliver. And then I was appalled by the embarrassed constraint of the comment. I'd have walked across the field of Waterloo, wouldn't I, the morning after the battle, and through the gag of my queasiness have opined that it was 'rather remarkable'?

A few days later we sat in the cinema and looked down with Churchill on the cheering crowds in Whitehall. But 'crowd' would hardly do as a word for this enormous congregation of heads. It was impossible, watching the newsreel, not to be filled with an almost uncontainable elation – not, for one incredible moment, to experience vicariously the ecstasy known only to history's idols – an ecstasy that must be close to madness. Could mortals survive, without derangement, a reception fit only for gods?

The news camera then travelled slowly through Berlin ... one vast grey wreck, obscenely absolute. My neighbours, two pleasant-looking, middle-aged women, applauded throughout: and one commented, with great heartiness: 'Well, that's worth a clap, anyway ...'

Of course, of course. But what had we done to ourselves?'

3

And now came the long end of it all ...

I think of that impatient period, the waiting for something else to begin, in terms of the German prisoners of war. Their waiting was particularly blank.

A group that was driven to the Quarry daily from their nearby camp, and put to work among us, was headed by a musician, Rudi. 'Der Musiker', the others called him. He was tall, thin, and desperately sad. His family had played the French horn for more than two hundred years in one Kapelle or another. Before the war Rudi had been happily a permanent member of a great Dutch orchestra. He was called up in the summer of 1939, and played in a military band until the German collapse. Then, he said, 'My French horn was taken away, and I was given a rifle.' He was instantly captured. It was now months since he'd played a note: perhaps the longest period of musical inaction experienced by any member of his family during those two centuries.

But his sadness was not simply that of a musician deprived of practice, and with no immediate prospect of even seeing a French horn. Like many of the prisoners, he had heard nothing for a long time from his family. He was engaged to a ballet dancer, but had no news of her. And his people lived in Thüringia, in the Russian-occupied zone. He had a great dread of being sent back.

'They will cut my throat,' he would say, and his terror was real as he sketched out this death with a long finger. 'Before they did that, I would do it myself.'

I was deeply uneasy when this cultivated man, in his ill-fitting chocolate-brown prisoner's clothes, talked of the Russians – and the Poles. They were unclean, he said: beastly – *tierisch*. And when I suggested that the Russians had no reason to love the Germans, he would make a thin, bitter face and cry:

'But I didn't start the war!'

I didn't know what answer to give. Platitudes about responsibility seemed weak enough, I thought, from one unheroic being to another.

There was a sailor, Fritz, a big, quiet man, placidly strong, who'd been a fisherman before the war, and was distressed by the need to confess that he'd been captured, not on the high seas, but in a helplessly trapped gunboat on the River Seine. And there was Karl, only seventeen, with a serious, long, thin boy's face: a boy deeply shocked who had fits of pointless giggling, when Rudi and Fritz would grasp his arms and murmur soothingly to him. And another boy, of twenty, with a small, cheerful face, who enjoyed giving the history of the wrinkled bullet wound on his left arm, just above the elbow, and the other across the knuckles of his right hand. He would put the two wounds together, showing that they were part of a common track, and demonstrate how he'd been squatting down at Monte Cassino, resting on his elbows, and the bullet had flashed across his chest.

'They saw my head,' he would explain, delightedly. 'But I am little. Luckily, I have a little head. The bullet could not find it. The bullet looked for my head but it could not find it.'

The biggest of all the gangs of prisoners was working on the marshes, among those sugar beets that so soon became an obsession. One of them, who'd been a designer of bridges on the autobahns, was a caricaturist of skill. He showed us his notebooks – full of camp scenes observed with wry comedy, each with a border of barbed wire – but also of scenes on the marshes: the black flatness of the place, with its stark vistas of receding telegraph poles, inhabited by prisoners who were all cap-peaks and monstrously baggy trousers. By wearing a coloured silken scarf, Hermann managed to maintain an appearance that was faintly debonair. He shared the musician's startling view of things:

startling, that is, to an Englishman who had vaguely imagined that intelligent Germans could only mumble cosmic apologies. There'd be another war, Hermann held, firmly: Russia was so aggressive. It would really have been better if the Germans had won. About that he was entirely matter of fact. Under Hitler the German people had been free.

Hotly I asked why, if the Germans were so free, Thomas Mann and Einstein and Freud and so many other remarkable men and women had been driven to flee the country. Ah, said Hermann, deboniar, convinced – ah, that was the regime's sole error. In any case, the exiles were mostly actors and actresses ... But he himself, I must understand, was not a Nazi. He was politically neutral. He could only say, standing there in the icy east wind that whistled like war across the black marsh, he could only say that under Hitler there had been freedom.

There was a bank cashier – even in his prisoner's clothes, as clearly a bank cashier as my old threshing companion Pringle had been. But in his grave face a sudden dry smile would appear, as we wrestled with the endless tons of beet: those roots that the caricaturist had made so much of in his notebook, where they marched alongside the prisoners, armies of oval, malicious, bewhiskered vegetable faces. 'I have never,' the bank cashier would say, plucking at beet caught between the tines of his fork, 'I have never known finer work than this!' He told me of the violent farce of his capture, as others did of theirs. 'Your watches, your watches!' his captors had cried. 'Come on, your watches!' The cashier had no watch: but he wore a ring. They tried to tug this off, but it would not budge. 'They said they would cut off my finger – ugh! – but then it came. It was my wedding ring but I was glad that it came!'

I drew desperately on my schoolboy German for many of these conversations. Once Jim Mead asked me to complain to a group on the marshes about his sleepless nights during the blitz. But the jest turned very sour. London! they cried. London had suffered hardly at all compared with the German cities. Sleepless nights! in Wuppertal, in one raid, 17,000 persons killed in forty-five minutes ... In Dresden...

Jim told them that I'd been a newspaper reporter. They were delighted, as if they'd been informed that I was once a performing bear. I was surrounded by Germans deliriously happy in the most curious way: '*Propaganda!*' they shouted. '*Goebbels!*' But, I said angrily, there *were* English newspapers that had a reputation for integrity ... Howls of glee! '*Propaganda!*' I tried my hand at driving a lorry, across the sticky marsh, and it foundered and sank to the hubs. I was surrounded at once. '*Propaganda! Propaganda!*' And for all my grinning, I was appalled oddly that this term, one of the crazy nerve-ends of our language during the thirties, had come home to roost, here on these English marshes, in the mouths of men from whom all faith in any information, any bulletin whatever, had been removed.

In our mixing with them there was a very simple, naïve element of moral relief, of all kinds of relief, on both sides. The long formal enmity had been so much to bear. Though the views of life we brought together in this way could not be made to match, still in the eager talking lay the nearly hysterical relief it was impossible not to feel: the relief of a German speaking to an Englishman, an Englishman unimportantly conversing with a German. The War Ag officials were vaguely alarmed by the impossibility of limiting this contact. They brandished at us the word 'fraternization', which was felt to have sinister undertones. Fish said: 'Look, men, don't fuss round the Jerries!' His use of the word 'men' was intended, clearly, to separate us from our ex-enemies, by stressing our human and virile character as compared with ...

There was a former surveyor, quiet-voiced, pipe-smoking, who said: 'When you go back to writing on a newspaper – tell your readers that the young Germans have never been able to form a picture of the situation. They had no experience to draw upon. But the older men have known democratic government. They didn't want war. But their democratic government was too weak.'

He told me, gravely, that life in the German Army had been intolerable. The British Army was very different. 'You see the English soldiers – they look ... independent, they have their own minds – yes? – their own opinions? You see them with cigarettes in their mouths – ah ... they look *free*! And the officers – so *freundlich* – so friendly – if you compare them with *our* officers.'

I'd read, I said, *All Quiet on the Western Front*, and —

Ah, he said, it was worse than that. It was a good thing the war was over. They could not have borne it much longer. They could not much longer have endured the life of a German soldier.

It was the older men who spoke in such ways. The young prisoners – if they were not mere boys, like the one who was so amused by his survival at Monte Cassino, or the profoundly shocked boy who suffered from outbursts of uncontrollable giggling – were often perky fantasists: their illusions impervious to defeat, even to the unspeakably dreadful nature of the defeat inflicted on Germany. A little, strutting ex-sailor on the marshes was naïvely aggrieved that German soldiers had been treated in France with murderous anger. And by this terrifying youth I was addressed in terms of pure Aryanism. The Dutch and the English, he proclaimed, were very similar peoples – but then, they and the Germans and the Scandinavians were all Nordic people. Why, then, had we fought one another? Was I not amazed at that?

I said there were reasons why I was not amazed.

But come – I would not marry an *Italian*, would I?

But why not? Of course I might do so.

'*Glaub*' *es nicht!*' he said, smiling as victoriously as if I'd said No. 'Don't believe it!' But I certainly would not marry a Jew?

Why not? I asked again – trying not to tremble.

Knowing smile, '*Glaub*' *es nicht!*'

There was Erich, too, an ex-marine, who worked alongside us as we unloaded drainage pipes in a park that was part of a large aristocratic estate, and was being ploughed. Erich, short and thick-necked, added natural braggadocio to his Aryan certainties. His talk was one anecdote after another intended to demonstrate German superiority over all other peoples whatever. He told, for example, how a group of prisoners had built a model cannon: and how, when they fired it off, the English people standing around had jumped out of their skins. It was natural, that. It was to be expected. Now, in Germany . . .

And his accounts of German excellence ended always with his making a ring of thumb and forefinger and brandishing it triumphantly under your nose: this accompanied by a cry of '*Fein! Wunderschön!*'

He looked around, once, at the park – gestured towards the tractors that were drawing ploughs between the trees that stood, everywhere, in ancient islands.

In Germany, said Erich to his fellow-prisoners, it was so different! There, if you had a field, it was a field! Only the English were so stupid as to grow trees in the middle of ploughland, to break up their acres with hedges.

I intervened, Must he not agree that her trees and hedges were among England's greatest beauties?

'*Schönheit!*' Erich scoffed. 'Beauty!'

Another, older prisoner attempted to excuse his compatriot. '*Wer liebt seine Heimat . . .*' he murmured.

It wasn't a question of loving your country, Erich snapped. If it came to that, he thought Holland was the loveliest country he'd ever seen. No, it was a question of commonsense.

Hell, I said, patriotism red in my face. This park was not, in any case, a typical example of English ploughland. It was being ploughed in an emergency: it had been a park, and would be again.

'*Er hat recht,*' muttered the older prisoner; but Erich was black-browed: he seemed about to order, for his apologetic fellow-countryman, instant court martial and execution. It was not sense, he said noisily.

A moment later he was cheerful again, telling me of the glorious uniform he had worn in his very remarkable regiment, not to be rivalled by any regiment in any other army.

'*Fein! Wunderschön!*' he crowed.

But the German who disturbed me most was one who helped us to load sugar beet at an icy farm one morning, under a sky onto which the clouds seemed to have been fixed by freezing. This man, with a lumpy, good-natured face and a rural accent, had been a farmworker before the war. He complained that German prisoners had less freedom than English prisoners had enjoyed in Germany. I said I didn't know about that, but more freedom might come later: at the moment, they were not much liked by the English. It might be as well that they were rather confined, for the time being.

'But I was not a Nazi,' he cried, with sudden passion. 'I was not a Nazi!'

He stabbed his fork into the frozen hill of beet so hard

that a whole yellow section broke away and for a moment there was a tumbling of roots about us. Then he said:

'What could we do? In a village of five hundred people, the eyes of the Nazis were everywhere. I am very religious! I am a Baptist! All my people are Baptists! Why should I shoot my brothers in other lands! Why should I wish to do that?

'All we wanted was to earn our living. We wanted only to look after our farms.

'But what could we do? *Man musste tot oder Soldat sein!* One had to choose between being a soldier and a corpse!'

The long end of it all was bad for most people. I remember it as a time when self-despisal bled from me – from that remote unformed person who was myself – as from a fatal wound. The personal helplessness that war created had been a support: there was so little one could do, anyway, that the sense of guilt was held in check. Now, in the no-man's-land between war and peace, one seemed again to have the power to determine one's own fate, but there was no reality in it. Still there was almost total helplessness. Or as George put it, navally, the wind was quite out of our sails.

'EVERY YOUNG MAN' – I copied Auden's lines in block letters into my diary – 'FEARS HE IS NOT WORTH LOVING.' I feared, indeed, that I was worth any man's contempt. There was nothing I did that I was not ready to regard as despicable. There was a girl driver in the Quarry, Hilda Grimes – known as 'La Grimes' – a painted bone of a girl, shrill and direct and greatly given to belching. The Queen of Eructation, I called her in my mind, and then beat myself for that, for the priggishness of it: for the way the word 'vulgar' kept suggesting itself. 'Went to bleeding church,' she shouted at me one Monday morning. 'Not that I go very often, but the preacher was very nice, he spoke ever so beautifully – but oh, I was bloody bored – it was all about God and all that.' Then – a favourite action based on her belief that I was 'too bloody shy' – 'nice but much too bloody shy!' – she made a grab at my genitals and released a great belch of laughter.

I thought I was a fool, a villain, an idler, a coward, a prig ... constant manufacturer of silly snatches of daydreams

... And even my discontent with myself made me angry. I turned discontent, I thought, into a comfortable way of life.

It was all at its worst at weekends – when I was simply set upon by all my unfocused aspirations. I felt taunted, then, by the richness of the world. Moving through the public library, I'd be positively startled by the names that snapped at me from the shelves. Behind each name the astounding existence of someone confident enough (what on earth could that be like?) to buttonhole the world with a book!

It did not at all occur to me that my fate was the common one of people whose early youth is swallowed up by a modern war. I should have drawn my metaphor from the Quarry's first-aid kit. Apply to a growing person the tourniquet of total warfare, then remove it, and allow the puzzled blood to grope its way through unfamiliar veins...

Something like that. Huge pins and needles.

Suddenly, there was politics once more. Early notions die hard: for me, at the heart of politics were posters, exhibiting the heads of party leaders. I even felt there was an element of playground rivalry between such men, simply because I'd first become aware of the whole business as a little boy going to school, at some time in the twenties, and seeing pinned to gate and fence the faces of men who clearly held the world on their shoulders: Baldwin, Mac-Donald, Lloyd George. They scrapped, these men, and grown-ups cheered them on; and the scrap was called an election. And now, for the first time, and as a sort of bonus for enduring the boring unanimity of war, I was to be part of an election.

I had already done some canvassing, the year before, for Richard Acland's Common Wealth Party, which was a product of impatience with the electoral truce. There'd been a tiny, ancient woman who'd looked up at me with curiously childlike, round brown eyes. The Common Wealth Party? She'd never heard of it. She trembled with alarm. 'Why? Have they altered it?' She always voted for those people round in Pepys Street – the Conservatives, weren't they? (In Pepys Street, in fact, was the polling booth.) With a guilty giggle, she said she voted Conservative because other people did. 'Some people vote Labour, don't

216

they?' She looked unhappy – wondering, perhaps, if she'd chosen wrong: perhaps it was Labour one should vote. 'I don't understand it.' Then, with sudden slyness: 'What's that old lady voted for next door?'

During the week before the election George – home from the Pacific – and I went to a Tory meeting together. Our local candidate was a brasshat: a man with a voice that sounded like a form of flagellation. That voice alone, slapping away at the buttocks of some meagre idea, had the place in an uproar. 'I think the best way to heckle,' George whispered, 'is to shout "Nonsense" at short intervals.' He did this. My heart pounded and I clenched my fists, but I found I didn't yet possess a heckler's voice. Churchill, said the candidate, was the only man who could get on with Stalin. Look at the success of their meetings! I was astounded to hear my old friend chant: 'Vodka! Vodka!' The secret, I told myself, was not to be afraid of a little crudity. 'Winston Churchill ... Winston Churchill!' the brasshat rapped and slapped, over and over, during his peroration.

'What's that name again?' carolled my unrecognizable companion.

Afterwards George said: 'Seeing a man like that – a typical backbencher – makes it clear that Labour, if they get in, will have to keep their fingers on the trigger. He's a fascist waiting for his opportunity and he'd have no hesitation in taking up arms – or rather, in ordering others to take up arms.'

And so, indeed, it seemed, in that exploding year.

It was strange: canvassing, declaring an allegiance, politically coming alive again. On the eve of the poll, a large audience, very quiet, very serious, addressed by J. B. Priestley. An unaccustomed sense of having done all one could, in the way of licking envelopes and knocking at doors: a nervous general feeling of hope: a most unfamiliar air of plans for the morrow...

On polling day itself: cycling, more knocking at doors, and another unfamiliarity in the spectacle of crowds making their way to the polling booths ... Many simple things were fresh and astonishing, then – like crowds walking through the streets for purely civil purposes ... Then the

217

long wait, while postal votes were counted ...

We were delivering equipment for a harvest camp: the farmer hustled across to us, with the air of a man who had a great deal of aimless and angry bustling to get through that afternoon, and said: 'Well, in a few hours we shall have a Labour Government!' His tone was that of a man who was really saying: '*That*'ll make you sorry you did it!' Then he walked round the lorry as though when he'd completed the circuit he might have quite the opposite message to deliver: but his detour was to no effect, and he hurried away – 'to hang himself', Jim Mead suggested.

Astonishing sensation! The wonder and strangeness of having a government to support! 'I don't care,' said the friend who called to take me to the local celebration, 'if it snows blue snow tonight.' I'd never known such solemn elation. All my life it had been the National Government, the Tories, and then the wartime coalition, and I think I'd never really imagined that the Labour Party might gain power. It was as far away, as improbable, as the victory of the third son in a fairy story. I believed then, on that amazing night, that something quite like ultimate political felicity had arrived. I was moved almost to tears by the thought of all the talented and humane men who would now surely be able to shape our affairs. Oh, it was like having a bad father replaced by a gentle, witty, disinterested and broadminded uncle! And oh, that old devil, History, which all my life had been pointed towards disaster, calamity, infamy, had now been given such a sharp twist, and was facing altogether in the other direction ... It was a great bewilderment, all of it!

At one of the schoolboys' harvest camps, the headmaster was ironic about our arrival with a stove he'd indented for. 'Amazed you've come. Frankly didn't expect it. There'll be no discipline now. I suppose it hasn't sunk in, yet – that from now on you can do just what you like!' He went to such pains to look physically at our mercy that Ralph Tarbox said: 'I'm sorry – is there something you'd like us to – ah...?' The headmaster bared the most formidable dentures and hurried away to brood over the decline of all decency.

And the proprietress of our favourite café told Reggie Gordon:

'It's started!'

'What's started, Mrs B?'

'My friend up the street – she went to the Post Office to get a withdrawal form for her savings. You know what they told her? They told her they're not issuing any more withdrawal forms ... Oh, it's all very well for you to laugh, Mr Gordon. They've changed the wavelengths on the wireless, too.'

'But that's a change that's been planned for a long time, Mrs B. Do cheer up! It's got nothing to do with politics.'

'Then tell me, Mr Gordon – *why can we only get the Labour station?*'

In my diary I wrote, solemnly: 'Each one of us has a responsibility to understand what our government is doing, to explain it to the ignorant, to combat misrepresentation and misunderstanding.'

Unaccustomed language for someone who elsewhere had concluded that he was silly even about his silliness.

On August 7, 1945, news of Hiroshima. The newspapers were full of excited articles, most of them of a rather wayward-sounding scientific character, accompanied by many photographs of physicists.

I passed the news on to a schoolteacher I knew, who was asleep in a tent in a harvest camp. The tent smelt powerfully of imprisoned bananas. My friend woke and heard me out. Then he swore, using a range of angry language partly drawn from his literary education, partly from a wartime experience of working in a coalmine.

Over Mollie Nunn's shoulder, back in the Quarry, I read a headline that said: BING CROSBY HELPED TO MAKE THE BOMB.

Suddenly the War Ag seemed to become a dazed and dying source of riches, to be plundered by anyone with the very smallest gift for dishonesty. The stories that were told of disappearing tractors and other large pieces of machinery may have been the legends that arise whenever corruption is in the air. Certainly small depredations were now part of the daily round. There had always been some element of this: I remember an urban lorry driver I once heard haranguing a countryman in a café. He didn't know, he said, how to make off with a bale of straw, or how to milk a bag of corn – 'I'm not conversant with these moves' – but he had his own townsman's skills ... He shouted with laughter. 'I can deal with a gasmeter,' he said.

But this immemorial workman's habit of quietly draining off some of his employer's wealth – this quality of the mod-est Robin Hood that certainly many countrymen had – was not of the order of the systematic stealings and confiscations that now began. Demobilized soldiers appeared among us, as drivers: and many of them had learned a special rapacity, in the forces. The moribund Committee seemed at their mercy. There was one of these drivers to whom I was mate for two quite startling days. Our first load was of wheat: five tons of it. And our first call, well off our route, was at a bungalow in a obscure village where, with the boldest precision, the driver unloaded three two-hundred-weight bags. I watched in stupefaction. We had begun to drive away when he braked the lorry hard, cursing his own thoughtlessness. He leapt briskly on to the load, picked up the folded tarpaulin that was part of the impedimenta of all our lorries, and hurried round to the back of the bungalow with it.

And so it went, throughout those two days. The official deliveries themselves that lay at the end of our piratical journeys became busy whisperings: winks, gestures with thumbs. And perpetually the lorry was skidding to a halt, and the driver vaulted into a cabbage field here, or assaulted a potato clamp there. It was one busy round of robbery, conducted with the utmost coolness and concentration.

George had said: 'A terrible thing about being in the Navy is that after a time you find yourself becoming ashamed of being decent.'

The conchies among the veteran drivers were taken aback by all this. When in convoy with their new-type colleagues, they were bound to demur at the curious view of their occupation held by these busy thieves. Ralph Tarbox met with violence when he protested against a particularly bold scheme hatched by two other drivers with whom, during a potato shortage, he was sacking, loading and delivering pig potatoes.

'Christ Almighty, though,' said one of these drivers to Ralph. 'I'm putting half a ton on for myself, every load!

Make a fortune, boy!'

'Why don't you make a real killing and flog the lorry too?' said Ralph. 'I mean, you could always go back into the Quarry making engine noises. They're too punch-drunk to notice anything wrong.'

'Trying to be clever?' one of the drivers inquired: then took one look at Ralph's pale, disgusted expression, decided that cleverness was indeed Ralph's intention, and smashed a fist into his face.

'So he had one of my teeth, too,' said Ralph. 'I looked for it but – of course – not a hope! He'll have flogged *that*, somewhere.'

Indifferent though they'd been at first to our ideological status, our new colleagues now began to direct their attention to this. 'Fucking yellow-bellies!' One or two attempted to influence opinion against us in the weary office. And a curious extra alignment made itself apparent. The Germans, with so little to do but observe, became sensitive to every twist and turn of this queer struggle.

'*Können Sie boxen?*' Fritz the sailor asked me one morning.

'*Nein. Warum?*'

'*Ach! Ich habe Angst für Sie!*' There was a conspiracy, he said, to round us all up in some dim corner of the Quarry and to teach us a lesson in terms of squashed noses and broken teeth. He was, Fritz anxiously explained, a reasonable boxer himself, and was willing to give any of us who desired it a crash course in self-defence.

It was a curious thought – that our ex-enemies should offer to teach pacifists to defend themselves against former members of the British forces. But it was not for this reason that I refused. I knew I'd make a ludicrous boxer . . .

Bob Doyle was quite explicit about his own hopes from the dissolving war. Soon, he said, there'd be more demobilized fools buying poultry and rabbit farms and failing after a year or two.

'There'll be plenty of pickings then,' said Bob, as gravely as if he were addressing a board meeting.

'I don't think so, Bob. They've been well warned, this time.'

'Oh yes, there will. Always are. Always are fools. I don't know what the silly sods expect . . .'

'But Bob – it's understandable, isn't it? After years in the open air they want an open-air life. Haven't you any sympathy for them?'

'Not me, mate.'

'If you had some land to sell that you knew was the wrong sort of land, you'd sell it to a demobilized soldier? You'd fleece him?'

'Of course I would,' said Bob, as if insisting on some obvious point of respectability. 'Of course I bloody would. They shouldn't be such bloody fools.'

Among the demobilized men who came to work at the Quarry was an ex-sailor who was perfectly honest, but perhaps the most horrifically brash man I've ever met. He came among us one day, huge and rolling, as though he were still treading a deck. 'The name's Sidney,' he cried. 'Sidney with an "i". I've come to join you lucky people. Give, give, give! What's the drill?' We stared at him, a shrinking tatty huddle of drivers and mates, and he went up to Tom Rush, a man of great reserve, and grabbed Tom's small grey hand. Pumping this up and down, he said: 'Cheer up, Tiny! The worst is over now that Sidney's here!' Tom, whose only vehemences were that he tended his garden with speechless love, and his lorry as if it had been his garden – Tom looked dazed. 'Deaf!' cried the ex-sailor. 'Deaf as a post! Take him away, someone!' He turned to me. 'You, sir,' he cried. 'You with the tasteful green jacket! Put me in the picture!' I smiled insipidly, and the ex-sailor brought up his knee and punched it with an immense fist. The leg of a lesser man would have been clean broken. 'They're dead! They're dead! They're all dead!' he carolled.

He spent little time with us, but it was long enough for a great deal of damage to be done. Even men like Bob Doyle, who might have flattered themselves that they led the way in brashness, felt pale and modest in his vast dark shadow. He ruined Ralph Tarbox's relations with Ralph's favourite café, making leviathan jokes about the food, the tea, the owner's wife ('Last word of advice, old lady: dust them sandwiches at least once a year!'). He also made poor Tom Rush deeply unhappy. Tom and I went out to fetch a load of linseed, and because of the notorious instability of such a

222

load, Sidney was sent with us as second mate. I got ready to be bawled to death by this horribly merry newcomer. And the savaging began even as we drew out of the Quarry. 'Hi – let 'em know we're going!' Sidney cried. As senior mate, I'd taken the mate's seat, and Sidney had installed himself on the engine cover, between Tom and me. Now he leaned over, crushing me against the back of the cab, and with his drumstick of a fist beat a furious tattoo on the cab door. We were going past the office as this happened. 'Leave it to us!' Sidney bellowed. 'Task force on its way! Over and out!' I caught sight of Fish's narrow face, aghast, and Mollie Nunn's marvellous little plain one, streaming with tears: and then we were out in the street, and Sidney had slumped back on the engine cover with a cry of: 'Well, mateys, this is it! And the best of luck to us all!' Tom said, changing gear: 'Don't bash my lorry about, mate. If you don't mind. And don't shout, either. I'm not deaf.' There came from the sailor a most awfully resonant burst of laughter. 'You're a marvel, mate,' he said fondly. 'You're a pure marvel. Keep it up. I love to hear you.' Tom looked as if he meant to reply, but Sidney converted his last remark into the first line of a song. 'I love to heaaaar you!' he sang; and then, deeply bass, 'To heaaar you!'

It was an extraordinary morning. Sidney was louder and livelier even than I'd feared. He gave out a constant flow of cheerful ejaculations. Whenever we passed a girl – indeed, whenever we passed anyone in skirts – he whistled: shrill variations on the wolf whistle such as I'd never imagined. At times, despite Tom's plea, he'd lean over and drum up on the door such feminine attention as his whistling had failed to evoke.

It was as we made our way over the last few miles to the farm where the linseed was to be fetched that I began to feel I'd met Sidney before somewhere. He'd half-slid off the engine cover, now, and I was having to shrug and twist for a fair share of my seat: I feared for my teeth, crouched there in the shadow of his enormous restless elbow. What was I reminded of? This gross giant beside me, with his shattering joviality ... Then he leaned over me and lowered the window and – it was a cold day – gallons of bitter air were thrown in my face. 'That's – that's too much for me,' I murmured: and I pulled the window up again. Sidney said nothing: but he gave me the full twinkle of his big black eyes: then his ham of a fist passed me and the window was down again. I raised my hand – and how slight it looked! – and let it hover there, and then I darted it out ... but *his* hand was there first, and it fell heavily on the edge of the window frame and remained there. Then I knew who Sidney reminded me of. It was in those Charlie Chaplin films – those great, bearded, amiably brutal oppressors who were attracted to Charlie like ... *elephants* to a flame. Sidney was absolutely of their kind. And Tom Rush and I were – yes, true enough – we were a couple of Charlies ...

The farm people had never met anyone like him. They were particularly taciturn, the farmer and his men. And anyway, they were saving their breath for the linseed. Economy of breath was not in Sidney's line. He began with a series of highly undiplomatic remarks about farming and farmers, evidently believing that these would give amusement: as they did not. Then he turned his tactless attention to the linseed. He'd never before encountered anything that came two hundredweight at a time and had to be carried on the back. He expressed loud and boisterous disbelief in the feasibility of carrying so much, on the back or in any other way. And he had certainly not met linseed before – this grain that slides and slithers, so that carrying it is like trying to dance with rubber men who've been vaselined all over. Tom and I and the farm people were used to this, and we knew the degree of patient doggedness that was required to get those sacks on the lorry and make a sane load of them. Sidney watched one sack performing, on Tom Rush's back, in its characteristic fashion – and at once he withdrew from the operation, devoting his whole energy to denouncing the very existence of linseed. It was crazy stuff, he suggested, and only a crazy industry would cultivate it, and only crazy men would try to carry it about. From the madness of linseed he progressed to the madness of agriculture in general, comparing it with life at sea, which we gathered was also mad, because of all the water that was involved, and the instability of water, and the wetness of water, and the danger of drowning in water, and of being made sick by the movement of water. But life at sea, with water, wasn't half so mad, he took the liberty of declaring, as life on land, with linseed.

We'd finished loading, grim and silent: and Sidney was still leaning on the tailboard of the lorry, shouting and laughing and throwing in an occasional inquiry as to where all the milkmaids were, that he'd been promised were such a feature of life in the countryside. Tom Rush, looking more grey even than usual, signed a chit, and the farmer counter-signed, and we silently got ready to move away: and Sidney paused for a moment to take in this fact: whereupon the farmer said, with all the intensity of indignation that the last hour had built up within him: '*I shall be phoning your transport officer about this.*' Sidney began to express his noisy, elaborate astonishment that the telephone should have reached a spot so primitive, that someone who had truck with linseed should also have a phone: but Tom and I somehow shrugged and shoved him into the cab, and amid a flow of new insults from our companion we drove out of that deeply shocked farmyard.

Perhaps the farmer did ring Fish, and perhaps that did play a part in bringing about the ex-sailor's departure: but before he went, Tom Rush and I (I was Tom's regular mate at the time) had the curious pleasure of seeing the sailor's abominable merriment countered by an exhibition of dole-fulness that was quite as formidable.

Sidney was again our mate when we took a load to a Ministry of Food store. This place, new to us, was staffed with a score or so of very old, very seedy men. They were really like so many cloth-capped skeletons, *very* old – and *very* slow. They were opposed to work in a thin, dismal way as Sidney was opposed to it fatly and jovially. And the whole occasion proved that the bully, cheerlessness, given half a chance, could always triumph over that other bully, cheerfulness. The sacks of corn were hauled up to a high store-room by hook and chain. The process was regulated by a very grey thin old man, whose entire object was to pinch out the first sign of energy on the part of anyone whatever. The ex-sailor, seeing that no carrying at all was involved, was on the back of that lorry in a flash, throwing out happy aspersions on the appearance of the store and its staff, and digging the hook into the first sack. 'Ready!' he called. Whereupon the old man above let go of the chain, stepped back and snapped: 'I'll pull when *I*'m ready, mate. There's always tomorrow, you know.' And another old man

near at hand called out, 'We've got one of *them*, have we?'
And still another shrilled: 'We know your kind, mate!' Proceedings were at a standstill for at least ten minutes: and
Sidney already looked actually smaller. He made one more
grand error. 'Do you want any help up there, my old
mate?' he called. This was good for a much longer stoppage, while, thin-voiced, bitter, they – all twenty of them –
told him what they thought of people who made a mock of
their age, and used sarcasm as an element in workaday
intercourse.

We had a silent ride home, apart from a few half-hearted
whistles and some very feeble affabilities. And we never saw
Sidney again in the Quarry. We never knew if the office had
warned him off or if he'd decided that this wasn't his kind
of ... well, perhaps *work* was not the word. It was possibly
a case of Fish's inclination chiming in perfectly with Sidney's.

A letter came from George: a few phrases in his crabbed
hand on a scrap of notepaper. He was married and it was
Jeanne who'd been chosen. Or was it, perhaps, Jeanne
who'd chosen? ... As usual, he had pinched his delight into
a single phrase: 'I imagine,' he wrote, 'that life with Jeanne
will hardly be dull.' I sat looking at this sentence and thinking how characteristic it was of George: and thinking, too,
how much I owed to this abstention of his from lavish
affirmations. Always, because I had known George, there
was an instinct in me to take my pleasures a little more
healthily dry than was natural.

He was to return to his ship after a short holiday. 'I
should imagine,' he wrote, 'that few honeymooners manage
in normal times to get away not only with their wives after
the marriage but from their wives after the honeymoon.
That assurance makes my position one of unusually careless abandon. Indeed, in general I feel a cautious buoyancy
as to the state of marriage. Later I will let you know if it is
a condition I can wholly recommend to more ascetic creatures like yourself.'

No, I thought regretfully: I could never have carried
dryness as far as that.

Everything happened now with a painful abundance. The

new postwar worlds, the public and the private ones, took rapid shape, and it became very hard to be tethered to a wearisome job. It wasn't simply that we were tired of log-sheets and lorries ... of carting hardcore to make paths so that the tedious sugar beet could, when the time came, be carried away from the tedious marshes ... It was also that this work was no longer, as it had been in wartime, part of a greater nightmare from which none could escape.

There was the interminable, dull expectation of release. George (at home and waiting for his own liberation, having left Jeanne in the West Indies till he had lodging for her) had outlined a statement of principles, in this respect, which secretly I . . found a grim one. 'I should think,' he said, 'they'll keep you there till the last soldier is demobilized. After all, though it's a queer situation, it would be an anomaly if you fellows should be released and profit from the dubious gains of this war before the men who've been fighting for you.' He'd added, sternly reflective: 'I reckon half the fellows in the Navy are conchies. They hate brutality and are very soft-hearted, but they simply hadn't the religious or political convictions to stand out.'

The government was less harshly logical than George. It drafted a Bill that would set us free with the Army groups to which we should have belonged. The House of Lords disliked this enormously, and amended it in George's vein: my Lord Swinton called it 'a very silly Bill'. We felt the greatest dejection: it seemed a kind of last straw (and for us the cliché wasn't mechanical) that our fate should be the subject of a Bill that was very silly.

Then there was talk of a world famine, and it was given out that possibly no agricultural labour might be released for years to come ...

Our vast naïve enthusiasm for the Labour government was soon dulled. I'd expected a warm and candid relation-ship with the people: the government would chat with us, informally, perhaps even wittily, explaining every step in the voice of, say, Kingsley Martin in the New Statesman's London Diary. Instead – here it was being applauded by the Tories: here it was, showing a strong distrust for intellec-tuals. Where were the world-changing bold strokes we'd looked for? George said he had a feeling – which he could support with no evidence whatever – that Attlee was waiting for something. 'It doesn't sound a very bright suggestion – but I believe it might be so. I believe they might be like men who are pushing a very heavy table – once it starts running it'll be all right.'

We waited for the table to gather speed ... But I was really of the mind of a friend, a compositor in the printing works of the suburban weekly I'd worked for, who wrote in a letter: 'A little while ago, there was a general appreciation of the fact that the effect of five years of war could not be cleared up in six months. The government could have drawn upon that understanding and mobilized the people behind a two-year plan of austerity. After that could have come Victory Day – victory in the sense of achievement.'

On the other hand, it was necessary to take up a posture of defence against those who talked as if the inevitable aftermath of a great war were something invented by a Labour government. It caused curious anger – to encounter people who would not accept the effects of causes that they had wholeheartedly embraced.

And the post-war world in general took its frightening shape. Even the care George had taken to instruct himself in realities ('Read Marx and Engels for five minutes and you'll know more about the way the world ticks than ninety-nine people out of a hundred') did not protect him from shock when the Americans brought Lend-Lease to an end. 'I think the way they've done this makes the next world war inevitable,' he brooded. 'They must believe they can emasculate the sterling area and still reap benefits from a ruined Europe ... Don't you think so?' I shook my head, not with disagreement, but in the hope of rearranging meaningfully its haphazard contents. 'But perhaps one good result of it all will be to oblige us to make common cause with New Zealand and Australia. Perhaps I'll take Jeanne to New Zealand. After all, Europe will be no place to invite a woman to make her home in ...'

Swiftly the allied world had fallen into its fearful halves, and we'd understood for the first time that, from now on, all the important dialogue would be spoken over our heads. George said: 'I can't help feeling that some of our left-wingers are pleased that Russia is being so cussed. They say: "Now we can get back to our liberalism." Eh?'

It became almost a relief to talk to Jim Mead, who as a

228

Jehovah's Witness believed that behind everything that happened was an immense ubiquitous conspiracy of Roman Catholics. It was pleasant to think that Stalin and Truman and the rest of our masters were really of one mind and, in this bashfully secret unanimity, were bent on the single, prodigious goal of bringing to an end the publication of *Watchtower*...

Daily intimacy with the German prisoners sharpened the drab anguish of that last year. Their own frustration gave off a smell, almost, which I associate with the acridity of chemical fertilizers. Off and on I was in charge of a gang of them at Beechall Park, loading the sulphates and phosphates onto lorries: attempting, in a blizzard of chemicals, to soften the sacks that had petrified in the damp air of the Park's old stabling. I was 'Herr Foreman'. They would sing for me – but really for themselves – and on some shabby November afternoon, in that shabby November of the mind that was then the mental weather of us all, I'd be aware of the tears falling. Did we cry, in fact? I'm sure I and Rudi the musician did, once when he was staggering out of the stable door with a sack on his back, and exclaimed: '*Du bist in meinem Wege!*'

'*Was ist Ihr Weg?*' I asked.

'*Nach Hause – nach Deutschland,*' sighed Rudi, '*das ist mein Weg.*' And I remembered the infinite sadness of the words that Shakespeare puts into the mouth of the exiled Bolingbroke, in *Richard II: Save back to England, all the world's my way.*

And suddenly there was great theatre again – and paintings to be seen. George and I walked dumbfounded round the reopened National Gallery. An exhibition of Picasso and Matisse came to the Victoria and Albert. It opened to cries of rage from the conservative: to go to it was, in a sense, like having a second chance of voting Labour. The gallery burst with people, and we glimpsed astonishing colour and – in Picasso's case – astonishing images over khaki shoulders. We left with a particular sea anemone, orange and red, burning in our heads. 'I'm glad I saw those,' George said. 'I could do with such things in my dreams. So often I feel I ought to apologize to Jeanne for the sordid world she has to pick her way about in, when I'm dreaming. I suppose we *shall* get used to colour again...'

And great theatre ... Oliver's Oedipus, for example ... the chorus of citizens stretched across the stage, a rippling green stream of sorrow ... and the groping shadow of the blinded Oedipus entering, with a slowness that seemed outside time, long before the torn body of the actor. And then, a half an hour later in the same programme, this ruined king becoming Puff in Sheridan's *The Critic*, a Puff of the most ingenious lightness ... removing with unspeakable delicacy an absurd hatpin from an absurd hat ... What a night that was! what a yoking of the most painful tragedy, the most intoxicating comedy!

My own private essay in post-war advance was to fall in love with a returned lady warrior. In all directions, for months on end, I saw her earrings, which were of that blue colour that flax is when it opens under the sun. I'd spent so long staring at her face, trying to understand the spirit resident within its bright oval: staring into a small world of which those earrings were the furthest points, and so made the edge of my own world, at that time. *This little narrow world, where I am lost*, I'd written, *And being lost, would not be shown my way* ... 'I love your letters,' she'd said about the one that contained this couplet. 'They're so original!' Ah, once again I found it impossible to mention a love affair to George. It was difficult to imagine him in the same room with Kate. She had a positive dislike of ideas. She wanted all those she loved to be held together by a blissful refusal to form opinions. By my habit of attempting to think about things, and then confessing to my thoughts, she was nervously drawn – so long as it was trapped in a boudoir. It was all 'original'. She was even, at the beginning, taken by my compulsive need to make notes of her conversation, on the backs of envelopes. And though the physical acts of love were as serious to her as ideas were to me, she laughed when I'd pause at some pleasant moment to record an image or sensation. Some of the images, indeed, she provided herself. Of my workman's hand on her thigh: it was like chocolate spilt on a cloth ... Oh, she was lovely! Her small coiling body, her lips parting in a kiss, one hand moving blindly at the back of my head ... her tiny feet, her slender wrists ... the evident fact that it was all a nonsense was drowned when we touched, when those star-like blue earrings blurred as I kissed her warm neck ... it was drowned in delight, all my doubt, and for a day or so I'd walk about, smiling to myself, and counting our children before they were hatched. I had never realized that two human beings might be like two horses, content to rest their chins on each other's shoulders for long minutes on end. George would certainly not have approved of such mindless sensuality and idleness.

Then the magic would grow fainter, my diffidence would strengthen. I'd tell myself that I was paying the price – and exacting it from her, too, sweet calamity that she was – for not accustoming myself sensibly to the company of women, as George had done. I told myself that our strong physical feeling for each other was complicated, in my case, by a shyness – the result of years of inhibition – about the acts of sexual love: the major ones of which we had not yet achieved, since I'd discovered that all my bold literary knowledge was no guide at all to erotic realities. The subject of our spiritual and mental affinity remained outside this matter, an affair of doubt.

'To me,' I said, 'the body is all myth and legend.' 'Oh,' she sighed. 'You make me feel I'm seducing you.'

I clumped around in my workmen's boots, at Beechall Park, reflecting that it was all a matter of Bottom and Titania, surely. She would be wakened, soon, by her true lover, and would see me for what I was ... a scarred coward with immense boots and a headful of clumsy ideas ...

At times, I was grateful for the work of the Quarry, roughly disbursing my energies, keeping me keyed up in a crude way by a timetable. But at other moments, weak and faint with physical affection, or torn between love and dread, I'd brood my way unseeingly through a day, imagining forms of suicide and tragic death, having myself summoned for sudden urgent expeditions to one or other of the Poles ... Brainsickly – that was the word, I used to think. The whole affair had induced a morbid exaggeration of my disbelief in myself. Kate, I thought wildly, make a fool of me: for no effort of mine will prevent me from being a fool.

And then the Commons expressed considerable distaste for the Lords' treatment of our Bill – it was an interference with the democratic decision of the elected House. The wicked amendment was accepted, but the Minister of Labour promised that 'administrative action would mitigate the problem'.

It was at this point that Fish offered me and Oliver permanent posts with the War Ag – or Peace Ag, as presumably it would become.

Fish had sent me with my Germans to patch some of the roadways through Beechall Park. 'We'll show some *austerity* here,' he'd mumbled. 'Put a lot of gravel down.' Then he didn't go away, but stood swishing at his coat tails as if he thought that by constant activity in that quarter he might cause himself at last to be airborne. The dull, difficult conversation turned to the subject of our release. Reggie Gordon and Ralph Tarbox had simply absented themselves from the War Ag's service, for ever. 'They've no right,' murmured Fish. 'But.' His habit of creating whole sentences out of single conjunctions was famous. He'd once said that he'd not wanted the job of Transport Officer. 'Though,' he'd added ... 'And Noon,' he said now. I knew what he meant by that. Leonard Noon had at last accepted a formula of release as between him and the War Ag. It stated that the Committee 'finds itself reluctantly compelled to regard Mr Noon's services as redundant.' I was certain that it was those two fine words, 'reluctant' and 'redundant', that had satisfied Leonard's vanity – as ever, entirely a matter of vocabulary – and had brought about his consent to the arrangement. He'd spent his last week in the War Ag's employment littering the Quarry with small, rather handsomely lettered notices that said: 'WARNING. Work is not appreciated here.'

But as to the rest of us, Fish had his own idea how our release was to be arranged. We would be set free only if it was thought that we'd done good work in the War Ag's service. 'But parliament —' I said: and then decided not to spoil Fish's simple notion. But I said: 'It may, I think, depend on whether we have a job to go back to.' 'Haven't you got one?' asked Fish, turning violet.

He came to fetch me at the end of the day. 'You come back with me,' he said. 'I've asked someone else to look after the Germans.' I climbed into his small, tongue-tied van and, as we drove towards the Quarry, watched his face redden. At last he mumbled: 'About what we were saying this morning – about your finishing. How would you like to stay on? Permanent job.' He cleared his throat, as though the emotional strain of making such a moving offer had almost been too much for him. I sat appalled while he worked out his shyness on the gear lever and outlined the plan: which was that I should become an assistant clerk in the Quarry office. 'We know we can't hold you if you want to go,' said Fish. 'But you know the Committee work pretty well.'

I felt very dizzy indeed. For the first time for nearly six years I was being actually solicited, sought after, offered a choice ... But any sense I might have had of the luxury of it foundered in my sense of its grotesqueness, and both in my feeling of sharp embarrassment. There sat Fish, taking out on the engine of the van all the difficulty this little interview had cost him, forcing his words out as if he'd been proposing to a girl. How could one say bluntly: 'No'? How could one even say it gently, to such a man? In a panic of soft-heartedness I told him – I gabbled – that I'd thought of trying to become a teacher – but I did, oh I certainly did, appreciate the offer ... 'Anyway, think it over,' he made himself say. 'Let me know soon. I mean, we don't want to fill the vacancy and then you say you'd have liked the job.' He jabbed the van into a gap between two lorries and became, for him, expansive. 'We've made up Oliver Cragg in charge of bikes,' he said.

It was difficult for me, at that moment, not to fall, writhing with laughter, from my seat. Oliver was to be in charge of bikes! This was a practical job of a kind that even to think of drove me to the edge of craziness. It involved the maintenance of some hundreds of machines. You did nothing but repair chains, straighten handlebars, replace cotterpins, mend punctures. I had myself a bad way with bikes: they fell to pieces under me. But Oliver was far worse.

Back in the Quarry I hunted Oliver down, bursting with my news. The lavatory was the safest place to pass this on. That thin-walled shack was still shaking with our amusement, and Oliver was saying: 'You almost feel you can't let them down,' when the door came abruptly open and in walked Fish. He marched red-faced to his place and Oliver said quickly, with that elaborate guile of his that was worse than plain clumsiness: 'Can't let them down – Charlie and all the other fellows.' Over his shoulder Fish grunted: 'You know what you're going to be given, Cragg?'

Oliver gabbled: 'Yes, but I don't think I'll take the job for two reasons. One is that I don't know anything about bikes – not that that matters, ha ha – and the other is – perhaps you've heard about our group numbers?' Fish continued, stolidly uncomprehending, with his task. 'Unfortunately,' Oliver went on wildly, '*unfortunately*, I have this job to go back to. I'd like to stay, but ... well, you see, my firm has been paying me, all through the war.' Fish turned and buttoned himself and his face became positively vermilion. 'Then it's your *duty* to go back,' he asserted. He advanced towards Oliver as though he meant to seize him by the scruff of the neck and haul him there and then back to the headquarters of that building society in the City of London. 'You *must* go back, Cragg,' he urged.

Cycling home that night, Oliver and I gloomily examined our characters. How ridiculously sentimental we both were! Here had we, through the anguish caused us by Fish's bashful benevolence, very nearly committed ourselves to employment of a kind the very thought of which filled us both with horror. We must watch ourselves very closely now that the enormous unfamiliarity of a world making offers, rather than a world making demands, was before us ...

Soon after this, Oliver followed in the footsteps of Reggie Gordon and Ralph Tarbox. But before he went he added a last service to that which his companionship had provided all those years. For a time I'd been persecuted by a perfectly witless driver, who was moved entirely by a desire to humiliate other human beings. The agonies of requited love – the fatigue that came from having for months been possessed by a mania of translation, as I worked alongside my Germans – despair at the general witlessness into which the War Ag had fallen – all these things made me bow with ineffective anger under the torments that Triggs provided. Take a sack off his lorry, and quick as one of the farts with which he punctuated his conversations he'd seat himself upon it, and your spine would snap dangerously. Place your hand on the frame of a door and he'd have the door closed on it. He became, for me, a symbol of the War Ag's dying stupidity. I came masochistically close to finding him welcome as such a symbol. But one day Oliver came to Beechall Park as his mate, and when Triggs made to trip him up as he bent under a sack, Oliver let the sack go and swung round at immense speed with his elbow advanced; and Triggs fell to the ground, as dreadfully winded as any man I've seen. He made no further attempt on Oliver, and when I borrowed this beautifully simple notion of defence by elbow, I won my own immunity, too.

The last winter had gone ... last of those tidied winters, when the fields were turned over and tucked up anew, like beds, and the roadmen had trimmed the ragged rims of the lanes ... All the weathers I'd known on the land! And here was the last day when from beginning to end it was a down-drift of sleet, slanting under a low grey sky across the cold, half-invisible fields ... And the last day of fog – and we in convoy, lorry following lorry through the smoky greyness, which breathed in and out as if behind it were strange mouths, blowing and sucking ...

And carting the sugar beet, from which all our sugar was made in those years. Collecting it from the marshes: or from farmyards where under the sun it would lie shining like butter. And so to the factory with it – which spread the sickly smell of boiling beet across the countryside, and re-leased great explosions of smoke into the cold sky. There was always a long queue of lorries, waiting to be unloaded, and we'd inch forward, through the nauseous air, and sugar beet became a kind of delirium in our minds. I would worry at the idea that someone might make me count those roots, the millions upon millions of them heaped in lorries, in railway trucks, in great storage bays – being washed out of our lorry, when at last we were inside, by a great jet of water. And all round the factory grounds, in fast-flowing channels, the beet raced.

And the coldness. All that water held the factory in the grip of the most intense frost, the next day, setting out to fork another load of those obsessive roots into the lorry, I'd feel I was breaking my arm out of the icy lock of its rheumatism.

But then came the last spring – a June-like April ... and in mid-summer Jeanne arrived in England.

Jeanne was as beautiful as George had almost confessed

that she was – and a composite of several nationalities ...

'I really don't see,' I said, 'why I should get a job. I could join your ménage as a sort of seedy hanger-on. Or as your Jeeves, George? Your Figaro?'

'Jeanne was afraid of that,' said George. 'She thought that, judging your character from what she'd heard of you, the temptation might be dangerous, and you might be shielded from your legitimate ambitions.'

'It's nice to be back with George,' said Jeanne, 'and to be reassured that, in fact, *that* is precisely how he *does* talk.'

'I know what you mean,' I said.

'We shall be glad to get the growing pains of marriage over,' said George. 'That is, if one ever does get over the growing pains of marriage ...'

He was demobbed now: and a flat had been ready for Jeanne, furnished and decorated in the laconic style of living quarters in a destroyer. 'I hope you are not expecting great luxury on your visits,' he said. 'There's not much more than a bed, a chamber pot and a breadknife. Anything else would represent a falling among the bourgeois, don't you think?'

Every day he was looking up five or six unfamiliar words in the dictionary, writing down the names of half a dozen men in the news, and finding out what he could about each. 'You'll think it very sordid, I daresay. But I've concluded that I've done nothing that's academic since I left school. I think my mind needs some systematic feeding. And – don't you think? – if you set out to do something pretentious, like writing a book or an article, you'd only make a fool of yourself ...'

We agreed that we had simply no sense of style, as yet. We'd hardly begun to be converted into civilians of our own natural sort – whatever that was. Jeanne would help him, he said. 'Of course, it won't be an English sense of style ...

'Don't you think if you'd not gone on the land, but had gone straight from school into some ... literary profession, you'd have become rather rarefied? I think that's what happens to lots of people. Do you think it's possible we might look back and count the land and the Navy in their crooked ways, as strokes of luck?'

It was July; and England was most beautiful for Jeanne's arrival. I told George my release had come.

'Well – now we can get on with things,' he said. 'After what counts, I suppose, as a rather rude interruption.'

My last task on the land took me across the flat plains of Cambridgeshire, with its horizons of feathery trees, to a farm where harvested flax stood, the source of the subtle linseed, twisted into witch-hat shapes, the palest bronze. I remembered long before watching a field of flax in Cold Clapton turn colour as the light fell upon it: a bright wash of blue, amazing, that spread in the wake of the sunshine. I thought dizzily of Kate's earrings, of all that fearful fever of fascination and recoil. In the quiet evening we drove back to the Quarry through Essex villages; and at the end of my days on the land I looked back to the beginning, five and a half years before, and felt a certain satisfaction in the symmetry of things: both opening and close having been in flat, phlegmatic Essex.

On my last day, there was no work at all. It was, as it happened, the thirty-second anniversary of the day when my father's war broke out. When I look back now, I think it was my father's war that I refused to fight. Of course, it was so easy to build up the case for declaring the Second World War ... a paroxysm in the death-throes of capitalism: a murderous hoax at the expense of the common people of the world ... I was under the spell of a dozen different views of what was happening: and I had the strongest feeling that none of us was able to stretch his mind over the whole dizzying complexity. I'd said so to George, once, when he'd made a sharp reference to my being on National Disservice: and I'd half-expected that he'd accuse me of rationalizing my own ignorance and lack of study: but he murmured, 'Yes, we all fall into pockets.' Although much of my feeling about myself and my conduct, as the war went on, gathered round the notion of my guilt – of the awful guilt of standing aside – I remained in fact deeply uncertain till the end. And, inevitably, conchies developed a very great sense of loyalty to the unpopular group they formed. In the first great war, they had been martyrized: in this one, they were put into positions of obscure discomfort. Both kinds of fate held the dissidents together, powerfully.

Had I been two or three years older when it all began, I

think I could not have been a pacifist. I should then perhaps have been able to accept the grim logic of the case: that the only way to bring the obscenity of Hitlerism to an end – and there was otherwise no hope of health for the world – lay in fighting. The need to do that overrode every revulsion, all the terrible doubts one might have about the real ends for which a vast war was fought ... But this isn't a story of ideal decisions taken with reference to purely disinterested perceptions. It's quite another – quite the *usual* sort of human story. George and I were driven to our different actions by forces of temperament and inheritance quite as powerful as what went on in our minds...

I hope there seems no complacency in this. That's not what I feel. I look back over the years and sigh for the way things were as they were. Thus it was, and at any later point one might wish to return with a blue pencil, to work on one's past life as if it were the manuscript of a novel. But there it lies, beyond editing. I say only that this was how it was, as I remember it. I feel rather small attachment to the fellow at the centre, and even shudder a little at the thought of him. Into what shames and perils the young fool took us, me and him, in his helpless gaucherie and inexperience!

That last day was suddenly hot: I chatted with Rudi, the musician, and Fritz, the sailor, and smiled at Mollie Nunn. I felt as though I were, for the moment, in a sort of no-where. Soon, unimaginably, I'd have to pretend to be a teacher. In my longing for clean hands and for a job exotically situated indoors, I'd applied for – and, astonished, been given – a post in a prep school in Hampstead: which in all senses was far from the Quarry.

Halfway through the afternoon, feeling dull and forlorn, I shook hands with Rudi and Fritz and clasped Mollie's warm fingers: was not very successfully carried for a few staggering yards on the Germans' shoulders: and ran out of the Quarry gates.

Other Panthers For Your Enjoyment

Outsize Heroes